JACK O'KEEFE'S
PROPERTY
DEC. 1980

Collectors' Guide to

Britains
Model Soldiers

by
John Ruddle

**Model and Allied Publications,
Argus Books Ltd,
14 St James Road,
Watford, Herts**

Model and Allied Publications,
Argus Books Ltd,
14 St James Road,
Watford, Herts,
England

ISBN 0 85242 568 6

Photography by
Jack Casement

Typeset by Inforum Ltd,
Portsmouth

Printed and bound in Great Britain by
A. Wheaton & Co., Ltd., Exeter

Contents

Introduction

WHEN this book was originally conceived it was hoped that it might have been possible to produce a sequel to the work written on early lead toy figures by L.W. Richards. This would have covered all makes, but the decision was finally made to deal with only one manufacturer's products. Britains were chosen as the firm which seemed to attract more collectors than any other in the lead toy industry.

To include all the photographs needed to cover the enormous range of figures produced in seventy years of manufacture would have proved an impossible task with the limited number of plates allowed in this publication. Eventually it was decided to concentrate on the unusual items rather than the very old which are, and have been, reproduced elsewhere. This book is really a "super catalogue" listing as many of the items known to the author as having been produced by Britains, together with a brief decription. Inevitably there will be omissions, but as Britains themselves never kept any comprehensive records, this will not be surprising considering that the numbers were issued and re-issued in a very haphazard way.

When William Britains first produced toy soldiers, in 1893 they were already well established as manufacturers of the conventional mechanical playthings prevalent at that time. Most lead toy soldiers were made on the Continent by German or French manufacturers and were usually of solid lead. When Britains entered the market they were first in the field with a hollow figure. This method (known as slush casting) was soon to be copied but somehow Britains quality was never equalled by the many imitators who came into the market as the trade in England developed. If one studies the production of foreign troops issued from 1900 onwards it can be seen as a record of the military history taking place at that time. It started with the Boer War, was followed by the Boxer Rebellion, the Turkish Greek conflict followed and the Russo-Japanese, Spanish American conflicts were all marked by the production of Britains figures. After the Great War of 1914-18 the struggle brought about a drop in the inter est in military items. To keep up sales a new civilian side of the toy market was developed. Although the title of this book indicates model soldiers only, most collectors have an interest in all sides of the lead models produced by William Britains. Even in this section of the products a bit of history is captured in the dress and trappings of these models of rural and town life. Except for the short break from 1940 to 1946 Britains continued to produce lead toys until events in 1966 affected manufacturer's everywhere who worked in this medium. For a long time cost had been reducing the number of items in the catalogue, and the number of figures in the boxes had been getting smaller with each issue. The final blow came with the Government's Lead Safety Act which forbade the use of lead in items made for children. Britains had already for over a year, been producing plastic soldiers along side the lead and they quickly changed over entirely.

It is ironic however that at the time of writing one of the fastest growing cottage industries is the new collectors' range of gloss painted figures, which are attempting to follow where Britains left off. The lines still portray the British Red Coat and other colourful uniforms but none as yet equal the excellence that was BRITAINS.

Scheme of Book

and Figure

Identification Guide

WITH THE VAST output of metal figures over about 70 years of miniatures from the firm of Britains, there is an inevitable problem when it comes to providing any type of listing of the models produced. Almost every year Britains produce an illustrated catalogue of some kind, occasionally a leaflet, but more often a substantial book which listed all existing models, illustrated most of them, and included 'New Lines' for the coming year. Some 'New Lines' were taken off the market after only a year or so, while some stayed in the catalogue for years – indeed right up to the end of metal figure production, and beyond in the case of some guns and farm accessories.

As a further complication some models were withdrawn then reintroduced later (sometimes after a gap of many years) under another number. Others were re-introduced but in a different series altogether. In this book we have made some cross-references where models are the same or a similar casting. In addition there are cross-references where models were intended to complement each other or were in some other way related. For example when Picture Pack single models were released, without exception they were simply individual models already available in established boxed sets. As a Picture Pack item, however, the model was itself given a new number.

Numbering of the models themselves did not immediately follow any obvious plan other than that 'New Lines' for a given year were just numbered chronologically in the next batch, at least as far as the Main List was concerned. This was quite obvious so long as soldiers only were produced, though some early items, like the original 4.7

inch Naval Gun did not, apparently have numbers when first issued. Some items, like the Evzones, No 196, stayed in the list until the 1960s under this old number. In 1931 the first Farm Series issues were issued, by which time model soldier output had reached nearly 500. The Farm, and subsequent Zoo, Hunt, and Railway figures then took numbers in the 501-1000 band, and subsequent Soldier releases jumped to 1201 onwards to leave room for expansion for Farm and Zoo items, etc. Various non-military items were then once again issued in the continuing sequence, such as the Coronation models of 1936-37 and Racing Colours. By the 1940-41 catalogue the sequence had reached No 1918, the Home Guard appropriately enough, and the last new item of all before production ceased 'for the duration' was a chess set.

In 1946 production started again in a block commencing with 2002 as far as 'New Lines' were concerned, and pre-war items reintroduced took their old numbers. Conventional boxed sets were issued until about 1960 with new issues, by which time plastics had taken over.

The year 1962 was something of a turning point. By the time the Farm and Zoo series had been converted almost entirely to plastic as far as figures were concerned. Plastic Soldiers, Cowboys and Indians, and others were firmly established (plastic items are not included in this book) and the remaining metal soldiers were then all renumbered in the 9000 series to facilitate more modern ordering and accounting techniques. It has not proved possible to trace all the renumbered sets, but where known, the 'new' 1962 number has been added in brackets after the original number. The other point of interest here was that for 1962 the metal soldier sets were put into window boxes in the same style as the plastic figures, so this marked the end of the 'traditional' lidded strawboard box which had been so much of the Britains scene since the 1890s.

Originally many of the early boxes had the figures slid into slots in the boxes or were laid into the compartments fixed inside. In the late 1930s they had been stitched in. The first boxes had very elaborate printing and decoration, called by some printers, flowers. In 1913 or thereabouts an artist living in Southend called Fredrick Whistock was commissioned to work on designing a more up to date cover. Pictures of the Regiments to be found in the box started to appear on the lid. Even when he was called up he must have continued to work during his leave as boxes are to be found signed Private, and Corporal Whistock. He retired, according to Britains, around 1928.

When Britains started to come on to the market again in 1947 the boxes were more formal with about four basic covers. They showed either a dismounted Scots Grey one side and Life Guard Trumpeter the other, or the traditional 'Toy Soldier' peering round a Fir Tree. The only indication as to content was on the end of the lid. There were of course a few exceptions to this, but something of the old individuality and charm had been lost. Over the years the contents of the boxes were gradually reduced. Some of the very early infantry boxes had ten figures. These gradually dropped to six and in some cases only five.

In 1966 the manufacture of metal figures ceased altogether, though in the 1970s a few die-cast Zamak figures were made, and most of the accessories, such as farm carts and guns, remained in metal. Because of the chronological nature of the numbering, no attempt has been made to segregate the Farm, Zoo, Soldier categories in the Main List which forms the first part of this book. By the mid-1930s, however, with the range expanding fast, Britains produced some new number series for certain lines – thus there were separately numbered Farm items with an F suffix, Zoo items with a Z suffix, and many others. All these ranges are entered separately in this book after the Main List but it must be remembered that they were actually produced, at various times, concurrent with Main List items. The 'A' series and 'Crown' series figures were features of the range, being basically normal quality castings with simpler paintings for sale in chain stores and non-toyshop outlets. There were a few castings which were included in these cheaper series, however, which were either old 'fixed arm' era types, or simplified models not found in later years in the Main List.

Britains figures originally had no identifying marks on them. The only way to date them is by the round or rather oval bases. As other firms entered the field a certain amount of copying went on. Several successful law suits took place and until a more permanent method came in a paper label was glued to the base of the figures. In 1900 the copyright date came cast on to the bottom of the pieces with the date of registration. With the issue of the first square based figures this was continued up till about 1914.

In the case of horse-drawn transport the best way to date this is by the type of horse or harness. Many of the early horses had the ears cast in one piece. Also the harness was the old collar harness type, used by farmers for many years after the army, but it caused much suffering to the horses in the Boer war so that by the beginning of the First World War it had been replaced by the breast harness. Britains introduced this in about 1918 in the gun teams and G.S. wagons. It will be noted that many of the figures were so similar to each other that only a coat of paint was used to change their appearance. In some cases they look identical. In others they changed the figures' appearance by altering the head. This was a simple matter as the top section of the moulds could be unscrewed and an entirely new section substituted.

This gave Britains a wonderful range of figures at a very economical cost. An example of this can be seen in the casting used for the walking Royal Canadian Mounted Policeman. This was used for the German No 432, the Polish soldier No 1856, the New Zealander No 1542, the Australian No 1544, the Netherlands Infantry as No 1850, and so on. The same of course applied to mounted figures as well.

The painting of Britains figures is also worth a mention. Although considered rough by todays' high standards of 'model soldiers' the detail is surprisingly good when you consider that the pay for a painter in 1950 was about 50p a gross (144).

The richer customer could persuade the firm to give them to more skilled painters for an extra sixpence, and so one had the 'Britains Specially Painted'. This also meant you could acquire a set not currently in the catalogue. One can always recognise these figures by the fineness of the lines, but it is impossible to find them in any makers list. An example of these models can be seen in the photos of the Black Watch Band on page 000 painted to order as that of the Gordon Highlanders.

Another intriguing subject is the mysterious and cryptic word on many bases: 'Depose'. An examination of the records at Britains reveals that in 1912 it was becoming expensive to send toy soldiers to the continent. This being so, the agents in France were instructed to set up a subsidiary company. Messrs Laudriew and Rousseau did this and the moulds were duly produced with this one word in French to protect them from the dreaded pirates.

By 1918 as well as a head office in Paris there were factories in St Leu and Cosque as well. Many confusing head changes took place but there is no evidence of any French Catalogue, so we must presume that the English one was used. Interesting notes appear in the company records, such as 'Mr Silvester called to the colours', so Mr Fred Britain was dispatched to carry on. The Paris office continued to operate until 1923 when to quote the minutes 'Due to the inability to run properly' it was wound up. The moulds of course along with other equipment came home and were used till they were worn out, which explains all those Britains toys in the U.K. with this mark on them.

In the photographic section there has been an attempt to show as many as possible of the main figures, though there is a physical limitation since many more pages would be needed to have shown every single item, even if the rarer pieces could have been procured. To simplify the captions each individual figure is identified by the number of the set in which it first appeared and an illustrated item is indicated in the writing by the serial number in bold. Bear in mind, however, that many figures appeared with simpler painting in one of the cheaper ranges, and then appeared again with yet another number as an individual item (eg, Picture Pack). Cross reference between entries in this book will show where this has occurred.

The author would like to thank Major E. Roche-Kelly for his invaluable assistance in the preparation of this work.

This Guide has been compiled for 'quick access' to the more detailed entries that form the bulk of this book. Named sets have been listed as such, with cross-references to their appearance in larger boxes, or in different guise given in the main text. Entries in bold indicate illustrated items, and the entire Guide is in alphabetical (or numerical for numbered units) rather than by Corps or Regimental seniority.

2nd Dragoon Guards (The Queen's Bays)	44, 54, 250
2nd Dragoon (The Royal Scots Greys)	**32**, 41, **55**, 58, 59, **73**, 129, 131, 132, 246, 302, 309, 345, 1267, 1350, 1607, **1720**, 1721, 2036, 2119, 695A, 734A, 748A, 767A, 775A, 782A, 790A, 6B, 41B, 668B, 1344B, 55N, 65P, 6S, 26S, 35S, 42S, 53S, 61S, 63S, 67S, 69S, 146W, 166W
2nd Life Guards	**43**, **73**, 84, 129, 132, **7B**
3rd Hussars	29, 55, 2120
4th Queen's Own Hussars	8, **50**, 53
(Later 5th Iniskillings Dragoon Guards)	3, 85, 131, 1267, **2087**, 3B
5th (Princess Charlotte of Wales's) Dragoon Guards 6th (Carabiniers) Dragoon Guards 1685–1922, **106**	
6th Dragoons (The Iniskillings)	**108**
7th Dragoon Guards (Later 4th/7th)	127, 132
7th Queen's Own Hussars	**2075**
9th Queen's Royal Lancers	**24**, 29, 54
10th Royal Hussars	**215**
11th (Prince Albert's Own Hussars)	12, 21, 51, 129, 131, 132, **182**, 270, 1267, 1350, 10B, 48B, 647B, **883B**, **1345B**
12th (Prince of Wales's) Royal Lancers	128, 129, 132, 1267, **2076**, 2169, 1346B, **1347B**, 1348B, 1349B
13th Hussars	13, 87, **99**, 9B
16th Lancers (Later 16th/5th)	33, 51, 52, **55**, 12B
17th Lancers (Later 17th/21st)	**73**, **81**, 131, 13B
21st Lancers (Later 17th/21st)	**94**, 100, 251, 1407
Infantry Argyll and Sutherland Highlanders, The	15, 2063
Bedfordshire and Hertfordshire Regiment, The	1558
Black Watch, The	11, 22, 122, 449, 480, 2036, **2109**, **2111**, 2126, 2179
Border Regiment, The	1590

Other Arms and Services

Scales and Sizes

BRITAINS FIGURES featured in this guide were made in a number of scales but by far the greatest output was in the so-called 'standard' size of 2 ¹/₈ inches (54mm) which is still the most popular size among model soldier collectors and manufacturers. The scale is ³/₈ inch to 1 ft or 1:32.

However, Britains made figures in several other sizes and these are also indicated on the diagram so that this will, in fact, serve as a useful check for the category of any unknown figure. In some cases the size was related to popular model railway sizes, and the 54mm size 'standard' figure was, in fact, scaled to match gauge 1 model railways which were in vogue when Britains first introduced their figures. The Lilliput size, in turn, matched HO gauge railways which were appearing in the late 1930s when these small figures were first introduced. The diagram shows actual heights for infantrymen in each of the scales or series and can thus be used as a gauge (by placing the figure on the page) to check the scale and/or possible series of any unidentified figure. Bear in mind that headgear variations may cause an apparent discrepancy in measureable height.

Though Britains made a good number of figures in informal poses or motion poses, most of the soldiers were produced in formal drill or parade positions. The most usual are shown in the diagram below, but in addition to these some regimental figures were produced in kneeling, and prone firing positions. In the numerical listings, the descriptions, where applicable, correspond to the positions shown here unless otherwise stated. Officers were produced with swords drawn, sheathed or at the carry to correspond with the action of the men.

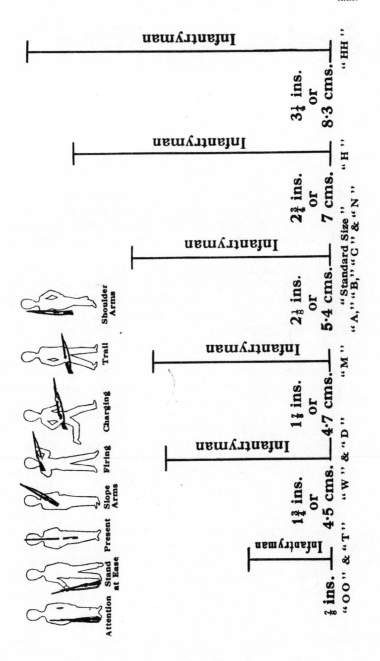

Infantryman

3¼ ins.
or
8·3 cms.
"HH"

Infantryman

2¾ ins.
or
7 cms.
"H"

Infantryman

2⅛ ins.
or
5·4 cms.
"Standard Size"
"A,""B,""C" & "N"

Infantryman

1⅞ ins.
or
4·7 cms.
"M"

Infantryman

1¾ ins.
or
4·5 cms.
"W" & "D"

Infantryman

⅞ ins.
"OO" & "T"

Attention   Stand   Present   Slope   Firing   Charging   Trail   Shoulder
             at Ease   Arms   Arms

Serial No: 1. (9206)
Title: 1st Life Guards.
Pieces in box: 5.
Issued: 1893.
1st change: 1899.
Remarks: Tin sword as originally
issued. Horses at trot. Replaced
by single piece moulding and
officer on trotting horse added in
1899. In catalogue until the end of
metal production. Renumbered in
1962, latterly with 4 figures in
box.

Serial No: 2. (9209)
Title: Royal Horse Guards (The
Blues).
Pieces in box: 5.
Issued: 1893.
1st change: 1899.
Remarks: Tin sword as originally
issued. Horses at trot. Altered to
all lead moulding in 1899. Later
issues of this and No. 1 had no
carbine. Other remarks as above.
See also 1343, 2085, 783A, 281B.

Serial No: 3.
Title: 5th (Princess Charlotte of
Wales's) Dragoon Guards.
Pieces in box: 5.
Issued: 1893.
1st changed: 1902.
Remarks: Tin sword as originally
issued. Horses at trot. Title
changed to 5th Royal Inniskilling
Dragoon Guards on
amalgamation of the Regiments in
1922. See also 2087.

Serial No: 4.
Title: 1st Life Guards.
Pieces in box: 5.
Issued: 1893.
Remarks: Gilt paint on figures
otherwise as No 1.

Serial No: 5.
Title: 1st Life Guards.
Pieces in box: 10.
Issued: 1893.
Remarks: Gilt paint, otherwise
basic figures as No 1.

Serial No: 6.
Title: Boer Cavalry.
Issued: 1899.
Remarks: Fixed arm, figures;
horses at trot. See also 26, 38, 104
and 105.

Serial No: 7.
Title: 7th Royal Fusiliers.
Pieces in box: 8.
Issues: 1893.
1st change: 1897.
2nd change: 1905.
Remarks: Marching at the slope,
with officer. Various detail and
painting changes in 1897 and
1905. See also 84, 251, 440, 448,
1323, 1394 and 8B.

Serial No: 8.
Title: 4th Queen's Own Hussars.
Pieces in box: 5.
Issued: 1896.
1st change: 1901.
2nd change: 1902.
Remarks: At gallop in Review
Order. Slight painting and detail
changes in 1901-1902. See also 50
and 53.

Serial No: 9.
Title: The Rifle Brigade.
Pieces in box: 8.
Issued: 1897.
1st change: 1902.
Remarks: Marching at the slope
with officer. Slightly altered in
1902.
See also 1618 and 2091.

Serial No: 10.
Title: The Salvation Army.
Pieces in box: 8.
Issued: 1903.
1st change: 1906.
Remarks: With marching officers,
band and Colours. Figures slightly
altered in 1906. First version had
open coats.

Serial No:11 *00*. (9135)
Title: The Black Watch (Royal
Highlanders).
Pieces in box: 8.
Issued: 1893.
1st change: 1903.
Remarks: Running, plug handed.
Officer same figure with plug
sword. Later changed to charging
figure. See also 22 and 2126.

Serial No: 12.
Title: 11th (Prince Albert's Own)
Hussars.
Pieces in box: 5.
Issued: 1893.
1st change: 1903.
Remarks: Fixed arm figure on
trotting horse as originally issued.
Horse moulding changed in 1903.
See also 182 and 270.

Serial No: 13.
Title: 13th Hussars.
Pieces in box: 5.
Issued: 1893.
1st change: 1903.
Remarks: Basic figure as No. 12.
Changed to proper trotting horse
1903. See also 87, 99, and 9B.

Serial No: 14.
Title: The Salvation Army.
Pieces in box: 8.
Issued: 1893-1910.
Remarks: Women officers,
timbrel band, and 'War Cry'. See
also 10.

Serial No: 15.
Title: Argyll and Sutherland
Highlanders.
Pieces in box: 8.
Issued: 1893.
Remarks: Charging figures.

Serial No: 16 *00*.
Title: East Kent Regt (The Buffs).
Pieces in box: 10.
Issued: 1894.
1st change: 1905.
2nd change: 1910.
Remarks: In 'On Guard' position.
Officer added 1905, bugler and
drummer 1910. Khaki Service
Dress version sold, 1901-02 under
same box bumber. See also 1582.

Serial No: 17 *00*.
Title: Somerset Light Infantry.
Pieces in box: 8.
Issued: 1894.
1st change: 1910.
Remarks: In Review Order with
Drummer Boy. Officer with
binoculars and bugler added in
1910. See also 40 and 1578.

Serial No: 18.
Title: Worcestershire Regt.
Pieces in box: 10.
Issued: 1894.
1st change: 1910.
Remarks: Review Order in On
Guard position, with officer and
drummer added in 1910. See also
22, 131 and 1598.

Serial No: 19.
Title: West India Regt.
Pieces in box: 9.
Issued: 1894.
1st change: 1910.
Remarks: Marching at the
shoulder. Mounted officer added
in 1910. See also 21.

Serial No: 20.
Title: Russian and Japanese
Infantry and Cavalry.
Pieces in box: 26.
Issued: 1904.
Remarks: With mounted officers.
Issued for Russo-Japanese war.

Serial No: 21.
Title: Display Box.
Pieces in box: 27.
Issued: 1893-1910.
1st change: 1918.
Remarks: With 1, 12, 16 and 19.
75 replaced 19 in 1918. Contains
Life Guards, 11th Hussars, West
India Regiment and Buffs.

Serial No: 22.
Title: Display Box.
Pieces in box: 27.
Issued: 1893-1910.
Remarks: Contains Royal Horse
Guards, 5th Lancers, Black
Watch, and Worcesters. As 2, 11,
18 and 23.

Serial No: 23.
Title: 5th Royal Irish Lancers.
Pieces in box: 5.
Issued: 1894.
1st change: 1903-1922.
Remarks: At the halt in Review
Order with officer. Known as
'bent leg' type. Detail alterations
to mouldings of horse from
1903-1922. See also 22. First
version had fixed arm.

Serial No: 24 *00*.
Title: 9th Queen's Royal Lancers.
Pieces in box: 5.
Issued 1894.
1st change: 1903.
Remarks: 'Bent leg' type as
originally issued. Officer turned in
saddle at the halt added in 1903.
See also 29 and 54.

Serial No: 25.
Title: Soldiers to Shoot.
Pieces in box: 4.
Issued: 1895.
Remarks: Kneeling firing. Regt.
not known. Hollow rifles with
spring at back.

Serial No: 26.
Title: Boer Infantry.
Pieces in box: 8.
Issued: 1899.
1st change: 1906.
2nd change: 1907.
Remarks: 1906 On Guard: 1907
Marching at the slope. See also 6,
38, 104 and 105. Also issued at
halt, sloped arms. All withdrawn
in 1912.

Serial No: **27** *00*.
Title: Band of the Line.
Pieces in box: 12.
Issued: 1895.
1st change: 1908.
2nd change: 1911.
Remarks: 1st version slot arms.
New figures added as above.
Replaced by 2114, 1950-54. See
also 1287, 1290 and 1458.

Serial No: 28 (9420).
Title: Mountain Battery R.A.
Pieces in box: 11.
Issued: 1895.
1st change: 1910.
2nd change: 1915.
Remarks: Contained 4 mules and
handlers, Officer, gun and limber
as 79 and ammunition. Various
detail changes in 1910 and 1915.
See also 29, 132, 1893 and 1903.
Earlier figure is the smaller type.

Serial No: 29.
Title: Display box.
Pieces in box: 41.
Issued: 1895.
Remarks: With Queen's Royal
West Surreys 'on guard' and at the
slope as 447. As boxes 1, 24 and
28.

Serial No: 30. (9137)
Title: Drums and Bugles of the
Line.
Pieces in box: 8.
Issued: 1895.
Remarks: Small figures. Similar
to 'B' size. See also 321.

Serial No: 31 *00*.
Title: 1st (The Royal) Dragoons.
Pieces in box: 5.
Issued: 1895.
1st change: 1902.
Remarks: Originally issued with
tin sword. Troopers on trotting
horses; Officer on rearing horse.
Mouldings slightly altered in
1902. See also 40, 129, 162,
696A, 735A, 750A, 754A, 766A,
777A, 791A and 59N.

Serial No. 32 *00*. (9210)
Title: The Royal Scots Greys (2nd
Dragoons).
Pieces in box: 5.
Issued: 1895.
1st change: 1902.
Remarks: At the walk with tin
sword and plug arm as originally
issued and no box number.
Altered to single piece moulding
in 1902. Later altered to moving
sword arm.

Serial No: 33.
Title: 16th Lancers.
Pieces in box: 5.
Issued: 1895.
Remarks: Set included officer. All
in Review Order at halt. As other
lancer regiments, with fixed arm in
first version.

Serial No: 34 *00*.
Title: Grenadier Guards.
Pieces in box: ?
Issued: 1895.
1st change: 1901.
2nd change: 1905.
Remarks: First issued standing
firing, not in the aiming position.
Altered to full aiming position in
1901. Officer and drummer added
in 1903.

Serial No: 35 *00* (9140).
Title: Royal Marine Artillery.
Pieces in box: 8.
Issued: 1895.
4th change: 1922.
Remarks: Fixed arms. Marching
at the slope. Same basic figure in
all sets but with rifle arm or gaiters
and painting altered on each
change. See also 97, 1284, 1288,
1291, 1610, 1619, 1620, 1622,
2071, 2115, 2127, 2153, 67B,
488B, 1021B, 1353B-1357B.

Serial No: 36 *00*. (9142)
Title: Royal Sussex Regt.
Pieces in box: 7.
Issued: 1895.
1st change: 1910.
Remarks: Fixed arm figures
marching at the slope in Review
Order. Mounted officer added in
1910.

Serial No: ·37 *00*.
Title: Band of the Coldstream Guards.
Pieces in box: 21.
Issued: 1895.
1st change: 1911.
Remarks: Slot arm band with
Bombardon and Drum Major.
Included in box 131. See also 93,
2108 and 2113. Other
instruments added later.

Serial No: 38.
Title: Dr Jameson and the South
African Mounted Police.
Pieces in box: 5.
Issued: 1895.
1st change: 1911.
Remarks: Fixed arm cavalry. Dr
Jameson figure with pistol. Title
changed to South African
Mounted Infantry in 1911. See
also 6, 26, 58, 15B, 1900-1901
and 1293.

Serial No: **39** *00* (9419)
Title: Royal Horse Artillery.
Pieces in box: 13.
Issued: 1895.
1st change: 1922.
Remarks: Issued in Review Order
with collar harness. Issued as 39A
when in khaki. Early version had
gunners seated on limber.
Changed to trace harness in 1922.

Serial No: 40.
Title: 1st (The Royal) Dragoons
and Somerset Light Infantry.
Pieces in box: 15.
Issued: 1893-1910.
Remarks: Both Regiments in
Review Order. See also 17, 31 and
1578.

Serial No: 41. (9310)
Title: Display set.
Pieces in box: 15.
Issued: 1893-1910.
Remarks: Scots Greys and
Grenadiers as 32 and 34.

Serial No. 42.
Title: Display Box.
Pieces in box: 12.
Issued: 1893-1910.
Remarks: Life Guards and Royal
Sussex. See also 1 and 36.

Serial No: **43** *00*.
Title: 2nd Life Guards.
Pieces in box: 5.
Issued: 1893-1910.
Remarks: 4 Troopers at the gallop
in Review Order with carbines in
the right hand. Trumpeter on
galloping horse in first version,
trotting in later one.

Serial No: 44.
Title: The Queen's Bays (2nd
Dragoon Guards).
Pieces in box: 5.
Issued: 1893-1910.
Remarks: In Review Order. 4
Troopers on galloping horses with
lances and a Trumpeter on a
trotting horse. Early version
trumpeter as set 43.

Serial No: 45.
Title: 3rd Madras Cavalry.
Pieces in box: 5.
Issued: 1893-1910.
Remarks: In light blue tunics with
trumpeter. See also 61, 64, 67 and
252.

Serial No: 46.
Title: 10th Bengal Lancers (*but
see below*).
Pieces in box: 5.
Issued: 1893-1910.
1st change: 1927.
Remarks: In brown coat.
Originally issued as 10th Bengal
Lancers until title change in 1927
to Hodson's Horse (4th Duke of
Cambridge's Own Lancers).

Serial No: 47. (9261)
Title: 1st Bengal Native Cavalry
(*but see below*).
Pieces in box: 5. Mtd.
Issued: 1893-1910.
Remarks: Title of set later
changed to 1st Bengal Lancers,
then Skinner's Horse, 1st Duke of
York's Own Cavalry. First issued
in brown kurta.

Serial No: 48. (9265)
Title: Egyptian Camel Corps.
Pieces in box: 6.
Issued: 1892-1910.
Remarks: Early version of camel
had wire tail. Removable riders.
See also 115-117, 123, 131, 918
and 68N.

Serial No: **49** *00*.
Title: South Australian Lancers.
Pieces in box: 5.
Issued: 1893-1910.
1st change: ?
Remarks: In spiked helmet at the
gallop. Small size with plug arms.
Earlier version had bush hats. See
also 1544, 1545, 2030 and 2031.

Serial No: 50. (9305)
Title: Display Box.
Pieces in box: 10.
Issued: 1893;1910.
Remarks: 1 and 8 combined.

Serial No: 51.
Title: 11th (Prince Albert's Own)
Hussars, 16th Lancers.
Pieces in box: 10. Mtd.
Issued: 1893-1910.
Remarks: As 33 and 51.

Serial No: 52.
Title: Display Box.
Pieces in box: 10.
Issued: 1893-1910.
Remarks: 2nd Life Guards
galloping, and 5th Lancers at halt.

Serial No: 53.
Title: Display set.
Pieces in box: 20.
Issued: 1893-1910.
Remarks: Containing Royal
Horse Guards, 4th Hussars and
Grenadier Guards. As 2, 8 and 34.

Serial No: 54.
Title: Display Box.
Pieces in box: 15.
Issued: 1893-1910.
Remarks: 1st Life Guards,
Queen's Bays, and 9th Lancers as
24 and 44.

Serial No: **55** *00*.
Title: Display Box.
Pieces in box: 15.
Issued: 1893-1910.
Remarks: Scots Greys, 3rd
Hussars and 16th Lancers as 13,
32 and 33.

Serial No: 56.
Title: Display Set.
Pieces in box: 15.
Issued: 1893-1910.
Remarks: Grenadier Guards and
Buffs as 16 and 34.

Serial No: 57.
Title: 1st King's Dragoon Guards.
Pieces in box: 12.
Issued: 1893-1910.
Remarks: 'B' size figures. See also
2074, 5B.

Serial No: 58.
Title: Display Set.
Pieces in box: ?
Issued: 1893-1910.
Remarks: 'B' size figures of Royal
Horse Guards, Scots Greys, and
Mounted Infantry as 2, 32 and
15B.

Serial No: 59.
Title: The Royal Scots Greys (2nd Dragoons).
Pieces in box: 10.
Issued: 1893-1910.
Remarks: Display box with officer.

Serial No: 60.
Title: 1st Bombay Lancers.
Pieces in box: 15.
Issued: 1893-1910.
Remarks: See also 66 and 68.

Serial No: 61.
Title: 3rd Madras Cavalry.
Pieces in box: 15.
Issued: 1893-1910.
Remarks: Troopers with swords. Officer included.

Serial No: 62.
Title: 1st Bengal Native Cavalry.
Pieces in box: 10.
Issued: 1893-1910.
Remarks: As 47 with same title and colour changes. Double size box. With swords.

Serial No: 63.
Title: 10th Bengal Lancers (*but see below*).
Pieces in box: 10.
Issued: 1893-1910.
Remarks: Title later changed (1927) to Hodson's Horse (4th Duke of Cambridge's Own Lancers). See also 46, 47, 62, 64 and 271.

Serial No: 64.
Title: 2nd Madras Lancers and 7th Bengal Native Infantry.
Pieces in box: 13.
Issued: 1893-1910.
1st change: ?
Remarks: Cavalry on galloping horse. Trumpeter's mount was different colour and position to the troopers. Infantry were at the trail. Later figures were at the slope with modern tunic.

Serial No: 65.
Title: Russian Cavalry and Infantry.
Pieces in box: 13.
Issued: 1904-1910.
Remarks: Cossacks and Infantry.

Serial No: 66. (9262)
Title: 1st Bombay Lancers (*but see below*).
Pieces in box: 5.
Issued: 1893-1910.
Remarks: Title later changed (1927) to 13th Duke of Connaught's Own Lancers. See also 60 and 68.

Serial No: 67.
Title: 1st Madras Native Infantry (*but see below*).
Pieces in box: 8.
Issued: 1893-1910.
1st change: 1929.
Remarks: Originally issued as marching at the trail in Review Order. Later changed to marching at the slope and title changed to Corps of Madras Pioneers.

Serial No: 68.
Title: 2nd Bombay Native Infantry.
Pieces in box: 8.
Issued: 1893-1910.
Remarks: Marching at the trail arms with officer.

Serial No: 69.
Title: Pipers of the Scots Guards.
Pieces in box: 7.
Issued: 1893-1910.
Remarks: See also 75 and 1722.

Serial No: 70.
Title: Scots Guards.
Pieces in box: 7.
Issued: 1893-1910.
Remarks: Running at the trail with officer on galloping horse.

Serial No: 71.
Title: Turkish Cavalry.
Pieces in box: 5

Serial No: **72** *00*.
Title: Life Guards of Waterloo
and Present Time.
Pieces in box: 12.
Issued: 1893-1910.
Remarks: This is catalogue title.
Actual box was issued for Jubilee
1897 with uniform of 1837 (60
years).

Serial No: **73** *00*.
Title: Display Box.
Pieces in box: 73.
Issued: 1893-1910.
Remarks: Box contained Welch
Fusiliers, Scots Greys, Gordon
Highlanders, 2nd Life Guards,
17th Lancers, R.F.A., with
General officer. See also 27, 32,
43, 74, 77, 81, 144 and 201.

Serial No: **74** *00*. (9144)
Title: Royal Welsh Fusiliers.
Pieces in box: 8.
Issued: 1893-1910.
Remarks: Marching at the slope
with officer and Goat mascot.

Serial No: **75** *00*. (9126)
Title: Scotts Guards.
Pieces in box: 8.
Issued: 1893-1910.
Remarks: Marching at the slope
with officer and piper. See also
2122.

Serial No: **76** *00*. (9136)
Title: Middlesex Regiment
Pieces in box: 8.
Issued: 1893-1910.
Remarks: Marching at the slope
with officer.

Serial No: **77** *00*. (9131).
Title: The Gordon Highlanders.
Pieces in box: 8.
Issued: 1893-1910.
Remarks: Marching at the slope in
Review Order with Slade Wallace
equipment. First release had two
pipers.

Serial No: **78** *00*.
Title: Royal Navy Bluejackets.
Pieces in box: 8.
Issued: 1893-1910.
Remarks: Running at the trail,
with Petty Officer.

Serial No: **79** *00*. (9455)
Title: Royal Navy Landing Party.
Pieces in box: 11.
Issued: 1893-1910.
Remarks: With Petty Officer as
78, 8 marching men, 3 part gun as
28. Small limber with opening
cover and shells. Men with holes in
hands to pull ropes.

Serial No: 80.
Title: Royal Navy Whitejackets.
Pieces in box: 8.
Issued: 1893-1910.
Remarks: Running at the trail
with Officer.

Serial No: **81** *00*.
Title: 17th (Duke of Cambridge's
Own) Lancers.
Pieces in box: 5.
Mtd/Officer/Tptr.
Issued: 1893-1910.
Remarks: In Foreign Service
Order. Troopers on galloping
horses, officer at the halt. Later
version was on trotting horses.

Serial No: **82** *00*.
Title: Colours and Pioneers of the
Scots Guards
Pieces in box: 8.
Issued: 1893-1910.
Remarks: Pioneers with axes,
Colour at the carry.

Serial No: **83** *00*.
Title: Middlesex Yeomanry.
Pieces in box: 5.
Issued: 1893-1910.
Remarks: Marching carrying
Carbines with officer. Officer on
rearing horse and men on trotting
horses.

Serial No: 84.
Title: 2nd Life Guards and 7th
Royal Fusiliers.
Pieces in box: 11.
Issued: 1893-1910.
Remarks: 'B' size figures.
Fusiliers at trail arms.

Serial No: 85.
Title: Display Set.
Pieces in box:
Issued: 1893-1910.
Remarks: Contained 3, 32, 75, 85
and 21B. 'B' size figures.

Serial No: 86.
Title: Lancashire Fusiliers.
Pieces in box: 14.
Issued: 1893-1910.
Remarks: 'B' size figures with
officer. See also 1559 and 17B.

Serial No: 87.
Title: 13th Hussars.
Pieces in box: 8.
Issued: 1893-1910.
Remarks: 'B' size figures with
officer.

Serial No: **88***00*.
Title: Seaforth Highlanders.
Pieces in box: 16.
Issued: 1893-1900.
1st change: 1903.
2nd change: 1912.
Remarks: 1st issued plug handed
running at the trail with two
pipers. Changed in 1903 to
charging figures and new piper
types added in 1912.

Serial No: 89.
Title: Queen's Own Cameron
Highlanders.
Pieces in box: 28.
Issued: 1893.
1st change: 1901.
Remarks: Box contained 7
standing, 10 lying, 9 kneeling, 2
pipers, 1 kneeling officer, 1
standing officer. Piper mouldings
changed in 1901.

Serial No: **90** *00*.
Title: Coldstream Guards.
Pieces in box: 27.
Issued: 1901.
Remarks: 3 positions firing.
Number later reduced.

Serial No: 91.
Title: U. S. Infantry.
Pieces in box: 8.
Issued: 1893-1910.
Remarks: In Federal Dress 'On
Guard' with officer.

Serial No: **92** *00*.
Title: Spanish Infantry.
Pieces in box: 8.
Issued: 1898.
1st change: 1914.
Remarks: Marching figures in
Review Order at the slope. Officer
added in 1914. See also 218.

Serial No: 93.
Title: Display Box.
Pieces in box: 71.
Issued: 1893-1910.
Remarks: With 2 Companies of
the Coldstream Guards as 90. 37
with Officer, Colours and
Pioneers.

Serial No: 94.
Title: 21st (Empress of India's)
Lancers.
Pieces in box: 5.
Issued: 1898.
Remarks: With officer all in
Active Service Dress with lance
and sun helmet on galloping
horse. Originally issued on a small
horse this was later changed to the
single ear type to be superseded by
a two eared version as casting
techniques improved.

Serial No: 95.
Title: Japanese Cavalry and
Infantry.
Pieces in box: 13.
Issued: 1904.
Remarks: With officer. All in
Review Order. Infantry charging.

Serial No: 96.
Title: York and Lancester Regt.
Pieces in box: ?
Issued: 1899.
1st change: 1913.
2nd change: 1920.
Remarks: Running at the trail in
Review Order. Various detail and
painting changes over the years.
See also 1567.

Serial No: 97.
Title: Royal Marine Light
Infantry.
Pieces in box: 8.
Issued: 1899.
1st change: 1913.
2nd change: 1922.
Remarks: Running at the trail
with officer, sword in hand. Slight
detail and painting alterations.
Reboxed as Royal Marines on
amalgamation of Regiment.

Serial No: 98.
Title: King's Royal Rifle Corps.
Issued: 1899.
1st change: 1913.
2nd change: 1920.
Remarks: Running at the trail
with officer. First version had
spiked helmets. All versions
issued in Review Order.
See also 2072 and 18N.

Serial No: **99** *00*.
Title: 13th Hussars.
Pieces in box: 5.
Issued: 1899.
1st change: 1903.
Remarks: with officer, trumpeter
and 4 troopers with sabres.
Originally issued on 'rocking
horse' replaced by trotting horse
in 1903.

Serial No: 100.
Title: 21st (Empress of India's)
Lancers.
Pieces in box: 5.
Issued: 1898.
1st change: 1903.
Remarks: In Review Order with
officer all on the small Britain's
horse. Altered to trotting horse
with trumpeter instead of officer
in 1903.

Serial No: **101** *00* (9406)
Title: Band of the Life Guards.
Pieces in box: 12.
Issued: 1899.
1st change: 1911.
Remarks: 1st version had slot, 2nd
version moving arms. Last
version, post 1947, had no sword.

Serial No: 102.
Title: Grenadier, Coldstream,
Irish and Scots Guards.
Pieces in box: 32.
Issued: 1901.
Remarks: With Officer on
galloping horse, Guardsmen at
attention, running at trail, sloped
arms, and half aim firing.

Serial No: 103.
Title: Band of the Royal Horse
Guards.
Pieces in box: 12.
Issued: 1899.
Remarks: Slotted arm figures.

Serial No: **104** *00*.
Title: City Imperial Volunteers.
Pieces in box: 10.
Issued: 1900.
1st change: 1907.
Remarks: 'On Guard' position in
Service Dress. Officer figure firing
pistol added in 1907. Also issued
was a C.I.V. Waggon with figures;
see illustration and sets 6, 26, 38
and 105.

Serial No: 105.
Title: Imperial Yeomanry.
Pieces in box: 5.
Issued: 1900.
Remarks: In Service Dress. See
also 6, 26, 38 and 104.

Serial No: **106** *00*.
Title: 6th (Carabiniers) Dragoon
Guards.
Pieces in box: 5.
Issued: 1898.
1st change: 1901.
Remarks: Original issue had
swords. This was changed for
carbines in 1901 although still
moulded with the weapon in its
bucket on the saddle. Officers'
horse was similar to early RHA
with both ears moulded as a single
piece on top of the head.

Serial No: 107.
Title: Irish Guards.
Pieces in box: 8.
Issued: 1893-1910.
Remarks: Marching at the slope.

Serial No: **108** *00*.
Title: 6th Dragoons (The
Inniskillings) 1689-1922.
Pieces in box: 5.
Issued: 1901-1906.
Remarks: On trotting horse in
khaki with tropical helmet.

Serial No: 109.
Title: Royal Dublin Fusiliers.
Pieces in box: 8.
Issued: 1901-1906.
Remarks: In khaki at the trail.
See also 19B.

Serial No: 110.
Title: Devonshire Regt.
Pieces in box: 8.
Issued: 1901.
Remarks: Marching at the slope in
tropical helmets and Service
Dress. See also 1593.

Serial No: 111.
Title: Grenadier Guards.
Pieces in box: 7.
Issued: 1893-1910.
Remarks: At attention with
mounted officer. 'Sway back'
horse at the halt. See also 2065
and 2113.

Serial No: 112.
Title: Seaforth Highlanders.
Pieces in box: 8.
Issued: 1910.
Remarks: Marching at the slope in
Review Order.

Serial No: **113** *00*.
Title: East Yorkshire Regt.
Pieces in box: 8.
Issued: 1910.
Remarks: At attention with
movable right arms and gaitered
legs. See also 1557.

Serial No: 114.
Title: Queen's Own Cameron
Highlanders.
Pieces in box: 8.
Issued: 1893-1910.
Remarks: Marching at slope in
tropical helmets. Khaki uniform.
First version had Slade Wallace
packs.

Serial No: 115. (9264)
Title: Egyptian Cavalry.
Pieces in box: 5.
Issued: 1901-1906.
Remarks: Lancer figures with
officer. See also 48, 116, 117 and
68N.

Serial No: **116** *00*.
Title: Soudanese Infantry.
Pieces in box: 8.
Issued: 1901-1906.
Remarks: Marching at the trail.
See also 48, 115 and 117.

Serial No: 117.
Title: Egyptian Infantry.
Pieces in box: 8.
Issued: 1901.
Remarks: At attention. See also
48, 115, 116 and 68N. With
officer in later issues.

Serial No: 118.
Title: The Gordon Highlanders.
Pieces in box: 10.
Issued: 1893-1910.
Remarks: Lying firing with legs
together, and officer. See also
157, 1325, 60B and 63B.

Serial No: 119.
Title: Gloucestershire Regt.
Pieces in box: 10.
Issued: 1893-1910.
Remarks: Standing Firing in khaki
Service Dress and tropical
helmets. See also 1592 and 2089.

Serial No: 120. (9123)
Title: Coldstream Guards.
Pieces in box: 10.
Issued: 1893-1910.
Remarks: Kneeling firing and
kneeling officer with binoculars.
See also 1327.

Serial No: 121.
Title: Queen's Royal West Surrey R
Pieces in box: 10, later 8.
Issued: 1893-1910.
Remarks: Standing firing with
officer holding binoculars. See
also 29, 447, 1571 and 2086.

Serial No: 122.
Title: The Black Watch (Royal
Highlanders).
Pieces in box: 8.
Issued: 1901-1906.
Remarks: 1 officer with binoculars,
7 men standing firing in scarlet
coats with tropical helmet.

Serial No: 123.
Title: Bikanir Camel Corps.
Pieces in box: 3.
Issued: 1901-1906.
Remarks: British Indian Empire
Regiment. Though two figures,
riders were sometimes soldered
on. See also 48, 131, 918 and 68N.

Serial No: 124.
Title: Irish Guards.
Pieces in box: 10, then 8.
Issued: 1901.
Remarks: Lying firing with
officer.

Serial No: 125.
Title: Royal Horse Artillery.
Pieces in box: 13.
Issued: 1901.
Remarks: 'B' size figures in
Review Order with separate
mounted officer and four
outriders.

Serial No: 126.
Title: Royal Horse Artillery.
Pieces in box: 13.
Issued: 1901.
Remarks: 'B' size figures in Active
Service Dress with separate
mounted officer and four
outriders.

Serial No: 127.
Title: 7th Dragoon Guards.
Pieces in box: 5.
Issued: 1902.
1st change: 1922.
Remarks: With officer. All in Review Order. Box title changed in 1922 to 4th/7th on amalgamation of two regiments. See also 132, 1630 and 1631.

Serial No: 128.
Title: 12th (Prince of Wales's) Royal Lancers.
Pieces in box: 5.
Issued: 1903.
Remarks: On trotting horse with lance slung; officer on white horse with sword.

Serial No: 129.
Title: Display Box.
Pieces in box: Not known.
Issued: 1901-1905.
Remarks: Included 11th Hussars, 2nd Life Guards, 12th Lancers, Royal Scots Greys, 1st Dragoons. See also 12, 31, 32, 43 and 128.

Serial No: 130.
Title: Display Set.
Pieces in box: 118.
Issued: 1901-1905.
Remarks: With 82 plus Piper Drummer and Bugles. See also 69 and 1722.

Serial No: 131.
Title: Display Set.
Pieces in box: 275.
Issued: 1906.
Remarks: Contained 2, 3, 12, 18, 28, 32, 37, 39, 43, 75, 81, 137, 144, 145, 201, 1264, 1325 and British Camel Corps.

Serial No: 132.
Title: Display set.
Pieces in box: 167.
Issued: 1906.
Remarks: R.F.A., Scots Greys, 11th Hussars, 12th Lancers, 2nd Life Guards, 7th Dragoon Guards, Band of the Line, Seaforths, Welch Fusiliers, Coldstream Guards, Buffs, Mule Battery R.A., R.A.M.C. & General.

Serial No: 133.
Title: Russian Infantry.
Pieces in box: 8.
Issued: 1904.
Remarks: In Review Order marching at the slope in the first version and at the trail in later ones.

Serial No: 134.
Title: Japanese Infantry.
Pieces in box: 8.
Issued: 1904.
Remarks: In Review Order, charging figures. See also 20, 135, 1363, 11B and 25B.

Serial No: 135.
Title: Japanese Cavalry.
Pieces in box: 5.
Issued: 1904.
Remarks: With officer, troopers with carbines. See also 20, 134, 1367, 11B and 25B.

Serial No: 136. (9273)
Title: Russian Cavalry.
Pieces in box: 5.
Issued: 1904.
Remarks: Cossacks with lances and officer on charging horse. See also 20, 65, 133, 2027, 2028, 2032, 2144, 2187, 14B, 26B, 151-152P and 285.

Serial No: **137** *00*.
Title: Royal Army Medical Corps.
Pieces in box: 24.
Issued: 1901-1905.
Remarks: With Nurses, Doctors, Wounded, Stretchers and Bearers in Review Order. See also 320, 1300, 1723 and 122P.

Serial No: 138. (9266)
Title: French Cuirassiers.
Pieces in box: 5.
Issued: 1905.
Remarks: In Review Order with officer ex Paris Office figures.

Serial No: **139** *00*.
Title: Chasseurs à Cheval.
Pieces in box: 5 Mtd.
Issued: 1901.
Remarks: In Review Order with Carbines and officer.

Serial No: 140.
Title: French Dragoons.
Pieces in box: 5.
Issued: 1901.
Remarks: In Review Order with officer and detachable carbines plugged in their backs.

Serial No: **141** *00*.
Title: French Infanterie de Ligne.
Pieces in box: 8.
Issued: 1901.
Remarks: Marching at the slope in Review Order with officer. Early figure was without gaiters.

Serial No: **142** *00*. (9166)
Title: French Zouaves.
Pieces in box: 8.
Issued: 1901.
Remarks: Charging figures. Walking officer added later. See also 191 and 1360.

Serial No: **143** *00*.
Title: French Navy Matelots.
Pieces in box: 8.
Issued: 1901.
Remarks: Running at trail and marching at the slope.

Serial No: 144.
Title: Royal Field Artillery.
Pieces in box: 9.
Issued: 1905.
1st change: 1914.
Remarks: Walking in Review Order with separate officer. Khaki set with peaked caps also issued under same number. In 1914 mouldings changed from collar to breast harness. Gunners seated on gun and limber.

Serial No: 145.
Title: R.A.M.C. Ambulance Waggon.
Pieces in box: 7.
Issued: 1905.
Remarks: Issued in both Review Order and Service Dress with 2 seated figures.

Serial No: **146** *00*.
Title: Royal Army Service Corps Waggon (Review).
Pieces in box: 4.
Issued: 1905.
1st change: 1905.
Remarks: Two horse team at walk with two men seated on waggon. First issued in Review Order and then in Khaki Service Dress with peaked caps.

Serial No: **147** *00*.
Title: Zulus of Africa.
Pieces in box: 8.
Issued: 1908.
Remarks: Last round base figure. All figures running with assegai and shield and club.

Serial No: 148.
Title: Patent Display.
Pieces in box: 13.
Issued: 1905-1908.
Remarks: King's Own Royal
Lancaster Regt. in white helmets.
Set had 1 Mtd Officer, 1 Bugler, 7
men running, 3 marching at slope,
2 gunners and a small artillery
piece.

Serial No: 149.
Title: American Display Tray.
Pieces in box: 18.
Issued: 1907.
As box 148 but in blue uniforms
and kepi. See also 1572.

Serial No: 150. (9189)
Title: North American Indians.
Pieces in box: 8.
Issued: 1907.
Remarks: 4 Braves on foot with
rifles 'at the ready' and 3 Chiefs in
same position and 1 Chieftain.

Serial No: 151 00.
Title: Royal Naval Reserve.
Pieces in box: 8.
Issued: 1907.
Remarks: Shoulder arms with
bearded Petty Officer. PO first
issued with moving right arm later
changed for fixed arm.

Serial No: 152. (9289)
Title: North American Indians.
Pieces in box: 5.
Issued: 1905-1908.
Remarks: On horse back with
rifles and tomahawks.

Serial No: 153.
Title: Prussian Hussars.
Pieces in box: 5.
Issued: 1907.
Remarks: In Review Order with
officer. See also 154, 432 and
1895.

Serial No: 154.
Title: Prussian Infantry.
Pieces in box: 8.
Issued: 1908.
Remarks: Slant based figures in
Review Order with officer. Figure
changed later.

Serial No: 155.
Title: Railway Station Staff.
Pieces in box: 12.
Issued: 1905-1908.
Remarks: Included luggage. See
also 168, 800, 802, 812 and 816.

Serial No: 156.
Title: Royal Irish Regt.
Pieces in box: 10.
Issued: 1905-1908.
Remarks: Standing, kneeling and
lying firing.

Serial No: 157.
Title: The Gordon Highlanders.
Pieces in box: 10.
Issued: 1907.
Remarks: In white helmets, 3
positions firing. See also 118,
1325, 61B-63B.

Serial No: 158 00.
Title: Railway Station Staff and
Passengers.
Pieces in box: 25.
Issued: 1905-1908.
Remarks: 800 to 816.

Serial No: 159.
Title: Yeomanry T.A.
Pieces in box: 5.
Issued: 1908.
Remarks: Mounted figures with
officer all in Service Dress with
peaked caps and drawn swords.

Serial No: 160.
Title: Territorial Army.
Pieces in box: 7 plus Officer.
Issued: 1903.
Remarks: Marching at the trail in
peak caps and puttees. See also
304 and 311.

Serial No: 161.
Title: Boy Scouts with Scoutmaster.
Pieces in box: 9.
Issued: 1901.
Remarks: Walking with stick in right hand.

Serial No: 162.
Title: Boy Scout Camp.
Pieces in box: 23.
Issued: 1893-1910.
Remarks: With Scoutmaster, scouts, tree with gate, and scouts with hook hand to climb tree.

Serial No: 163.
Title: Boy Scout Signallers.
Pieces in box: 5.
Issued: 1910-1912.
Remarks: 'With moving flags'. Early figures had arms fixed.

Serial No: **164** *00*. (9291)
Title: Arabs.
Pieces in box: 5.
Issued: 1911.
Remarks: 3 figures with rifles, 2 with scimitars. All mounted on galloping horse with swivelling weapon arm.

Serial No: **165** *00*.
Title: Italian Cavalry.
Pieces in box: 5.
Issued: 1910.
Remarks: In Review Order with officer all at the halt. See also 1368.

Serial No: 166.
Title: Italian Infantry.
Pieces in box: 8.
Issued: 1910.
Remarks: Marching at the slope in Review Order with officer. See also 169, 1435-1438.

Serial No: 167.
Title: Turkish Infantry.
Pieces in box: 8.
Issued: 1910.
Remarks: In Review Order; 'On Guard' position.

Serial No: 168.
Title: Civilians.
Pieces in box: 8.
Issued: 1910.
Remarks: All in distinctive Edwardian clothes. See also 641, 645, 779, 780, 781, 1426, 1513, 1514, LB536, LB538-543, LB548, LV617 and Farm Series in general.

Serial No: **169** *00*.
Title: The Bersaglieri.
Pieces in box: 8.
Issued: 1910.
Remarks: Marching with slung rifles in Review Order. See also 1368.

Serial No: 170.
Title: Greek Cavalry.
Pieces in box: 5. Mtd.
Issued: 1910.
Remarks: At the trot in Review Order with officer and carrying carbines.

Serial No: 171.
Title: Greek Infantry.
Pieces in box: 8.
Issued: 1910.
Remarks: Running at the trail in Review Order with officer. See also 170, 196 and 2176.

Serial No: 172.
Title: Bulgarian Infantry.
Pieces in box: 8.
Issued: 1910.
Remarks: Marching at the trail with officer.

Serial No: 173.
Title: Serbian Infantry.
Pieces in box: 8.
Issued: 1910.
Remarks: Charging figures.

Serial No: **174** *00*.
Title: Montenegrin Infantry.
Pieces in box: 8.
Issued: 1910.
Remarks: Marching at the slope and trail with officer.

LEFT TO RIGHT   No. 116, No. 225 (three soldiers), No. 116,
No. 117, rare white officer for No. 225 issued in special sets,
No. 117, Hut from No. 188.

TOP   No. 2. No. 47 New and Old, 1 and 2 Skinners Horse,
3 and 4 1st Bengal Cavalry (Troopers with swords).

BOTTOM   Left to Right, 1856 1850 196 (Pre 1940), 196
(Post 1947), 219 1st version, 2035.

TOP   Japanese Cavalry and Infantry, Sets 134, 135, 95. Dark Blue same as Light Blue but only issued in small numbers. Heads indicate age, smallest being the oldest, 4th from left.

BOTTOM   3 Serial No. 172, 174 two versions, 178, 92 last version, 177, 166.

TOP   Special issued with no serial numbers. British Infantry
(Paris Office), Australian Infantry. No. 16 Buffs (figure that
many variations come from), thought to be also No. 16 but with
Tropical Helmet, Serial No. 104, Serial No. 26 (version).

BOTTOM   1 and 2 Variation painted for the Coronation
1911, 18N 122 1st version officer with smooth helmet, 11
Britain's version of an officer, charging with highlander with
gold collar, British Infantry (Paris office) using the chauffer
158.

TOP   Colour Bearers, two examples of last version No 14.,
2120, 182 (early version), back painting dropped in later
versions.

BOTTOM Sample of figures made for sale at Madame
Tussaud's Wax Works.

TOP   Band-master from last version 101, two figures from Set No. 72 (first issued without serial number for Diamond Jubilee 1897), Band-master for Set 1720 (Lyons Corner House display).

BOTTOM   587, 819R 801b last version passenger, 1R porter and Station-master all from last version 1R, 607 (Guide Mistress), 558.

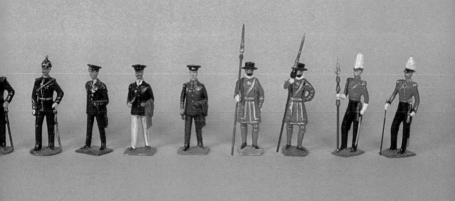

TOP   Scots Grey Drummer Pre 1947 with arms fixed. No. 1721, 1720, Queen's Colour Bearer Black Watch No. 2111, Officer Gordon Highlander 8458.

BOTTOM   RAMC Colonel 137, Doctor 137, three issues using same figure 1911, 158, 1081B, Naval Commodore, Yachtsman, Air Commodore, 1475, 1257, 2149, 1257 (officer).

Flight Sergeant and Officer Set 2011, Monoplane and pilot
No. 433, Pilot in Sidcot suit 333 and 66B, Pilot behind plane
in full flying suit No. 1894 and 1054B.

Serial No: 175.
Title: Austrian Lancers.
Pieces in box: 5. Mtd/Officer.
Issued: 1910.
Remarks: At walk with officer and
trumpeter.

Serial No: 176.
Title: Austrian Dragoons.
Pieces in box: 5.
Issued: 1910.
Remarks: At trot with officer and
trumpeter.

Serial No: 177.
Title: Austrian Infantry of the Line.
Pieces in box: 8.
Issued: 1910.
Remarks: Slant based; marching
at the slope with officer. Later
figure had no equipment.

Serial No: 178.
Title: Austrian Foot Guards.
Pieces in box: 8.
Issued: 1910-1912.
Remarks: Slant based figures;
marching at the slope with officer.

Serial No: 179. (9288)
Title: Cowboys.
Pieces in box: 5.
Issued: 1910-1912.
Remarks: Mounted on trotting
horse with pistol and lassoo.

Serial No: 180.
Title: Boy Scout Display.
Pieces in box: 22.
Issued: 1910-1912.
Remarks: With Scoutmaster,
Scouts, Signallers, trek carts and
ladders. See also 524, 527, 7F.

Serial No: 181.
Title: Boy Scout Encampment.
Pieces in box: 44.
Issued: 1911.
Remarks: Double box with all
scouting types.

Serial No: **182** *00*. (9114)
Title: 11th (Prince Albert's Own)
Hussars.
Pieces in box: 8.
Issued: 1913.
Remarks: 4 standing men with
mobile right arms and 4 horses.
See also 12 and 270.

Serial No: 183 (9188).
Title: Cowboys.
Pieces in box: 8.
Issued: 1912.
Remarks: 4 walking with rifles in
right hand, 4 walking with right
hand on holstered pistol.

Serial No: 184.
Title: Cowboys.
Pieces in box: 15.
Issued: 1911.
Remarks: Figures as 179 and 183
plus trees 521 etc.

Serial No: 185.
Title: Wild West Display.
Pieces in box: 30.
Issued: 1911.
Remarks: 150, 152 and 184
combined.

Serial No: 186.
Title: Mexican Infantry.
Pieces in box: 8.
Issued: 1912.
Remarks: Sub titled 'Rurales De
La Federacion'. Marching with
slung rifles in Review Order with
officer.

Serial No: **187** *00*.
Title: Arabs.
Pieces in box: 8.
Issued: 1914.
Remarks: Walking with musket
over left shoulder.

Serial No: **188**00.
Title: Zulu Kraals.
Pieces in box: 11.
Issued: 1912-1918.
Remarks: Scenic background, 2
Metal Beehive huts, 6 running
Zulus as 147, 1 coconut palm as
919, 1 date palm cluster as 920.
Later set had only 1 hut, 1 palm
and had monoplane as 433. See
also 704A, 725A and 21N.

Serial No: 189.
Title: Belgian Infantry.
Pieces in box: 8.
Issued: 1914.
Remarks: On guard position in
Review Order.

Serial No: **190** 00.
Title: Belgian Cavalry.
Pieces in box: 5.
Issued: 1914.
Remarks: 2nd Chasseurs Regt. at
halt in Review Order with officer
on trotting horse.
See also 1358, 1380 and 135P.

Serial No: **191** 00.
Title: French Turcos.
Pieces in box: 8.
Issued: 1914.
Remarks: As 142. See also 1388.

Serial No: 192.
Title: French Infanterie de Ligne.
Pieces in box: 8.
Issued: 1916.
Remarks: Marching at the slope in
steel helmets with officer.

Serial No: **193** 00.
Title: Arabs.
Pieces in box: 6 Mtd.
Issued: 1912-1918.
Remarks: on camels with musket
at the trail on swivelling arm.

Serial No:**194** 00.
Title: British Army Machine-gun
Section.
Pieces in box: 8.
Issued: 1912-1918.
Remarks: Lying position in
Service Dress with Vickers
machine-gun on tripod.

Serial No: 195.
Title: Infantry of the Line,
Pieces in box: 8.
Issued: Probably 1918.
Remarks: In steel helmets at the
trail with officer.

Serial No: **196** 00. (9170)
Title: Greek Infantry.
Pieces in box: 8.
Issued: 1912-1918.
Remarks: The Evzones in Review
Order marching at the slope.
Early set in scarlet. Last set in
Winter Blue.

Serial No: 197.
Title: 1st K.G.O. Ghurka Rifles.
Pieces in box: 8.
Issued: 1918.
Remarks: Subtitled 'The Malaun
Regiment'. Marching at the trail in
Review Order.

Serial No: **198** 00.
Title: Machine-gun Section.
Pieces in box: 12.
Issued: 1912-1918.
1st change: 1914.
Remarks: In sitting position
wearing Service Dress with
detachable Maxim. Changed to
Vickers machine-gun in 1914.

Serial No: 199.
Title: Machine Gun Corps.
Pieces in box: 3.
Issued: 1914-1918.
Remarks: Motor-cycle with
Vickers machine-gun in side car. 2
man crew with gunner removable.

Serial No: 200.
Title: Dispatch Riders.
Pieces in box: 4.
Issued: 1912-1918.
Remarks: On motor-cycles.

Serial No: 201.
Title: Officers of the General
Staff.
Pieces in box: 4. Mtd.
Issued: 1912-1918.
Remarks: All mounted in Review
Order with cocked hat; 2 on
walking horses and 2 at the halt
with binoculars. See also 73, 131,
132, 1907 and 1908.

Serial No: 202 00.
Title: Togoland Warriors.
Pieces in box: 8.
Issued: 1912-1918.
Remarks: Standing with nocked
arrow and strung bow.

Serial No: 203 00 and 204 00.
Title: Royal Engineers Pontoon
Section.
Pieces in box: 8.
Issued: 1912-1918.
Remarks: Four horse team with
203 in Review Order; 204 in
Service Dress with peaked caps.
Planks on pontoon were stitched
together. See also 1254, 1330 and
1331.

Serial No: 205 00.
Title: Coldstream Guards.
Pieces in box: 8.
Issued:
Remarks: At 'Present Arms' with
feet in correct position unlike 206.

Serial No: 206 00.
Title: Royal Warwickshire Regt.
Pieces in box: 8.
Issued: 1912-1918.
Remarks: As 205 at 'Present
Arms' but feet in wrong position.

Serial No: 207 00.
Title: Officers and Petty Officers
of the Royal Navy.
Pieces in box: 8.
Issued: 1912-1918.
Remarks: Midshipmen, Admiral
and Petty Officers.

Serial No: 208. (9389)
Title: North American Indians.
Pieces in box: 13.
Issued: 1912-1918.
Remarks: Foot and mounted
figures with Chieftain. See also
150, 152 and 272.

Serial No: 209. (9388)
Title: Cowboys.
Pieces in box: 13.
Issued: 1912-1918.
Remarks: With lassoos, rifles and
pistols as 179 and 183.

Serial No: 210.
Title: North American Indians.
Pieces in box: 15.
Issued: 1912-1918.
Remarks: Mounted, and on foot,
with trees as 521 etc.

Serial No: 211.
Title: 18 inch Howitzer No. 2.
Pieces in box: 13.
Issued: 1912-1918.
Remarks: Pulled by 10 horse team
and with lead shells included.

Serial No: 212 00. (9145)
Title: Royal Scots.
Pieces in box: 8.
Issued: 1912-1918.
Remarks: Marching at the slope in
Review Order with new type rifle
arm. See also 1267, 1324 and
1350.

Serial No: 213 00.
Title: Highland Light Infantry.
Pieces in box: 8.
Issued 1912-1918.
Remarks: Marching at the slope
with new rifle arm as 212.

Serial No: 214.
Title: Royal Canadian Mounted
Police.
Pieces in box: 8.
Issued: 1912-1913.
Remarks: Marching at the slope in
Winter Dress.

Serial No: 215.
Title: French Infanterie de Ligne.
Pieces in box: 14.
Issued: 1912-1918.
Remarks: 3 positions firing,
machine gunners and officer.

Serial No: **216** *00*.
Title: Argentine Infantry.
Pieces in box: 8.
Issued: 1912-1918.
Remarks: Marching at the slope in
Review Order.

Serial No: **217** *00*.
Title: Argentine Cavalry.
Pieces in box: 5.
Issued: 1912-1918.
Remarks: Granaderos a Caballo
in Review Order with lance arm
on trotting horse.

Serial No: **218** *00*.
Title: Spanish Cavalry.
Pieces in box: 5.
Issued: 1912-1918.
Remarks: Hussars with officer on
walking horse. See also 92.

Serial No: **219** *00*.
Title: Argentine Cadet Military
School.
Pieces in box: 8.
Issued: 1912-1918.
Remarks: Marching at the slope.

Serial No: **220** *00*.
Title: Uruguayan Cavalry.
Pieces in box: 5.
Issued: 1912-1918.
Remarks: See also 221-222 and
2051.

Serial No: 221.
Title: Uruguayan Cadets.
Pieces in box: 8.
Issued: 1912-1918.
Remarks: Marching at the slope
with officer. See also 2051.

Serial No: **222** *00*.
Title: Uruguayan Infantry.
Pieces in box: 8.
Issued: 1912-1918.
Remarks: Marching at the slope
with officer. See also 220-221 and
2051.

Serial No: **223** *00*.
Title: Arabs.
Pieces in box: 13.
Issued: 1912-1918.
Remarks: Figures from boxes 164
and 187.

Serial No: **224** *00*. (9491)
Title: Arabs.
Pieces in box: 11.
Issued: 1912-1918.
Remarks: 4 foot figures, 2
mounted on horses, 2 on camels, 2
date palm clusters as 920, 1 single
palm tree as 919.

Serial No: **225** *00*.
Title: King's African Rifles.
Pieces in box: 8.
Issued: 1924.
Remarks: Marching at the slope in
shorts and fez.

Serial No: 226.
Title: U.S. West Point Cadets.
Pieces in box: 8.
Issued: 1912-1918.
Remarks: Marching at the slope in
Winter Dress. All grey uniform.

Serial No: 227.
Title: U.S. Infantry.
Pieces in box: 8.
Issued: 1912-1918.
Remarks: Marching at the slope in
Service Dress with officer.

Serial No: **228** *00*. (9182)
Title: U.S. Marines.
Pieces in box: 8.
Issued: 1912-1918.
Remarks: Marching at the slope in blue uniform. Early figures had blue top to cap.

Serial No: 229.
Title: U.S. Cavalry.
Pieces in box: 5.
Issued: 1912-1918.
Remarks: In Service Dress on walking horse.

Serial No: 230.
Title: U.S. Sailors.
Pieces in box: 8.
Issued: 1912-1918.
Remarks: Bluejackets marching at the slope.

Serial No: 231.
Title: U.S. Infantry and West Point Cadets.
Pieces in box: 29.
Issued: 1912-1918.
Remarks: See also 91, 226 and 227.

Serial No: 232. (9381)
Title: Infantry, Marines and West Point Cadets.
Pieces in box: 24.
Issued: 1912-1914.
Remarks: See also 91, 226-228.

Serial No: 233.
Title: U.S. Infantry, Cavalry, Marines and West Point Cadets.
Pieces in box: 29.
Issued: 1912-1918.
Remarks: See also 91, 226-229.

Serial No: 234 (9655)
Title: 'The Meet'.
Pieces in box: 18.
Issued: 1925-1929.
Remarks: With 3 × 608, 609, 611 2 × 612, 2 × 613, 614.

Serial No: 235.
Title: 'Full Cry'.
Pieces in box: 20.
Issued: 1925-1929.
Remarks: With 4× 610, 3 × 611, 12 ×615, 616.

Serial No: 236.
Title: Hunting Display.
Pieces in box: 38.
Issued: 1925-1929.
Remarks: Combination of boxes 234 and 235.

Serial No: 237.
Title: Racing Colours.
Pieces in box: 12.
Issued: 1925-1929.
Remarks: 1 each of 1480-1485.

Serial No: 238.
Title: U.S.A. Civilians – Girl Scouts.
Pieces in box: 8.
Issued: 1925-29.
Remarks: See also 289, 293, 607 and 1332.

Serial No: 239.
Title: Motor Police and Road Signs.
Pieces in box: ?
Issued: 1925-1929.
Remarks: See also 319, 621, 659, 775, 776, 808, 824, 1413, 1427, 1430, 1477, 1511, 1792, 149P and LB 550.

Serial N: **240** *00*.
Title: R.A.F. Personnel.
Pieces in box: 8.
Issued: 1925-1929.
Remarks: Aircraftsmen figures. See also 433, 434, 1906.

Serial No: 241.
Title: Chinese Infantry.
Pieces in box: 8.
Issued: 1925.
Remarks: 'Boxers' with sword.

Serial No: 242.
Title: U.S. Infantry.
Pieces in box: 7.
Issued: 1925-1929.
Remarks: Marching at the slope
with mounted officer. See also 227.

Serial No: 243.
Title: Not Known.

Serial No: 244.
Title: North American Indians.
Pieces in box: 7.
Issued: 1925-1929.
Remarks: Mounted and on foot
with Chieftain as 150 and 152.

Serial No: 245.
Title: Cowboys.
Pieces in box: 7.
Issued: 1925-1929.
Remarks: 3 figures from 179, 2 of
each type from 183.

Serial No: 246.
Title: Display Set.
Pieces in box: 7.
Issued: 1893-1910.
Remarks: Royal Scots Greys and
Scots Guards. As 32 and 75.

Serial No: 247.
Title: Arabs.
Pieces in box: 7.
Issued: 1925-1929.
Remarks: Mounted and on foot.

Serial No: 248.
Titel: Display Box.
Pieces in box: 7.
Issued: 1929.
Remarks: Life Guards and
Middlesex Regt. as 1 and 76.

Serial No: 249.
Title: Modern Army British
Infantry and Cavalry.
Pieces in box: 7.
Issued: 1925-1929.
Remarks: In Service Dress.

Serial No: 250.
Title: Display Set.
Pieces in box: 7.
Issued: 1925-1929.
Remarks: Guardsmen standing
firing; 1 trumpeter on trotting
horse and 2 Troopers with lances
on galloping horses from Queen's
Bays.

Serial No: 251.
Title: 21st (Empress of India's
Lancers) and Royal Fusiliers.
Pieces in box: 7.
Issued: 1925-1929.
Remarks: See also 7, 84, 94, 100,
440, 448, 1323, 1394, 1407 and 8B

Serial No: 252.
Title: 3rd Madras Cavalry and 1st
Madras Native Infantry.
Pieces in box: 7.
Issued: 1925-1929.
Remarks: Cavalry as box 45, 1st
Madras marching at the trail in
Review Order. See also 45, 61, 64
and 67.

Serial No: 253.
Title: Welsh Guards.
Pieces in box: 9.
Issued: 1925-1929.
Remarks: Marching at the slope
with mounted officer. Basic
Guards figure. See also 329, 2083
and 2108.

Serial No: 254.
Title: Royal Navy Bluejackets and
Whitejackets.
Pieces in box: 9.
Issued: 1912-1918.
Remarks: At Shoulder Arms with
Petty Officer, all as 151.

Serial No: 255.
Title: Green Howards.
Pieces in box: 9.
Issued: 1925-1929.
Remarks: Officer with Colours,
drummer and 7 men all in Review
Order. See also 1595.

Serial No: 256.
Title: Cowboys.
Pieces in box: 17.
Issued: 1925-1929.
Remarks: Figures from 179 and 183.

Serial No: 257.
Title: North American Indians.
Pieces in box: 17.
Issued: 1925-1929.
Remarks: Mounted and on foot.

Serial No: 258.
Title: Modern Army British
Infantry.
Pieces in box: 8.
Issued: 1925-1929.
Remarks: In khaki wearing
gasmasks. Weapons at the trail.

Serial No: 259.
Title: U.S. West Point Cadets.
Pieces in box: 8.
Issued: 1925-1929.
Remarks: See also 226 and 299.

Serial No: 260.
Title: U.S. Infantry Squad.
Pieces in box: 16.
Issued: 1928-1929.
Remarks: See also 264.

Serial No: 261.
Title: U.S. Marines.
Pieces in box: 16.
Issued: 1928-1929.
Remarks: Marching at the slope in
Blue uniforms. See also 228.

Serial No: 262.
Title: U.S. Cavalry.
Pieces in box: 5.
Issued: 1928-1929.
Remarks: With officer. See also
229.

Serial No: 263.
Title: U.S. West Point Cadets.
Pieces in box: 24.
Issued: 1928-1929.
Remarks: See also 299.

Serial No: 264.
Title: U.S. Infantry Squad.
Pieces in box: 24.
Issued: 1928-1929.
Remarks: See also 260.

Serial No: 265.
Title: U.S. Marines.
Pieces in box: 24.
Issued: 1929-1929.
Remarks: Bluejackets and
Whitejackets marching at the
slope with officers. See also 228,
261 and 399.

Serial No: 266.
Title: U.S. Cavalry.
Pieces in box: 15.
Issued: 1928-1929.
Remarks: In slouch hats. See also
229 and 276.

Serial No: 267. (9380)
Title: U.S. Infantry and Cavalry.
Pieces in box: 13.
Issued: 1928-1929.
Remarks: In Service Dress as 227
and 229.

Serial No: 268.
Title: U.S. Sailors.
Pieces in box: 6.
Issued: 1928-1929.
Remarks: See also 230.

Serial No: 269.
Title: U.S. Sailors.
Pieces in box: 24.
Issued: 1928-1929.
Remarks: See also 230 and 268.

Serial No: 270.
Title: 11th (Prince Albert's Own)
Hussars.
Pieces in box: 12.
Issued: 1928-1929.
Remarks: Mounted and
dismounted figures from 12 and
182.

Serial No: 271.
Title: Skinner's Horse (1st Duke of York's Own Cavalry).
Pieces in box: 5.
Issued: 1928-1930.
Remarks: with lances. See also 46, 47, 62 and 63.

Serial No: 272. (9390)
Title: Wild West Display.
Pieces in box: 15.
Issued: 1928-1929.
Remarks: All figures mounted and on foot as 203 and 1252.

Serial No: 273.
Title: Wild West Display.
Pieces in box: 15.
Issued: 1928-1929.
Remarks: All figures mounted and on foot as 272.

Serial No: 274.
Title: North American Indians.
Pieces in box: 7.
Issued: 1928-1929.
Remarks: Mounted and on foot.

Serial No: 275.
Title: Cowboys.
Pieces in box: 7.
Issued: 1928-1929.
Remarks: Mounted and on foot. See also 179 and 183.

Serial No: 276.
Title: U.S. Cavalry.
Pieces in box: 5.
Issued: 1928-1929.
Remarks: In Service Dress with carbine in right hand on galloping horse. See also 229, 262, 266 and 339.

Serial No: 277.
Title: North American Indians.
Pieces in box: ?
Issued: 1928-1929.
Remarks: Mounted and on foot.

Serial No: 278.
Title: Cowboys.
Pieces in box: ?
Issued: 1928-1929.
Remarks: Mounted and on foot. See also 179 and 183.

Serial No: 279.
Title: U.S.A. Display.
Pieces in box: ?
Issued: 1928-1929.
Remarks: Contained Cavalry and Infantry. See also 91, 227, 229, 242, 260, 262, 264, 266 and 276.
Remarks: Contained Cavalry and Infantry. See also 91, 227, 229, 242, 260, 262, 264, 266 and 276.

Serial No: 280.
Title: U.S. Infantry and Cavalry.
Pieces in box: ?
Issued: 1928-1929.
Remarks: See also 91, 227, 229, 242, 260, 262, 264, 266 and 276.

Serial No: 281.
Title: North American Indians.
Pieces in box: 8.
Issued: 1928-1929.
Remarks: Mounted and on foot with tent as 2002.

Serial No: 282.
Title: Cowboys.
Pieces in box: 8.
Issued: 1928-1929.
Remarks: Mounted and foot figures with tent as 2002.

Serial No: 283.
Title: U.S. Infantry and Cavalry.
Pieces in box: 8.
Issued: 1928-1929.
Remarks: In Service Dress with bell tent as 2002.

Serial No: 284.
Title: U.S. Cavalry and Infantry.
Pieces in box: 21.
Issued: 1928-1929.
Remarks: In Service Dress as 227 and 229.

Serial No: 285.
Title: U.S. Cavalry and Infantry.
Pieces in box: 18.
Issued: 1928-1929.
Remarks: See also 227 and 229.

Serial No: 286.
Title: U.S. Cavalry and Infantry.
Pieces in box: 10.
Issued: 1928-1929.
Remarks: Cavalry both standing
and in action.

Serial No: 287.
Title: U.S. Cavalry and Infantry.
Pieces in box: 7.
Issued: 1928-1929.
Remarks: In Service Dress.

Serial No: 288.
Title: U.S. Marines and Sailors.
Pieces in box: 16.
Issued: 1928-1929.
Remarks: See also 228, 230, 261,
265, 268 and 269.

Serial No: 289.
Title: U.S. Boy and Girl Scouts.
Pieces in box: ?
Issued: 1928-1920.
Remarks: See also 161-163, 180,
181, 238, 293, 423, 607, 1332,
1761 and 1N. Export set produced
for U.S.A. market.

Serial No: 290.
Title: U.S. Cavalry and Infantry.
Pieces in box: 13.
Issued: 1928-1929.
Remarks: In Service Dress as 260
and 276.

Serial No: 291.
Title: U.S. Cavalry and Infantry.
Pieces in box: 26.
Issued: 1928-1929.
Remarks: In Service Dress.

Serial No: 292.
Title: Arabs.
Pieces in box: ?
Issued: 1928-1930.
Remarks: Mounted and on foot.

Serial No: 293.
Title: U.S. Boy Scouts and Girl
Scouts.
Pieces in box: ?
Issued: 1928-1930.
Remarks: See also 161-163, 180,
181, 238, 289, 423, 607, 1332,
1761 and 1N.

Serial No: 294.
Title: U.S. Infantry and Marines.
Pieces in box: 16.
Issued: 1928-1929.
Remarks: See also 227 and 288.

Serial No: 295.
Title: U.S. Infantry and Cavalry.
Pieces in box: ?
Issued: 1928-1929.
Remarks: See also 97, 227, 229,
242, 260, 262, 264, 266 and 2766.

Serial No: 296.
Title: Arabs.
Pieces in box: ?
Issued: 1928-1930.
Remarks: Mounted and on foot.

Serial No: 297.
Title: North American Indians.
Pieces in box: ?
Issued: 1928-1929.
Remarks: Mounted and on foot.

Serial No: 298.
Title: Cowboys.
Pieces in box: ?
Issued: 1928-1929.
Remarks: Mounted and on foot.
See also 184, 306, 1252.

Serial No: 299. (9178)
Title: U.S. West Point Cadets.
Pieces in box: 8.
Issued: 1928-1929.
Remarks: Marching at the slope in
Summer Dress. See also 226.

Serial No: 300.
Title: Arabs.
Pieces in box: 17.
Issued: 1928-1930.
Remarks: Mounted and on foot.

Serial No: 301.
Title: Arabs.
Pieces in box: 8.
Issued: 1929-1930.
Remarks: Mounted and on foot
with tent.

Serial No: 302.
Title: Display Box.
Pieces in box: 8.
Issued: 1928-1929.
Remarks: Royal Scots Greys and
Scots Guards as 32, 75 and 2002.

Serial No: 303.
Title: Display Box.
Pieces in box: 8.
Issued: 1928-1929.
Remarks: Life Guards, Middlesex
Regt, and tent as 1, 76 and 2002.

Serial No: 304.
Title: Territorial Army.
Pieces in box: 8.
Issued: 1928-1929.
Remarks: Mounted figures plus
infantry and tent.

Serial No: 305.
Title: North American Indians.
Pieces in box: 10.
Issued: 1928-1929.
Remarks: Mounted and on foot.

Serial No: 306.
Title: Cowboys.
Pieces in box: 10.
Issued: 1928-1929.
Remarks: Mounted and on foot.
See also 184, 298 and 1252.

Serial No: 307.
Title: Arabs.
Pieces in box: 10.
Issued: 1928-1930.
Remarks: Mounted and on foot.

Serial No: 308.
Title: U.S. Cavalry and Infantry.
Pieces in box: ?
Issued: 1928-1929.

Serial No: 309.
Title: Display Box.
Pieces in box: 10.
Issued: 1928-1930.
Remarks: Scots Guards and Scots
Greys as 32.

Serial No: 310.
Title: Display Box.
Pieces in box: 10.
Issued: 1928-1930.
Remarks: Life Guards and
Middlesex Regt.

Serial No: 311.
Title: Territorial Army.
Pieces in box: 10.
Issued: 1928-1930.
Remarks: Infantry and 2nd Cavalry
in peaked caps and Service Dress.

Serial No: 312. (9121)
Title: Grenadier Guards.
Pieces in box: 8.
Issued: 1928-1930.
Remarks: Marching at the slope in
Greatcoats with officer.

Serial No: 313 00.
Title: Modern Army Team of
Gunners.
Pieces in box: 8.
Issued: 1928-1930.
Remarks: Standing and kneeling
figures in peaked caps and Service
Dress. Officer standing with
binoculars. Later issued in steel
helmets.

Serial No: 314.
Title: Coldstream Guards.
Pieces in box: 8.
Issued: 1928-1930.
Remarks: At ease with marching officer.

Serial No: 315.
Title: 10th Royal Hussars (Prince of Wales's Own).
Pieces in box: 5.
Issued: 1928-1930.
Remarks: At halt with plain right hand and sword in scabbard. Sword added later.

Serial No: **316** *00*.
Title: Royal Horse Artillery.
Pieces in box: 7.
Issued: 1928-1930.
Remarks: Team at the halt in Review Order with separate mounted officer from 315 and gun No. 1201.

Serial No: 317.
Title: Royal Field Artillery.
Pieces in box: 9.
Issued: 1928-1930.
Remarks: Team at halt in Review Order with separate mounted officer and gun No. 1201. See also 73, 131, 132 and 144.

Serial No: 318.
Title: Royal Artillery Set.
Pieces in box: 17.
Issued: 1928-1930.
Remarks: RA team at halt with gun No. 1201 and standing and kneeling gunners in Service Dress and steel helmets. See also 1289, 1440 and 1730.

Serial No: 319.
Title: Police.
Pieces in box: 7.
Issued: 1928-1930.
Remarks: Mounted, foot and traffic. See also 239, 621, 659, 775, 776, 808, 824, 1413, 1430, 1477, 1511, 1792, 149P and LP550.

Serial No: 320.
Title: R.A.M.C.
Pieces in box: 8.
Issued: 1928-1930.
Remarks: With Doctors and Nurses as 137.

Serial No: 321.
Title: Drum and Fife Band of the Line.
Pieces in box: 17.
Issued: 1928-1930.
Remarks: See also 30.

Serial No: 322.
Title: Drum and Fife Band of the Coldstream Guards.
Pieces in box: 25.
Issued: 1928-1930.
Remarks: With Rank and File. See also 1555.

Serial No: 323.
Title: U.S. Display.
Pieces in box: 73.
Issued: 1928-1930.
Remarks: Included Artillery 200, 256, 276, 299, 330, 331 and an infantry set, 91 etc.

Serial No: 324.
Title: U.S. Display.
Pieces in box: 81.
Issued: 1928-1930.
Remarks: Included Infantry (91 etc), 226, 228, 229 etc, 230, 330, 331, 359 and 1623.

Serial No: 325-328.
Title: Not Known.

Serial No: **329** *00*. (9426)
Title: Sentry with Box.
Pieces in box: 2.
Issued: 1928-1930.
Remarks: Guardsman in Review Order standing 'at ease'. See also 1607 and 1859.

Serial No. **330** *00*.
Title: U.S.A. Aviation.
Pieces in box: ?
Issued: 1928-1930.
Remarks: Officers in short coats.
See also 323, 324, 331-334, 1904,
1905 and 2044.

Serial No: 331.
Title: U.S.A. Aviation.
Pieces in box: 8.
Issued: 1928-1930.
Remarks: Officers in overcoats.
See also 323, 324, 330, 332-334,
1904, 1905 and 2044.

Serial No: 332.
Title: U.S.A. Aviation.
Pieces in box: 8.
Issued: 1928-1930.
Remarks: Aviators in flying kits as
330.

Serial No: 333.
Title: U.S.A. Aviation.
Pieces in box: ?
Issued: 1928-1930.
Remarks: Aviators in Sidcot Suit
as 1899 and 2011.

Serial No: 334.
Title: U.S.A. Aviation.
Pieces in box: ?
Issued: 1928-1930.
Remarks: Privates in peaked caps.

Serial No: 335-337.
Title: Not Known.

Serial No: 338.
Title: Modern Army British
Infantry.
Pieces in box: 16.
Issued: 1928-1930.
Remarks: Service Dress in
gasmasks.

Serial No: 339.
Title: U.S. Cavalry.
Pieces in box: ?
Issued: 1928-1930.

Serial No: 340.
Title: U.S. Cavalry.
Pieces in box: ?
Issued: 1928-1930.
Remarks: In Service Dress.

Serial No: 341.
Title: British Army Machine-gun
Section.
Pieces in box: 16.
Issued: 1928-1930.
Remarks: Prone position as 194.

Serial No: **342** *00*.
Title: Argentine Cavalry &
Infantry.
Pieces in box: ?
Issued: 1928-1930.
Remarks: Probably combination
of boxes 216 and 217.

Serial No: 343.
Title: Argentine Cavalry &
Infantry.
Pieces in box: 26.
Issued: 1928-1930.
Remarks: No details.

Serial No: 344.
Title: Display Box.
Pieces in box: ?
Issued: 1928-1930.
Remarks: Middlesex Regt and
Life Guards as 1 and 76.

Serial No: 345.
Title: Display Box.
Pieces in box: ?
Issued: 1928-1930.
Remarks: Scots Guards and Scots
Greys.

Serial No: 346.
Title: U.S. Cavalry.
Pieces in box: ?
Issued: 1928-1929.
Remarks: With tent as 2002.

Serial No: 347.
Title: U.S. Infantry.
Pieces in box: 10.
Issued: 1928-1930.
Remarks: Marching at the slope in
Service Dress with officer and
tents as 2002.

Serial No: 348.
Title: U.S. West Point Cadets.
Pieces in box: 10.
Issued: 1928-1930.
Remarks: Marching at the slope in
Review Order with officer and
tent as 2002.

Serial No: 349.
Title: U.S. Marines.
Pieces in box: 10.
Issued: 1928-1930.
Remarks: Marching at the slope in
Review Order, with tent as 2002.

Serial No: 350.
Title: North American Indians.
Pieces in box: 10.
Issued: 1928-1930.
Remarks: On foot with Chieftain
and tent as 150 and 2002.

Serial No: 351-358.
Title: Not Known.

Serial No: 359.
Title: U.S. Machine-gun Section.
Pieces in box: 8.
Issued: 1928-1929.
Remarks: Men in prone position.
See also 324, 341, 1626 and 48N.

Serial No: 360-398.
Not Listed.

Serial No: 399.
Title: U.S. Marines.
Pieces in box: 8.
Issued: 1930.
Remarks: Marching at the slope in
active Service Dress. See also 228,
261 and 265.

Serial No: 400 (9205)
Title: 1st Life Guards.
Pieces in box: 5.
Issued: 1930.
Remarks: In Winter Dress with
cloaks and swords. Officer had
plain arm.

Serial No: 401-406.
Not Listed.

Serial No: 407.
Title: Royal Navy Whitejackets
and Bluejackets.
Pieces in box: 16.
Issued: Not known.
Remarks: Running at the trail.

Serial No: 408.
Title: Royal Navy Bluejackets.
Pieces in box: 8.
Issued: 1930-1931.
Remarks: Running at the trail
with Officer.

Serial No: 409.
Title: Royal Navy Whitejackets.
Pieces in box: 8.
Issued: 1930-1931.
Remarks: Running at the trail
with Officer.

Serial No: 410-416.
Not Listed.

Serial No: **417** *00*.
Title: Admiral with Squad of
Bluejackets.
Pieces in box: 8.
Issued: 1930-1931.
Remarks: Sailors running at the
trail.

Serial No: 418.
Title: Admiral with Squad of
Whitejackets.
Pieces in box: Not known.
Issued: 1930-1931.
Remarks: Figures from 80 and
207.

Serial No: 419-422.
Not Listed.

Serial No: 423.
Title: Boy Scouts.
Pieces in box: ?
Issued: 1930-1931.

Serial No: 424.
Title: U.S. West Point Cadets.
Pieces in box: 16.
Issued: 1930.
Remarks: In Winter and Summer
Dress as 226 and 299.

Serial No: 425.
Not Listed.

Serial No: 426.
Title: Ideal Flower Support.
Pieces in box: 1.
Issued: 1930.
Remarks: For real or artificial
flowers. See also 1526.

Serial No: 427.
Title: Cuirassiers and Infanterie
de Ligne.
Pieces in box: 13.
Issued: 1930.
Remarks: Combination of 138
and 141. See also 1365.

Serial No: 428.
Title: U.S.A. Civilians and Police.
Pieces in box: ?
Issued: 1930.
Remarks: See also 168, 238, 239
and 293.

Serial No: 429. (9306)
Title: Display Set.
Pieces in box: 13.
Issued: 1930.
Remarks: 400 and 431 in Winter
Dress.

Serial No: 430.
Title: 1st Life Guards.
Pieces in box: 10.
Issued: 1931.
Remarks: Summer and Winter
dress.

Serial No: 431.
Title: Scots Guards.
Pieces in box: 16.
Issued: 1931.
Remarks: Marching at the slope
with officers in Summer and
Winter Dress. See also 75.

Serial No: 432. (9169)
Title: German Infantry.
Pieces in box: 8.
Issued: 1931.
Remarks: New modern figure in
Active Service Dress and steel
helmets marching at the slope,
officer with drawn sword. Grey
uniform.

Serial No: 433 *00*.
Title: R.A.F. Monoplane.
Pieces in box: 3.
Issued: 1931-1935.
Remarks: With pilot and hangar
formed from box. See also 188,
434-436.

Serial No: 434 *00*.
Title: R.A.F. Monoplane.
Pieces in box: 7.
Issued: 1931.
Remarks: Aircraft from 433 with
6 Aircraftsmen probably from 240
and hangar formed from box.

Serial No: 435.
Title: U.S. Aviation Monoplane.
Pieces in box: 3.
Issued: 1931.
Remarks: Monoplane and pilot as
for 433 with different painting.
Hangar formed from box.

Serial No: 436.
Title: U.S. Aviation Monoplane.
Pieces in box: 3.
Issued: 1931.
Remarks: As 435 with 6
Aircraftsmen probably from
1904. See also 433 and 434.

Serial No: 437.
Title: Officers of The Gordon
Highlanders.
Pieces in box: 5.
Issued: 1931.
Remarks: Mounted and foot
figures. See also 118, 157, 2168,
60B, 292B, 461B, 845B.

Serial No: 438.
Title: Parade Series.
Pieces in box: ?
Issued: 1931.
Remarks: Grenadier Guards.

Serial No: 439.
Title: Parade Series.
Pieces in box: 8.
Issued: 1931.
Remarks: Middlesex Regt.
marching at the slope in Review
Order.

Serial No: 440.
Title: 7th Royal Fusiliers.
Pieces in box: 8.
Issued: 1931.
Remarks: Parade Series figures.

Serial No: 441 00.
Title: Parade Series.
Pieces in box:
Issued: 1931.
Remarks: The Gordon
Highlanders marching at the slope
in Review Order.

Serial No: 442.
Title: Parade Series.
Pieces in box: 8.
Issued: 1931.
Remarks: Britisn Infantry in
khaki.

Serial No: 443.
Title: Parade Series.
Pieces in box: 8.
Issued: 1931.
Remarks: U.S. West Point Cadets
in Winter Dress as 226.

Serial No: 444.
Title: Parade Series.
Pieces in box: 8.
Issued: 1931.
Remarks: U.S. Marines as 228.

Serial No: 445.
Title: Parade Series.
Pieces in box: 8.
Issued: 1931.
Remarks: U.S. Infantry as 227.

Serial No: 446.
Title: Parade Series.
Pieces in box: 8.
Issued: 1931.
Remarks: Scots Guards.

Serial No: 447.
Title: Parade Series.
Pieces in box: 9.
Issued: 1931.
Remarks: Queen's Royal West
Surrey Regt. marching at the slope
in Review Order. See also 29, 121,
1571 and 2086.

Serial No: 448.
Title: Royal Fusiliers.
Pieces in box: 9.
Issued: 1931.
Remarks: Parade Series figures.

Serial No: 449.
Title: The Black Watch (Royal
Highlanders).
Pieces in box: 9.
Issued: 1931-1935.
Remarks: Parade Series. See also
480, 2036 and 2111.

Serial No: 450.
Title: Parade Series.
Issued: 1931.
Remarks: British Infantry in
khaki.

Serial No: 451.
Title: Parade Series.
Issued: 1931.
Remarks: U.S. West Point Cadets
in Summer Dress as 299.

Serial No: 452.
Title: Parade Series.
Issued: 1931.
Remarks: U.S. Marines.

Serial No: 453.
Title: Parade Series.
Issued: 1931.
Remarks: U.S. Infantry.

Serial No: 454.
Title: Parade Series.
Issued: 1931.
Remarks: U.S. West Point Cadets
in Summer Dress.

Serial No: 455.
Title: Parade Series.
Issued: 1931.
Remarks: U.S. West Point
Cadets.

Serial No: 456.
Title: Parade Series.
Issued: 1931.
Remarks: U.S. Sailors.

Serial No: 457.
Title: Parade Series.
Issued: 1931.
Remarks: U.S. Sailors.

Serial No: 458.
Title: U.S. Infantry and Cavalry.
Issued: 1931.
Remarks: In Service Dress.

Serial No: 459.
Title: U.S. Infantry and Cavalry.
Issued: 1931.
Remarks: In Service Dress.

Serial No: 460.
Title: Colour Party of the Scots
Guards.
Issued: 1931.
Remarks: Colour Bearer possibly
with tin flag.

Serial No: 461-478.
Not Listed.

Serial No: 479.
Title: U.S. Marines and Sailors.
Issued: 1931.
Remarks: See also 228, 230 and
399.

Serial No: 480.
Title: The Black Watch (Royal
Highlanders).
Issued: 1931-1935.
Remarks: With officer and piper.

Serial No: 481.
Title: Parade Series.
Issued: 1931.
Remarks: Middlesex Regt. with
mounted officer, drummer and
bugler. See also 76, 439 and 490.

Serial No: 482.
Title: Parade Series.
Issued: 1931.
Remarks: The Gordon
Highlanders marching at the slope
in Review Order. See also 73, 77,
441, 28B.

Serial No: 483.
Title: Parade Series.
Issued: 1931.
Remarks: U.S. Infantry with
mounted and foot officers. See
also 227 and 242.

Serial No: 484.
Title: Parade Series.
Issued: 1931.
Remarks: U.S. West Point Cadets
in Winter and Summer Dress as
226 and 299.

Serial No: 485.
Title: U.S. Infantry.
Issued: 1931.
Remarks: With mounted and foot
officers. See also 227 and 242.

Serial No: 486.
Title: U.S. Infantry and Cavalry.
Issued: 1931.

Serial No: 487.
Title: U.S. Infantry and Cavalry.
Pieces in box: 13.
Issued: 1931.

Serial No: 488.
Title: U.S. Marines and Sailors.
Pieces in box: 16.
Issued: 1931.
Remarks: See also 228, 230 and
399.

Serial No: 489.
Title: West Point Cadets.
Pieces in box: ?
Issued: 1931.
Remarks: In Winter and Summer
Dress as 226 and 299.

B.G.M.S.— E

Serial No: 490.
Title: Middlesex Regt.
Pieces in box: ?
Issued: 1931.
Remarks: With mounted officer,
drummer and bugler.

Serials 438-489 probably had 8
pieces.

Serial No: 491-500.
Not Listed.

Individual item Farm Series starts.
See also F range on page 112.

Serial No: 501. (9660)
Title: Farmer.
Issued: 1931.
Remarks: Standing with stick and
wearing bowler hat. See also 502,
503, 554, 561, 598, 1430, 5010,
5016, 5023, 20F, L2, L4, L5, L52,
LP508, LB515.

Serial No: 502. (9663)
Title: Farmers Wife with Basket.
Issued: 1931.
Remarks: See also 501, 503, 554,
561, 5010, 5029, L2, L5, LB516.

Serial No: 503 00. (9668)
Title: Farmers Wife with
Umbrella.
Issued: 1931.
Remarks: See also 501, 502, 554,
561, 5010, 5029, L2, L5, LB516.

Serial No: 504 00. (9670)
Title: Carter.
Issued: 1931.
Remarks: Walking with plain arm.
See also 505.

Serial No: 505. (9865)
Title: Carter.
Issued: 1931.
Remarks: As 504 but with arm
holding whip. See also 4F, 5F and
LV606.

Serial No: 506.
Title: Shire Horse.
Issued: 1930.
Remarks: See also 507, 5001,
1F-3F, 55F, 63F, 77F and LB 514.

Serial No: 507.
Title: Shire Colt.
Issued: 1930.
Remarks: See also 506, 602, 2F,
3F, 16F, 77F and 55F.

Serial No: 508.
Title: Cow.
Issued: 1930.
Remarks: Available in assorted
colours. See also 656, 5008, 5019,
1F-3F, 36F, 38F, 52F, 56F, 63F,
72F, 74F, 77F, 111F, LP502,
LP507 and LB520.

Serial No: 509.
Title: Calf.
Pieces in box: 1.
Issued: 1930.
Remarks: Available in assorted
colours. See also 534, 786, 5008,
5012, 5017, 5027, 1F, 3F, 36F,
71F, 74F, 111F and LP507.

Serial No: 510.
Title: Sheep.
Issued: 1930.
Remarks: Walking with curled
horns. See also 577, 655, 658,
5006, 5009, 5016, 5018, 5031,
2F, 3F, 18F, 38F, 39F, 52F, 53F,
62F, 63F, 69F, 70F, 72F, 73F,
77F, 111F, LP501 and LB525.

Serial No: 511.
Title: Sheep.
Issued: 1930.
Remarks: Standing grazing. See
also 658, 5006, 5009, 5018, 2F,
39F, 53F, 63F, 70F, 77F, LP501
and LB526.

Serial No: 512.
Title: Lamb.
Issued: 1930.
Remarks: See also 536, 594,
5018, 5027, 5031, 2F, 18F, 39F,
62F, 111F, LP501 and LB528.

Serial No: 513OO.
Title: Collie Dog.
Issued: 1930.
Remarks: Standing. Available in
assorted colours.
See also 569-571, 576, 577, 658,
664, 5016, 5018, 5028, 5035, 1F,
3F, 16F, 18F, 36F, 38F, 63F, L52,
LP506, LP508, LP509, LB523.

Serial No: 514.
Title: Pig.
Issued: 1930.
Remarks: Available in assorted
colours. See also 546, 596, 664,
746, 5010, 5011, 5016, 5024,
5030, 1F-3F, 17F, 38F, 39F, 52F,
62F, 69F, 72F, 73F, 100F, 111F,
LP508 and LB527.

Serial No: 515.
Title: Turkey Cock.
Issued: 1930.
Remarks: With extended tail.
See also 655 and 102F.

Serial No: 516.
Title: Speckled Fowls.
Pieces in box: 2.
Issued: 1930.
Remarks: Cocks and hens. See
also 517, 518, 544, 545, 642-644,
660, 664, 1F-3F, 39F, 53F and
102F.

Serial No: 517.
Title: Fowls.
Pieces in box: 2.
Issued: 1930.
Remarks: White: as 516.

Serial No: 518.
Title: Fowls.
Pieces in box: 2.
Issued: 1930.
Remarks: Yellow: as 516.

Serial No: 519.
Title: Angry Gander.
Issued: 1930.
Remarks: With spread wings and
outstretched neck. See also 520,
565, 5010, 1F-3F, 111F and
LP505.

Serial No: 520.
Title: Goose.
Issued: 1930.
Remarks: Standing. See also 519,
565, 5010, 1F-3F, 111F, LP505
and LB524.

Serial No: 521.
Title: Oak Tree.
Issued: 1930.
Remarks: In full leaf. See also
522-524, 640, 1430, 3F and 58F.

Serial No: 522.
Title: Cedar Tree.
Issued: 1930.
Remarks: In full leaf. See also
521, 523, 524, 640, 3F and 58F.

Serial No: 523.
Title: Elm Tree.
Issued: 1930.
Remarks: In full leaf. See also
521, 522, 524, 640, 1430, 2F, 3F,
38F, 55F and 58F.

Serial No: 524.
Title: Fir Tree.
Issued: 1930.
Remarks: In full leaf. See also
162, 180, 521-523, 640, 1430, 2F,
3F and 58F.

Serial No: 525.
Title: Fallen Tree.
Issued: ?
Remarks: Trimmed tree stump.
See also 521-523 and 3F.

Serial No: 526.
Title: Hedge.
Issued: ?
Remarks: In full leaf. See also 639
and 11F.

Serial No: 527.
Title: Hurdle.
Issued: 1930.
Remarks: 5 barred. See also 162,
180, 5009, 5011, 5013, 2F, 3F,
63F, LP503 and LB530.

Serial No: 528.
Title: Large Trough.
Issued: 1930.
Remarks: See also 529, 655,
5011, 5023, 5024, 5030 and 18F.

Serial No:529.
Title: Small Trough.
Issued: 1930.
Remarks: See also 528, 655,
5011, 5023, 5024, 5030 and 18F.

Serial No: 530.
Title: Sheep.
Issued: 1930.
Remarks: Lying down.
See also 655, 70F and LP501.

Serial No: 531.
Title: Milkmaid.
Issued: 1930.
Remarks: With pail on head. See
also 508, 532, 537, 591, 652 and
63F.

Serial No: 532 00.
Title: Milkmaid.
Issued: 1930.
Remarks: Carrying pail.
See also 5012 and 39F.

Serial No: 533.
Title: Ducks and Drakes.
Pieces in box: ?
Issued: 1930.
Remarks: Standing. See also 575,
5033, LP505 and LB529.

Serial No: 534.
Title: Calf.
Issued: 1930.
Remarks: Lying down. See also
509, 786, 5017, 71F, 72F and
LB522.

Serial No: 535.
Title: Land Girl.
Remarks: Later replaced by 745
as fashion and war dictated. See
also 657, 54F, L1, L3, L5, L51
and LP505.

Serial No: 536.
Title: Sheep and Lamb.
Issued: 1930.
Remarks: Composite moulding.
Both lying. See also 512, 530, 594,
5005, 5006 and LP501.

Serial No: 537.
Title: Milkmaid.
Issued: 1930.
Remarks: Kneeling milking. See
also 508, 531, 532, 590, 591, 652,
657, 5008 and 77F.

Serial No: 538.
Title: Cow.
Issued: 1930.
Remarks: Lying down. See also
5005, 5017 and LP502.

Serial No: 539.
Title: Cow.
Issued: 1930.
Remarks: Standing grazing. See
also 656, 5021, 39F, 53F, 56F,
69F, LP502, LB521.

Serial No: 540.
Title: Goat.
Issued: 1930.
Remarks: Standing. See also 17F.

Serial No: 541.
Title: Cart Horse.
Issued: 1930.
Remarks: Walking wearing
harness. See also 5002, 4F, 5F, 8F,
12F, 16F, 55F and LV606.

Serial No: 542.
Title: Wheat Sheaves.
Issued: 1930.
Remarks: Stacked. See also 553,
655 and 144F.

Serial No: 543.
Title: Horse.
Issued: 1930.
Remarks: Standing grazing.
Similar type to Cob. See also 656,
5023, 38F, 62F and 71F.

Serial No: 544.
Title: Chicks.
Pieces in box: 3.
Issued: 1930.
Remarks: 3 assorted positions and
colours. See also 516-518, 545,
642-644, 660, 102F and 111F.

Serial No: 545.
Title: Hen.
Issued: 1930.
Remarks: Sitting: Available in
assorted colours. See also
516-518, 544, 642-644, 660, 664
and 102F.

Serial No: 546.
Title: Piglets.
Pieces in box: 2.
Issued: 1930.
Remarks: Available in two sizes
and assorted colours. See also
514, 596, 746, 5011, 5024, 5030,
3F, 17F, 38F, 39F, 62F, 100F and
111F.

Serial No: 547.
Title: Man with Wheel Barrow.
Pieces in box: 2.
Issued: 1930.
Remarks: See also 670, 678 and 022.

Serial No: 548.
Title: Hedges and Field Gate.
Pieces in box: 2.
Remarks: Hedges in full leaf. See also 549, 630-632.

Serial No: 549.
Title: Hedges and Garden Gate.
Pieces in box: 2.
Issued: 1930.
Remarks: Hedges in full leaf.

Serial No: 550.
Title: Cob.
Issued: 1930.
Remarks: Standing. See also 656, 007, 36F, 39F, 55F, 73F, LB519 and LP 504.

Serial No: 551.
Title: Scarecrow.
Issued: 1930.
Remarks: With removable hat.

Serial No: 552.
Title: Donkey.
Issued: 1930.
Remarks: Standing. See also 17F and 54F.

Serial No: 553.
Title: Sheaves of Wheat.
Issued: 1930.
Remarks: Single sheaves. See also 542, 566 and 144F.

Serial No: 554 *00*.
Title: Farmer Son.
Issued: 1930.
Remarks: Sitting.
See also 501, 502 and 561.

Serial No: **555** *00*.
Title: Old Man.
Issued: 1930.
Remarks: Sitting. Also listed as 'Aged Villager, Man'. See also 556, 567, 657 and 5026.

Serial No: **556** *00*.
Title: Old Woman.
Issued: 1930.
Remarks: Sitting. Also listed as 'Aged Villager, Woman'. See also 555, 567 and 5026.

Serial No: **557***00*.
Title: Village Girl.
Issued: 1930.
Remarks: Walking. See also 558 and 657.

Serial No: 558.
Title: Village Boy.
Issued: 1930.
Remarks: Walking with stick. See also 557, 657 and 17F.

Serial No: 559.
Title: Young Lady.
Issued: 1930.
Remarks: 'Flapper' type. See also 618 and 657.

Serial No: 560.
Title: Farm Hand.
Issued: 1930.
Remarks: Sitting, for driving farm machinery. See also 744 and 8F.

Serial No: **561** *00*.
Title: Farmer's Daughter.
Issued: 1930.
Remarks: Sitting. See also 501, 502, 554 and 657.

Serial No: **562***00*.
Title: Golfer.
Issued: 1930.
Remarks: Walking in 'plus fours' with club in hand. See also 1430 and LB543.

Serial No: 563.
Title; Stable Lad.
Issued: 1930.
Remarks: See also 657, 12F, 16F,
36F, 55F, 63F, L3, L4, L51,
LP506 and LB531.

Serial No: 564.
Title: Man with Swing Water
Barrow.
Pieces in box: 2.
Issued: 1930.
Remarks: See also 5034.

Serial No: 565.
Title: Goslings.
Pieces in box: 2.
Issued: 1930.
Remarks: In two positions. See
also 519, 520 and 5027.

Serial No: 566.
Title: Field Haystack.
Issued: 1930.
Remarks: See also 542, 553 and
144F.

Serial No: 567.
Title: Log Seat.
Issued: 1930.
Remarks: See also 556, 557 and
5026.

Serial No: 568*00*.
Title: Garden Seat.
Issued: 1930.
Remarks: See also 655.

Serial No: 569.
Title: Dog Kennel.
Issued: 1930.
Remarks: See also 513, 570-572,
637 and 5015.

Serial No: 570.
Title: Dog Kennel with
Baseboard.
Issued: 1930.

Serial No: 571.
Title: Dog.
Issued: 1930.
Remarks: Lying, for use with 569
or 570. See also 572, 637, 658,
5035 and 55F.

Serial No: 572.
Title: Dog.
Issued: 1930.
Remarks: Sitting, for use with 569
or 570. See also 571, 637, 664,
5015 and 5035.

Serial No: 573.
Title: Bull.
Issued: 1930.
Remarks: Standing pawing
ground. See also 758, 784, 5004,
17F, 38F and 62F.

Serial No: 574.
Title: Telegraph Pole.
Issued: 1930.

Serial No: 575.
Title: Dove Cote.
Issued: 1930.
Remarks: See also 533 and 622.

Serial No: **576** *00*.
Title: St. Bernard Dog.
Issued: 1930.
Remarks: Standing. See also 513,
605, 614, 658 and 5035.

Serial No: **577** *00*.
Title: Shepherd.
Issued: 1930.
Remarks: Standing with crook in
right hand. See also 594, 595,
5006, 5018, 1F-3F.

Serial No: **578** *00*.
Title: A A Scouts.
Pieces in box: ?
Issued: 1931-1935.
Remarks: Standing, walking and
saluting. Also sold with RAC
facings.

Serial No: 579 & 580.
Title: A.A. Signs.
Pieces in box: ?
Issued: 1931-1935.
Remarks: 579 circular destination
type. 580 triangular caution sign.

Serial No: 581.
Title: Rustic Stile.
Issued: 1930.
Remarks: See also 586 and 626.

Serial No: 582-585.
Title: Sign Posts.
Issued: 1931-1935.
Remarks: Wooden direction arm
types. 582 1 armed; 585 2 armed;
584 3 armed; 585 4 armed.

Serial No: 586.
Title: Wooden Fencing.
Issued: 1930.
Remarks: 5 barred. See also 581,
626, 630, 631, 1430, 30F and
111F.

Serial No: 586B.
Title: Dancing Couple.
Pieces in box: 2.
Issued: 1938.
Remarks: Doing the Lambeth
Walk from a popular London
show of the period. Number also
used for Wooden Fencing.

Serial No: 587.
Title: Village Idiot.
Issued: 1930.
Remarks: Standing with straw in
hand.

Serial No: 588.
Title: Milk Churns.
Pieces in box: 2.
Issued: 1930.
Remarks: With removable tops.
See also 45F and 131F.

Serial No: 589.
Title: Blacksmith with Anvil.
Issued: 1930.
Remarks: See also 650, 651 and
5034. Hammer in hand.

Serial No: 590.
Title: Pail.
Issued: 1930.
Remarks: See also 98F.

Serial No: 591.
Title: Dairyman.
Issued: 1930.
Remarks: With removable yoke
and pails. See also 531, 532, 587,
590 and 652.

Serial No: 592.
Title: Curate.
Issued: 1930.
Remarks: See also 593 and 657.

Serial No: 593 00.
Title: Country Clergyman.
Issued: 1930.
Remarks: See also 592 and 657.

Serial No: 59400.
Title: Shepherd.
Issued: 1930.
Remarks: Walking with lamb
under arm and crook in right
hand. See also 512, 536, 577 and 595.

Serial No: 595 00.
Title: Shepherd Boy.
Issued: 1930.
Remarks: With lantern in left
hand and crook over right
shoulder. See also 577 and 594.

Serial No: 596 00.
Title: Berkshire Pigs.
Pieces in box: 2.
Issued: 1930.
Remarks: Sow and Boar issued.
See also 514, 546, 658, 746, 5024,
5025, 36F, 38F, 77F and 100F.

Serial No: 597.
Title: 'Exmoor Horn' Sheep.
Issued: 1930.
Remarks: Ewes and Rams in full
fleece. See also 655, 5005, 54F,
62F and LP501.

Serial No: 598.
Title: Gentleman Farmer.
Pieces in box: 1. Mtd.
Issued: 1930.
Remarks: See also 501 and
LB565.

Serial No: 599.
Title: Jersey Cow.
Issued: 1930.
Remarks: 'Champion'. See also
5012, 5020, 54F, 62F, 70F and
LP502.

Serial No: 600.
Title: Boy on Shetland Pony.
Issued: 1930.
Remarks: See 618 and 619.

Serial No: 601.
Title: Hampshire Down, Ram.
Issued: 1930.
Remarks: See also 36F, 38F, 62F
and LP501.

Serial No: 602.
Title: Foal.
Issued: 1930.
Remarks: Standing. See also 507,
557, 55F, 73F, 77F, 111F, LP504
and LB518.

Serial No: 603.
Title: Rabbit.
Issued: ?
Remarks: Crouched on all fours.
See also 620, 636 and 101F.

Serial No: 604.
Title: Cat.
Issued: 1930.
Remarks: Sitting. See also 638
and 664.

Serial No: 605.
Title: Greyhound.
Issued: 1930.
Remarks: Standing. See also 513,
576, 606, 614 and 5035.

Serial No: 606.
Title: Greyhound.
Issued: 1930.
Remarks: Running.

Serial No: 607.
Title: Girl Guide Walking.
Issued: 1931-1935.
Remarks: or 'Girl Guides and
Guiders'. See also 238, 289, 299
and 1332.

Serial No: **608** *00*.
Title: Mounted Huntsman.
Issued: 1930.
Remarks: On walking horse. See
also 234, 236, 1445-1447 and
LB565.

Serial No: **609** *00*.
Title: Huntswoman.
Issued: 1930.
Remarks: Mounted side saddle on
standing horse. See also 234, 236,
811, 1445-1447 and LB 564.

Serial No: 610.
Title: Huntsman.
Issued: 1930.
Remarks: In top hat on galloping
horse. See also 235, 236, 1445,
1447 and LB 559.

Serial No: 611.
Title: Huntswoman.
Issued: 1930.
Remarks: Mounted side saddle on
galloping horse. See also 234-236,
609, 1447 and LB 560.

Serial No: 612.
Title: Huntsman.
Issued: 1930.
Remarks: Standing in top hat and
riding jacket with whip. See also
234, 236, 1445, 1447 and 5038.

Serial No: 613.
Title: Huntswoman.
Issued: 1930.
Remarks: Standing holding riding
whip. See also 234, 236,
1445-1447 and 5039.

Serial No: **614** *00*.
Title: Hounds.
Pieces in box: 2.
Issued: 1930.
Remarks: Standing with head
erect or walking sniffing the
ground. See also 234, 236, 615,
1445-1447, 5038 and 5039.

Serial No: **615***00*.
Title: Hound.
Issued: 1930.
Remarks: Running. See also
234-236, 614, 1445-1447,
LB561-562.

Serial No: 616.
Title: Fox.
Issued: 1930.
Remarks: Running. See also 235,
236, 1445, 1447 and LB563.

Serial No: 617.
Title: Table.
Issued: 1930.
Remarks: See also 663.

Serial No: 618.
Title: See-Saw with Boy and Girl.
Pieces in box: 4.
Issued: 1930.
Remarks: Balanced on log. See
also 557, 600 and 619.

Serial No: 619.
Title: Garden Swing with Boy.
Pieces in box: 3.
Issued: 1930.
Remarks: See also 600, 618 and
19F.

Serial No: 620.
Title: Running Hare.
Issued: 1930.
Remarks: Running. See also 603,
616 and 664.

Serial No: 621-00.
Title: Traffic Policeman.
Issued: 1930.
Remarks: With one moving arm.
See also 239, 319, 659, 775, 776,
808, 824, 1413, 1430, 1477,
1511, 1792, 149P and LB550.

Serial No: 622.
Title: Swan with Cygnets.
Pieces in box: 6.
Issued: 1930.
Remarks: All swimming. See also
575 and 655.

Serial No: **623** *00*.
Title: Huntswoman.
Issued: 1930.
Remarks: Mounted astride on
galloping horse. See also LB560
and LB564.

Serial No: 624.
Title: Flint Wall.
Issued: 1930.
Remarks: Straight section. See
also 625, 627-634.

Serial No: 625.
Title: Flint Wall.
Issued: 1930.
Remarks: Round Corner Section.

Serial No: 626.
Title: Stile.
Issued: 1930.
Remarks: See also 581 and 586.

Serial No: 627.
Title: Flint Wall.
Issued: 1930.
Remarks: Gate Post Section
without gate. See also 624, 625,
628-634.

Serial No: 628.
Title: Flint Wall.
Issued: 1930.
Remarks: Short Cross Section.
See also 624, 625, 627, 629-634.

Serial No: 629.
Title: Flint Wall.
Issued: 1930.
Remarks: Square Corner Section.
See also 624, 625, 627, 628,
630-634.

Serial No: 630.
Title: 5 Barred Gate.
Issued: 1930.
Remarks: Large version. See also
586, 631, 634, 7F, 19F and 30F.

Serial No: 631.
Title: 5 barred gate.
Issued: 1930.
Remarks: Small version. See also
586 and 630.

Serial No: 632.
Title: Tryst Gate Frame.
Issued: 1930.
Remarks: See also 630 and 631.

Serial No: 633 and 634.
Title: Stone Piers.
Issued: 1930.
Remarks: 634 has fitments for
gates. See also 624, 625, 627-632.

Serial No: 635.
Not listed.

Serial No: 636.
Title: Rabbit.
Issued: 1930.
Remarks: Sitting up on back legs.
See also 603, 620 and 101F.

Serial No: 637.
Title: Dog.
Issued: 1930.
Remarks: Begging. See also 589,
570-572, 664 and 5035.

Serial No: 638.
Title: Spiteful Cat.
Issued: 1930.
Remarks: With arched back. See
also 604 and 664.

Serial No: 639.
Title: Shrubs.
Pieces in box: 2.
Issued: 1930.
Remarks: 2 types. See also 526,
39F, 62F, 63F and 111F.

Serial No: 640.
Title: Tree.
Issued: 1930.
Remarks: In full leaf. See also
521-524, 38F, 39F, 55F, 56F, 62F
and 63F.

Serial No: 641.
Title: Motor Cycle and Side Car.
Pieces in box: 4.
Issued: 1930.
Remarks: Driver and Pillion
passenger removable. See also
653.

Serial No: 642.
Title: Rhode Island Reds.
Pieces in box: 2.
Issued: 1930.
Remarks: Cock and hen. See also
516-518, 544, 545, 643, 644, 660,
664, 69F, 71F and 102F.

Serial No: 643.
Title: White Leghorns.
Pieces in box: 2.
Issued: 1930.
Remarks: Cock and hen. See also
516-518, 544, 545, 642, 644, 660,
664 and 102F.

Serial No: 644.
Title: Black Plymouth Rocks.
Pieces in box: 2.
Issued: 1930.
Remarks: Cock and hen.
See also 516-518, 544, 545, 642,
643, 660, 664 and 102F.

Serial No: 645*00*.
Title: Navvy.
Issued: 1930.
Remarks: With pickaxe. See also
646.

Serial No: 646.
Title: Navvy.
Issued: 1930.
Remarks: With shovel. See also
645.

Serial No: 647 *00*.
Title: Highland Cattle.
Issued: 1930.
Remarks: Available in assorted
colours. See also 5014.

Serial No: 648 and 649.
Title: Field Horses.
Pieces in box: 2.
Issued: 1930.
Remarks: Both walking. See also
769, 6F, 12F, 40F and 45F.

Serial No: 650.
Title:Blacksmith.
Issued: 1930.
Remarks: See also 589, 651 and
5034.

Serial No: 651.
Title: Anvil.
Issued: 1930.
Remarks: See also 589, 650 and
5034.

Serial No: 652.
Title: Milk Roundsman.
Issued: 1930.
Remarks: See also 588, 1430,
45F, 131F, L7 and LV605.

Serial No: 653.
Title: Man on Motor Cycle.
Pieces in box: 2.
Issued: 1930.
Remarks: See also 641, LB536
and LB548.

Serial No: 654.
Not listed.

Serial No: 655.
Title: Assorted Farm Animals.
Pieces in box: 36.
Issued: 1930.
Remarks: Included 510, 515, 528,
529, 530, 542, 551, 568, 597 and
622.

Serial No: 656.
Title: Assorted Large Farm
Animals.
Pieces in Box: 36.
Issued: 1930.
Remarks: Included 508, 539, 543
and 550.

Serial No: 657.
Title: Assorted Farm People.
Pieces in box: 24.
Issued: 1930.
Remarks: Included 501, 502, 535,
537, 555, 557-559, 561, 563, 592
and 593.
See also 52F, 111F, L101, L102
and LP509.

Serial No: 658.
Title: Assorted Small Animals.
Pieces in box: 36.
Issued: 1930.
Remarks: Included 510, 511, 513,
571, 576 and 596.

Serial No: 659 *00*.
Title: Policeman.
Issued: 1930.
Remarks: In peaked cap.
Sometimes referred to as a
'Special Constable'. See also 239,
319, 621, 775, 776, 808, 824,
1413, 1430, 1477, 1511, 1792,
149p and LB550.

Serial No: 660.
Title: Prize Poultry.
Pieces in box: 2.
Issued: 1930.
Remarks: Assorted cocks and
hens feeding. See also 516-518,
544, 545, 642-644, 664, 5037,
63F and 102F.

Serial No: 661, 662.
Not Listed.

Serial No: 663.
Title: Folding Table.
Issued: 1930.
Remarks: For 'Garden or Cafe'.
See also 617.

Serial No: 664.
Title: Assortment of Farm
Animals.
Pieces in box: 36.
Issued: 1930.
Remarks: Included 513. 514, 516,
545, 572, 604, 620, 637, 638,
642-4 and 660.

Serial No: 665.
Not Listed.

Serial No: 666.
Title: Stone Pier.
Issued: 1930.
Remarks: For 671.

Serial No: 667.
Title: Garden Roller.
Issued: 1930.
Remarks: See also 680, 715, 5032
and 98F.

Serial No: 668.
Title: Crazy Paving.
Issued: 1930.

Serial No: 669.
Title: Sundial.
Issued: 1930.

Serial No: 670.
Title: Wheelbarrow.
Issued: 1930.
Remarks: See also 547, 678, 5022
and 98F.

Serial No: 671.
Title: Stone Walling.
Issued: 1930.
Remarks: See also 666.

Serial No: 672.
Title: Fencing.
Issued: 1930.
Remarks: Latticework type for
gardens, different to 586.
See also 1430.

Serial No: 673.
Title: Lawn Mower.
Issued: 1930.
Remarks: See also 679 and 98F.

Serial No: 674.
Title: Stone Balustrading.
Issued: 1930.

Serial No: 675.
Title: Cold Frame.
Issued: 1930.
Remarks: See also 112F.

Serial No: 676.
Title: Hose Reel.
Issued: 1930.
Remarks: See also 98F.

Serial No: 677.
Title: Pond.
Issued: 1930.
Remarks: With statue in centre.

Serial No: 678.
Title: Man for Wheelbarrow.
Issued: 1930.
Remarks: See also 547, 670 and
5022.

Serial No: 679.
Title: Man for Lawn Mower.
Issued: 1930.
Remarks: See also 673.

Serial No: 680.
Title: Man for Garden Roller.
Issued: ?
Remarks: See also 667, 715 and
5032.

Serial No: 681-714.
Not Listed.

Serial No: 715.
Title: Man with Garden Roller.
Pieces in box: 2.
Issued: 1930.
Remarks: See also 667, 680 and
5032.

Serial No: 716-743.
Not Listed.

Serial No: 744.
Title: Farm Hand.
Issued: 1939.
Remarks: Sowing seed.
See also 560.

Serial No: 745.
Title: Women's Land Army.
Issued: 1939.
Remarks: See also 535 and 747.

Serial No: 746.
Title: Berkshire Sow with Litter.
Pieces in box: 5.
Issued: 1930.
Remarks: Composite figure.
See also 514, 546, 596 and 100F.

Serial No: 747.
Title: Girl with Feeding Bucket.
Issued: 1930.
Remarks: See also 535, 5037 and
LB582.

Serial No: 748-51.
Title: Petrol Pumps.
Issued: 1931-1935.
Remarks: 748 Shell. 749 Shell
Mex. 750 B.P. 751 Power.

Serial No: 752-755.
Not Listed.

Serial No: 756.
Title: Wild Horse.
Issued: 1930.
Remarks: See also 156F.

Serial No: 757.
Not Listed.

Serial No: **758** *00*.
Title: Bullock.
Issued: 1930.
Remarks: Running with head
lowered. Also issued as a 'Steer'.
See also 573, 784 and 5004.

Serial No: 759-768.
Not Listed.

Serial No: 769.
Title: Field Horse.
Issued: 1930.
Remarks: See also 648 and 649.

Serial No: 770.
Not Listed.

Serial No: 771.
Title: Esso Petrol Pump
Issued: 1931-1935.
Remarks: See also 748-51and 'V'
series.

Serial No: 772-774.
Not Listed.

Serial No: **775** *00*.
Title: Mounted Policeman.
Issued: 1930.
Remarks: At the halt in peaked
cap with moveable right arm. See
also 239, 319, 621, 659, 776, 808,
824, 1413, 1430, 1477, 1511,
1792, 149p and LB550.

Serial No: **776** *00*.
Title: Policeman.
Issued: 1930.
Remarks: Previously with sets 158
and 1423. Figure wears what is
now the City Police helmet. See
also 239, 319, 621, 659, 775, 808,
324, 1413, 1430, 1477, 1511,
1792, 149P and LB550.

Serial No: 777-778.
Not Listed.

Serial No: 779.
Title: Painter's Ladder.
Issued: 1930.
Remarks: See also 780, 781 and
1495.

Serial No: 780.
Title: Painter.
Issued: 1930.
Remarks: To carry 779. See also
781 and 1495.

Serial No: 781.
Title: Painter.
Issued: 1930.
Remarks: See also 779, 780 and
1495.

Serial No: 782.
Title: Suffolk Mare.
Issued: 1930.
Remarks: See also 602 and 783.

Serial No: 783.
Title: Suffolk Foal.
Issued: 930.
Remarks: See also 507, 602 and
782.

Serial No: 784.
Title: Ayrshire Bull.
Remarks: See also 573, 758, 785,
786 and 5004.

Serial No: 785.
Title: Ayrshire Cow.
Issued: 1930.
Remarks: See also 784, 786 and
LP502.

Serial No: 786.
Title: Ayrshire Calf.
Issued: 1930.
Remarks: See also 509, 534, 784
and 785.

Serial No: 787.
Title: Garage Hand.
Issued: 1931-1935.
Remarks: See also 104V.

Serial No: 788-799.
Not Listed.

Note: In later catalogues the suffix
R was used for Railway items and
they also appeared as the 'Bulk'
lines. Only Main List items have
been dealt with here.
Railway Series usually Nos
800-817 single items in gauge 1
and gauge '0' Nos 818-825.

Serial No: 800.
Title: Porter.
Remarks: To push trolly 811.

Serial No: 801.
Title: Porter.
Remarks: To carry luggage
812-816.

Serial No: 802.
Title: Station Master.

Serial No: 803.
Title: Guard.
Remarks: With flag.

Serial No: 804.
Title: Guard.
Remarks: With lamp.

Serial No: 805.
Title: Ticket Collector.

Serial No: 806.
Title: Lady passenger.

Serial No: 807.
Title: Gentleman passenger.

Serial No: 808.
Title: Policeman.
Issued: 1930.
Remarks: Part of Railway Series.
See also 239, 319, 621, 659, 775,
776, 824, 1413, 1430, 1477,
1511, 1792, 149P and LB550.

Serial No: 809.
Title: Engine Driver.

Serial No: 810.
Title: Fireman.

Serial No: 811.
Title: Trolley.
Remarks: For station luggage.

Serial No: 812.
Title: Trunk.
Remarks: Travelling type.

Serial No: 813.
Title: Dress Basket.
Remarks: Wicker type.

Serial No: 814.
Title: Portmanteaux.

Serial No: 815.
Title: Golf Sticks.
Remarks: See also 562 and 819.

Serial No: 816.
Title: Rugs and Sticks.
Issued: 1930.

Serial No: 817.
Title: Yachtsman.
Remarks: Figure later issued as
Air Commodore 1081B.

Serial No: 818.
Title: Platelayer.
Pieces in box: 2.
Remarks: 'O' gauge size.

Serial No: 819.
Title: Golfer.
Remarks: See also 562 and 815.
'O' gauge size.

Serial No: 820.
Title: Guard with Flag.
Remarks: 'O' gauge size.

Serial No: 821.
Title: Porter for Trolley.
Remarks: 'O' gauge size.

Serial No: 822.
Title: Ticket Collector.
Remarks: 'O' gauge size.

Serial No: 823.
Title: Lady Passenger.
Remarks: 'O' gauge size.

Serial No: 824.
Title: Policeman.
Issued: 1930.
Remarks: 'O' gauge size standing.
See also 239, 319, 621, 659, 775,
776, 808, 1413, 1430, 1477,
1511, 1792, 149P and LB550.

Serial No: 825.
Title: 2 Trunks and Trolley.
Pieces in box: 2.
Remarks: For 821. 'O' gauge size.

Serial No: 826-900.
Not Listed.

Zoo Series starts. Usually
individual items. See also Z suffix
items on page 110.

Serial No: **901** *00*.
Title: Indian Elephant.
Issued: 1931-1935.
Remarks: Adult walking. See also
944, 952, 974, 1550, 4Z, 24Z,
25Z and 27Z.

Serial No: 902.
Title: Kangaroo.
Issued: 1931-1935.
Remarks: Adult standing. Great Grey or Red Kangaroo. See also 950, 972, 973, 2Z-4Z and 9004.

Serial No: 903.
Title: Penguin.   '
Issued: 1931-1935.
Remarks: Adult standing.
See also 916, 972, 1550, 1Z-4Z, 112, 20Z, 9007 and 9014.

Serial 904.
Title: Monkey.
Issued: 1931-1935.
Remarks: Gibbon to hange from cage bars. See also 973, 1Z-4Z, 6Z and 21Z.

Serial No: 905.
Title: Hippopotamus.
Issued: 1931-1935.
Remarks: 'Or Water Horse';
Adult standing.
See also 940, 959, 973, 974, 1550, 4Z, 11Z, 27Z and 9003.

Serial No: 906.
Title: Gorilla.
Issued: 1931-1935.
Remarks: Adult standing.
See also 954, 972, 973, 1Z, 3Z, 4Z and 9012.

Serial No: 907.
Title: Zebra.
Issued: 1931-1935.
Remarks: Adult standing. See also 974, 1Z-4Z, 11Z, 18Z and 9008.

Serial No: **908** *00*.
Title: Indian Rhinoceros.
Issued: 1931-1935.
Remarks: Adult standing. See also 951, 960, 973, 1550, 4Z and 18Z.

Serial No: 909.
Title: Pelican.
Issued: 1931-1935.
Remarks: Adult with open beak. See also 913, 972, 1Z-4Z, 23Z and 2013.

Serial No: 910.
Title: Lion.
Issued: 1931-1935.
Remarks: Adult standing.
See also 911, 962, 974, 1550, 1Z-4Z, and 9010.

Serial No: 911.
Title: Lioness.
Issued: 1931-1935.
Remarks: Adult lying. See also 910, 962, 1550, 1Z-4Z and 9010.

Serial No: 912.
Title: Giraffe.
Issued: 1931-1935.
Remarks: Adult standing. See also 961, 974, 4Z and 11Z.

Serial No: 913.
Title: Pelican.
Issued: 1931-1935.
Remarks: Adult with spread wings. See also 909, 1Z-4Z, 23Z and 2013.

Serial No: 914.
Title: Polar Bear.
Issued: 1931-1935.
Remarks: Adult sitting erect. See also 966, 967, 2Z-4Z and 19Z.

Serial No: **915** *00*.
Title: Chimpanzee.
Issued: 1931-1935.
Remarks: Adult standing on three limbs with left arm outstretched. See also 978, 3Z, 4Z, 6Z and 9012.

Serial No: 916.
Title: King Penguin.
Issued: 1931-1935.
Remarks: Adult standing.
See also 903, 972, 1Z-4Z, 20Z,
9007 and 9014.

Serial No: 917.
Title: Nile Crocodile.
Issued: 1931-1935.
Remarks: Adult lying with open
jaws.
See also 974, 958 and 4Z.

Serial No: **918** *00*.
Title: Bactrian Camel.
Issued: 1931-1935.
Remarks: Adult walking.
See also 123, 131, 943, 953, 1313,
1314 and 2Z-4Z.

Serial No: 919.
Title: Coconut Palm.
Issued: 1931-35.
Remarks: See also 920, 3Z and
4Z.

Serial No: 920.
Title: Date Palm.
Issued: 1931-1935.
Remarks: Cluster of four.
See also 919, 3Z and 4Z.

Serial No: **921** *00*.
Title: Guenon Monkey.
Issued: 1931-1935.
Remarks: Adult walking on all
fours.
See also 1550, 6Z, 11Z, 21Z and
9012.

Serial No: 922.
Title: Ostrich.
Issued: 1931-1935.
Remarks: Adult standing. See
also 973, 4Z, 6Z, 11Z and 17Z.

Serial No: 923.
Title: Llama.
Issued: 1931-1935.
Remarks: Adult walking. See also
1550, 4Z, 6Z and 11Z.

Serial No: 924.
Title: Gate with Posts.
Issued: 1931-1935.
Remarks: To fit 925-930, 993 and
994.

Serial No: 925-926.
Title: Railings.
Issued: 1931-1935.
Remarks: 925 straight section;
926 curved section. See also 924,
927-930, 993 and 994.

Serial No: 927-930.
Title: Standard Post.
Issued: 1931-1935.
Remarks: 927 Two way straight;
928 Two way right angle; 929
Three way; 930 Four way. See
also 924-926, 993 and 994.

Serial No: **931** *00*.
Title: Keepers.
Pieces in box: 2.
Issued: 1931-1935.
Remarks: In peaked caps;
standing and walking. See also
932. One shorter than the other.

Serial No: 932.
Title: Keeper.
Issued: 1931-1935.
Remarks: 'Seated astride'. To fit
901. See also 931, 24Z and 25Z.

Serial No: 933.
Title: Eland Bull.
Issued: 1931-1935.
Remarks: Adult grazing. See also
62, 11Z, 18Z and 9009.

50					Nos 934—949

Serial No: 934.
Title: Brown Bear.
Issued: 1931-1935.
Remarks: Adult walking. See also
936, 972, 1550, 6Z and 9005.

Serial No: 935.
Title: American Bison.
Issued: 1931-1935.
Remarks: Adult standing. See
also 6Z.

Serial No: 936.
Title: Cub Bears.
Pieces in box: 2.
Issued: 1931-1935.
Remarks: Brown Bear cubs sitting
erect and walking. See also 934,
6Z and 9005.

Serial No: 937.
Title: Giant Tortoise.
Issued: 1931-1935.
Remarks: Adult walking. See also
973, 17Z and 20Z.

Serial No: 938.
Title: Howdah for Elephant.
Issued: 1931-1935.
Remarks: To fit 901. See also 932,
939, 24Z and 25Z.

Serial No: 939.
Title: Boy and Girl for Howdah.
Pieces in box: 2.
Issued: 1931-1935.
Remarks: To fit 901. See also 932,
938, 24Z and 25Z.

Serial No: 940.
Title: Baby Hippopotamus.
Issued: 1931-1935.
Remarks: Squatting. See also 905,
959, 973 and 9003.

Serial No: 941.
Title: Tiger.
Issued: 1931-1935.
Remarks: Adult walking. See also
992 and 9015.

Serial No: 942.
Title: Wild Boar.
Issued: 1931-1935.
Remarks: Adult walking.
See also 17Z, 22Z and 9002.

Serial No: 943.
Title: Baby Bactrian Camel.
Issued: 1931-1935.
Remarks: Standing. See also 918,
953 and 9006.

Serial No: 944.
Title: Baby Indian Elephant.
Issued: 1931-1935.
Remarks: Standing. See also 901,
952, 973 and 9001.

Serial No: 945.
Title: Sable Antelope.
Issued: 1931-1935.
Remarks: Adult walking. See also
11Z and 17Z.

Serial No: 946.
Title: Stork.
Issued: 1931-1935.
Remarks: Adult standing. See
also 972, 1550, 17Z, 23Z and
9009.

Serial No: 947.
Title: Flamingo.
Issued: 1931-1935.
Remarks: Adult standing. See
also 972, 23Z and 9013.

Serial No: 948.
Title: Wart Hog.
Issued: 1931-1935.
Remarks: Adult walking. See also
973 and 22Z.

Serial No: 949.
Title: Malay Tapir.
Issued: 1931-1935.
Remarks: Adult walking. See also
973, 22Z and 9006.

Serial No: 950.
Title: Baby Kangaroo or Wallaby.
Issued: 1931-1935.
Remarks: Standing.
See also 902, 1550 and 9004.

Serial No: 951.
Title: Baby Rhinoceros.
Issued: 1931-1935.
Remarks: Standing grazing.
See also 908, 960 and 9002.

Serial No: 952.
Title: Young Indian Elephant.
Issued: 1931-1935.
Remarks: Standing. See also 901,
944, 11Z and 9001.

Serial No: 953.
Title: Bactrian Camel with Boy
Rider.
Pieces in box: 2.
Issued: 1931-1935.
Remarks: 918 plus rider. See also
943.

Serial No: 954.
Title: Gorilla with Pole.
Issued: 1931-1935.
Remarks: Adult standing holding
pole in right paw. See also 906,
972, 973, 1Z, 4Z, 172, 21Z and
9012.

Serial No: 955.
Title: Wolf.
Issued: 1931-1935.
Remarks: Grey wolf loping. See
also 972, 1550 and 17Z.

Serial No: 956.
Title: Walrus.
Issued: 1931-1935.
Remarks: Adult lying. See also
972, 11Z, 20Z and 9014.

Serial No: 957.
Title: Red Deer.
Issued: 1931-1935.
Remarks: Adult standing with full
spread of antlers. See also 972.

Serial No: 958.
Title: Young Nile Crocodile.
Issued: 1931-1935.
Remarks: Lying with open jaws.
See also 917 and 17Z.

Serial No: 959.
Title: Young Hippopotamus.
Issued: 1931-1935.
Remarks: Walking. See also 905,
940 and 9003.

Serial No **960** *00*.
Title: Young Rhinoceros.
Issued: 1931-1935.
Remarks: Walking. See also 908,
951 and 9002.

Serial No: 961.
Title: Young Giraffe.
Issued: 1931-1935.
Remarks: Standing. See also 912.

Serial No: 962.
Title: Lion Cub.
Issued: 1931-1935.
Remarks: Sitting. See also 910,
911, 972 and 9010.

Serial No: 963.
Title: Gazelle.
Issued: 1931-1935.
Remarks: Adult standing. See
also 972 and 9008.

Serial No: 964.
Title: Sea Lion.
Issued: 1931-1935.
Remarks: Adult lying with head
erect. See also 972, 20Z and 9014.

Serial No: 965.
Title: Himalayan Bear.
Issued: 1931-1935.
Remarks: Adult black bear sitting
erect. See also 972.

Serial No: 966.
Title: Polar Bear.
Issued: 1931-1935.
Remarks: Adult walking. See also 914, 967, 1550, 17Z, 19Z and 9007.

Serial No: 967.
Title: Polar Bear.
Issued: 1931-1935.
Remarks: Adult standing erect on hind legs. See also 914, 966, 1550, 19Z and 9007.

Serial No: 968.
Title: Indian or Water Buffalo.
Issued: 1931-1935.
Remarks: Adult walking. See also 182.

Serial No: 969.
Title: Giant Panda.
Issued: 1931-1935.
Remarks: Adult standing. See also 970, 971, 974 and 9001.

Serial No: 970.
Title: Baby Pandas.
Pieces in box: 2.
Issued: 1931-1935.
Remarks: Standing on all fours and sitting erect. See also 969, 971 and 9011.

Serial No: 971.
Title: The Panda Family.
Pieces in box: 3.
Issued: 1931-1935.
Remarks: 969 and 970. See also 9011.

Serial No: 972.
Title: Assortment of Zoo Animals.
Pieces in box: 37.
Issued: 1931-1935.
Remarks: Contained 902, 903, 906, 909, 916, 934, 946, 947, 954, 957, 962, 965.

Serial No: 973.
Title: Assortment of Zoo Animals.
Pieces in box: 24.
Issued: 1931-1935.
Remarks: Contained 902, 904, 906, 908, 922, 937, 940, 944, 948, 949 and 954.

Serial No: 974.
Title: Assortment of Zoo Animals.
Pieces in box: 12.
Issued: 1931-1935.
Remarks: Contained 901, 905, 907, 910, 912, 917 and 969.

Serial No: 975-977.
Not Listed.

Serial No: 978.
Title: Baby Chimpanzee.
Issued: 1931-1935.
Remarks: See also 915 and 9012.

Serial No: 979-985.
Not Listed.

Serial No: 986.
Title: Panther.
Issued: 1931-1935.
Remarks: Adult crouched.

Serial No: 987.
Title: Baboon.
Issued: 1931-1935.
Remarks: Standing on hind legs.

Serial No: 988.
Title: Spring Buck.
Issued: 1931-1935.

Serial No: 989.
Title: Bush Buck.
Issued: 1931-1935.

Serial No: 990.
Title: Vulture.
Issued: 1931-1935.

Serial No: 991.
Title: King Cobra.
Issued: 1931-1935.

Serial No: 992.
Title: Tiger.
Remarks: Adult sitting. See also
941, 9015 and 449 (bulk).

Serial No: 993-994.
Title: Railing.
Issued: 1931-1935.
Remarks: 993 Curved, see 926;
994 straight, see 925.
See also 924, 927-930.

Serial No: 995-1200.
Not Listed.

Serial No: 1201. (9715)
Title: Royal Artillery 18 pdr Gun.
Pieces in box: 1.
Issued: 1930.
Remarks: Also appeared in sets
9, 144, 316, 317, 1462, 1831 and
2077. Smaller version produced as
292.

Serial No: 1202.
Not Listed.

Serial No: **1203** 00.
Title: British Army Tank.
Pieces in box: 4.
Issued: 1930.
1st change: 1941.
Remarks: Carden-Lloyd type with
man Royal Tank Corps crew.
Issued in 1930 with rubber tracks
these were changed to the fixed
cast type in 1941.
See also 1322. Machine gun
separate from tank.

Serial No: 1204-1234.
Not Listed.

Serial No: 1235-1244.
Title: Hunting Series.
Pieces in box: ?
Issued: 1930.
Remarks: No details known. See
also 234-236, 1445-1447.
Believed to be each figure from
series sold individually.

Serial No: 1245-1249.
Not Listed.

Serial No: 1250.
Royal Tank Corps.
Pieces in box: 8.
Issued: 1930.
Remarks: In Service Dress with
black berets. Marching at the trail
with officer. See also 1322.

Serial No: 1251.
Title: U.S. Infantry.
Pieces in box: 9.
Issued: 1930.
Remarks: 3 positions firing in
Service Dress with officer in
peaked cap.

Serial No: 1252.
Title: Cowboys.
Pieces in box: 8.
Issued: 1930.
Remarks: Standing and kneeling
firing pistols. See also 298, 306,
707A, 274B and 275B, 256B.

Serial No: **1253** 00. (9184)
Title: U.S. Sailors.
Pieces in box: 8.
Issued: 1930.
Remarks: Marching at the slope in
Whitejackets with officer.

Serial No: 1254.
Title: Royal Engineers Pontoon
Section.
Pieces in box: 8.
Issued: 1930.
Remarks: Active Service Dress
with different heads and painting
to 20. See also 203, 1330 and 1331.

Serial No: 1255. Not Listed.

Serial No: 1256.
Title: Railway Station Staff and
Passengers.
Pieces in box: 17.
Issued: 1930.
Remarks: Numbered 800 to 816
when sold as separate items.

Serial No: **1257** *00*. (9300)
Title: Yeoman of the Guard.
Pieces in box: 9.
Issued: 1930.
Remarks: 'Historical Series'.
Governor and 8 'Beefeaters' with
movable pike arm.

Serial No: 1258. (9491)
Title: Historical Series.
Pieces in box: 6.
Issued: 1930.
Remarks: 2 mounted knights, 2
squires, standing Herald with
trumpet and mounted Marshal.

Serial No: 1259. Not Listed.

Serial No: 1260.
Title: Modern Army British
Infantry.
Pieces in box: 9.
Issued- 1930.
Remarks: Khaki in peaked caps;
standing, kneeling and lying
action positions.

Serial No: 1261-1262. Not Listed.

Serial No: 1263. (9700)
Title: Gun of the Royal Artillery.
Pieces in box: 1.
Issued: 1930.
Remarks: Small size piece with
fixed elevation still available in the
early 1970s.

Serial No: **1264** *00*. (9730)
Title: 4.7 inch Naval Gun.
Pieces in box: 1.
Issued: 1930.
Remarks: With spring loaded
breech and adjustable elavation
on field carriage. Updated version
of early gun without shield.
Earlier version had no catalogue
number.

Serial No: 1265.
Title: 18 inch Heavy Howitzer No.
Pieces in box: 8.
Issued: 1930.
Remarks: On Garrison Mounting
with 3 shells, 3 extra shell noses
and shell loader. No wheels.

Serial No: 1266.
Title: 18 inch Heavy Howitzer No.
Pieces in box: 8.
Issued: 1930.
Remarks: On Field Carriage with
tractor wheels. 3 shells, 3 extra
shell noses and shell loader.
See also 1211, 1265, 1725, 1726,
1861, 1863, 2008, 2106 and 2107.

Serial No: 1267.
Title: Display Box.
Pieces in box: 83.
Issued: 1930.
Remarks: Contained Royal Scots
Greys, Scots Guards, Gordons,
5th Dragoon Guards, Royal Scots,
Middlesex Regt, 12th Lancers.
Life Guards, and 11th Hussars.
See also 3, 12, 32, 52, 73, 76, 128,
175 and 212.

Serial No: 1268-1282. Not Listed.

Serial No: 1283. (9122)
Title: Grenadier Guards.
Pieces in box: 8. Dismtd.
Issued: 1933-1934.
Remarks: 3 action positions.
Trousered leg without gaiter
different to 34.

Serial No: 1284.
Title: Royal Marines.
Pieces in box: 16.
Issued: 1933-1934.
Remarks: Marching at the slope
and running at the trail with
officers.

Serial No: 1285.
Title: Territorial Army.
Pieces in box: 13.
Issued: 1933-1934.
Remarks: As 159 and 160.

Serial No: 1286.
Title: Modern Army Infantry.
Pieces in box: 25.
Issued: 1933-1934.
Remarks: Khaki in peaked caps; 3
firing positions with officer.

Serial No: **1287** *00*.
Title: British Military Band.
Pieces in box: 21.
Issued: 1933-1934.
Remarks: Khaki Service Dress
with peaked caps. All figures had
moving arms. Smaller set with
some of these figures was 1290.

Serial No: 1288.
Title: R.M.L.I. Band.
Pieces in box: 21.
Issued: 1933-1934.
Remarks: Special figures similar
to Salvation Army Box 10.

Serial No: **1289** 00.
Title: Royal Artillery Set.
Pieces in box: 17.
Issued: 1933-1934.
Remarks: Gun No. 1201, officer
with binoculars and men in
peaked cap. Steel helmets on 1st
change.
See also 313, 318, 1730 and 1440.

Serial No: **129000**.
Title: Band of the Line.
Pieces in box: 12.
Issued: 1933-1934.
Remarks: Khaki Service Dress
with peaked caps. Smaller version
of 1287.

Serial No: 1291.
Title: Royal Marine Band.
Pieces in box: 12.
Issued: 1933-1934.
Remarks: See also 2115 and
2153.

Serial No: 1292. (9710)
Title: Gun of the Royal Artillery.
Pieces in box: 1.
Issued: 1933-1934.
Remarks: Similar to but smaller
than 1201.

Serial No: 1293.
Title: Durban Light Infantry.
Pieces in box: 8.
Issued: 1933-1934.
Remarks: Marching at the slope
with officer. Stepping off with
right foot, wearing shorts.

Serial No: 1294.
Title: Modern Army Infantry.
Pieces in box: 8.
Issued: 1933-1934.
Remarks: Tropical Service Dress
at the slope with officer. Same
figure as 1293.

Serial No: 1295-1299. Not Listed.

Serial No: 1300.
Title: Display Set.
Pieces in box: 42.
Issued: 1933-1934.
Remarks: as 137 plus 145 and
2005.

Serial No: 1301.
Title: U.S. Military Band.
Pieces in box: 12.
Issued: 1933-1934.
Remarks: With Drum Major all in
Service Dress.
See also 1302, 2110 and 2117.

Serial No: 1302.
Title: U.S. Military Band.
Pieces in box: 21.
Issued: 1923-1934.
Remarks: In Service Dress with
Drum Major.

Serial No: 1303-1306. Not Listed.

Serial No: 1307. (9398)
Title: Historical Series.
Pieces in box: 7.
Issued: 1933-1934.
Remarks: 16th Century knights; 2
mounted with lance on charging
horse, 5 standing in armour with
lance in right hand. Standing
figures had no base.

Serial No: 1308.
Title: Historical Series.
Pieces in box: 11.
Issued: 1933-1934.
Remarks: 16th Century knights: 5
mounted, 6 standing.
See also 1307 and 1530.

Serial No: 1309-1310.

Serial No: 1311.
Title: North American Indians
and Cowboys.
Pieces in box: 8.
Issued: 1933-1934.
Remarks: As 150 and 183 with
Chief.

Serial No: 1312.
Title: Wild West Display.
Pieces in box: 5.
Issued: 1933-1934.
Remarks: All mounted pieces as
209 and 142.

Serial No: **1313** *00*.
Title: Eastern Man, Boy,
Shepherd and Woman.
Pieces in box: 12.
Issued: 1933-1934.
Remarks: With animals and
palms. As 918, 2 × 919, 508, 510,
552 and 597. See also 1314 and
1550.

Serial No: **1314** *00*.
Title: Eastern Men and Women.
Pieces in box: 20.
Issued: 1933-1934.
Remarks: Larger box contains
same as 1313 plus 920.

Serial No: 1315-1317. Not Listed.

Serial No: **1318***00*. (9149)
Title: British Army Machine-gun
section.
Pieces in box: 7.
Issued: 1933-1934.
Remarks: Lying and sitting
positions. See also 194, 198, 1319
and 1608.

Serial No: 1319.
Title: British Army Machine-gun
section.
Pieces in box: 14.
Issued: 1933-1934.
Remarks: 1318 plus officer with
movable binocular arms as 1289.

Serial No: 1320.
Title: Modern Army Infantry.
Pieces in box: 9.
Issued: 1933-1934.
Remarks: Khaki, peaked caps;
lying firing with officer.

Serial No: **1321** *00*.
Title: British Armoured Car.
Pieces in box: 1.
Issued: 1933-1934.
Remarks: With swivelling turret.
See also 1203.

Serial No: **1322** *00*.
Title: Army Tank with Squad of
Royal Tanks Corps.
Pieces in box: 7. Dismtd/Officer.
Issued: 1933-1934.
Remarks: 1203 and 1250
combined.

Serial No: 1323. (9345)
Title: Display Box.
Pieces in box: 23.
Issued: 1933-1934.
Remarks: Contained 7th Royal
Fusiliers. Seaforth Highlanders
and Royal Sussex Regt. with
mounted and foot officers.
See also 7, 36 and 88.

Serial No: 1324.
Title: Display Box.
Pieces in box: 24.
Issued: 1933-1934.
Remarks: Contained 76, 212 and
a Scots Guards set.

Serial No: 1325.
Title: The Gordon Highlanders.
Pieces in box: 16.
Issued: 1933-1934.
Remarks: In Tropical Helmet, 3
positions firing.

Serial No: 1326.
Title: Display Box.
Pieces in box: 16.
Issued: 1934.
Remarks: Irish Guards and
Gordon Highlanders.

Serial No: 1327. (9321)
Title: Coldstream Guards.
Pieces in box: 17.
Issued: 1933-1934.
Remarks: Standing, kneeling,
firing and lying.
See also 90 and 120.

Serial No: 1328.
Title: Modern Army Display Box.
Pieces in box: 18.
Issued: 1933-1934.
Remarks: Active Service Dress;
Infantry 3 position firing.

Serial No: 1329.
Title: Royal Army Service Corps
General Service Waggon.
Pieces in box: 4.
Issued: 1933-1934.
Remarks: Two horse team at walk
in Review Order.

Serial No: 1330 and 1331.
Title: Royal Engineers General
Service Waggon.
Pieces in box: 5.
Issued: 1933-1934.
Remarks: Two horse team at walk
with outrider. 1330 in Review
Order, 1331 in Service Dress.
Some later issued with steel
helmets.

Serial No: 1332.
Title: Girl Guides with Guider.
Pieces in box: ?
Issued: 1933-1934.
Remarks: See also 238, 289, 293
and 607.

Serial No: 1333.
Title: Half-tracked Army Tender.
Pieces in box: 1.
Issued: 1933-1934.
Remarks: With driver and mate.
See also 1335, 1433, 1462 and
1727. Changed to modern cab
post-war.

Serial No: 1334.
Title: Army Lorry.
Pieces in box: 1.
Issued: 1933-1934.
Remarks: 4 wheeled type with
tipping body. See also 1335, 1432,
59F and 90F. Changed to modern
(Commer) cab post-war.

Serial No: 1335.
Title: Army Lorry.
Pieces in box: 1.
Issued: 1933-1934.
Remarks: 6 wheeled tipper with driver. See also 1334, 1432, 60F and 91F. Changed to modern cab post-war.

Serial No: 1336.
Title: Miniature Golf.
Pieces in box: 6.
Issued: 1933-1934.
Remarks: With Bunker, Green, etc.

Serial No: 1337-1338. Not Listed.

Serial No: 1339.
Title: Miniature Archery.
Pieces in box: 10.
Issued: 1933-1934.
Remarks: With Archer, Bow, Arrows and Target.

Serial No: 1340-1341. Not Listed.

Serial No: 1342.
Title: 3/7th Rajput Regt. (Duke of Connaught's Own).
Pieces in box: 8.
Issued: 1933-1934.
Remarks: In Khaki marching at the slope.

Serial No: 1343.
Title: Royal Horse Guards (The Blues).
Pieces in box: 5.
Issued: 1933-1934.
Remarks: In Winter Dress with cloaks.

Serial No: 1344-1348. Not Known.

Serial No: 1349. (9256)
Title: Royal Canadian Mounted Police.
Pieces in box: 5.
Issued: 1933-1934.
Remark: In Summer Dress with officer. On galloping horse with carbine in right hand; officer had plain arm.

Serial No: 1350.
Display Box:
Pieces in box: 64.
Issued: 1933-1934.
Remarks: With Gordons, Scots Greys, Royal Scots, pipers, Scots Guards, Life Guards, and 11th Hussars.

Serial No: 1351-1356. Not Listed.

Serial No: 1357.
Title: French Infanterie de Ligne.
Pieces in box: 16.
Issued: 1933-1934.
Remarks: With officer. See also 141.

Serial No: 1358.
Title: Belgian Infantry and Cavalry.
Pieces in box: 16.
Issued: 1933-1934.
Remarks: Review Order. Figures from 189 and 190.

Serial No: 1359.
Title: French Infanterie de Ligne.
Pieces in box: 16.
Issued: 1933-1934.
Remarks: With steel helmets.

Serial No: 1360.
Title: French Zouaves.
Pieces in box: 16.
Issued: 1933-1934.
Remarks: See also 142.

Serial No: 1361. Not Listed.

Serial No: 1362.
Title: Belgian Infantry.
Pieces in box: 24.
Issued: 1933-1934.
Remarks: 23 infantrymen and an officer in Review Order.
See also 134P.

Serial No: 1363-1364. Not Listed.

Serial No: 1365.
Title: French Cuirassiers and
Infanterie de Ligne.
Pieces in box: 13.
Issued: 1933-1934.
Remarks: In Review Order.

Serial No: 1366.
Title: French Infanterie de Ligne.
Pieces in box: 7.
Issued: 1933-1934.
Remarks: Including
machine-gunner and in action.

Serial No: 1367.
Title: Japanese Infantry and
Cavalry.
Pieces in box: 21.
Issued: 1933-1934.
Remarks: With officer. Charging
figures.

Serial No: 1368.
Title: The Bersaglieri and Italian
Cavalry.
Pieces in box: 13.
Issued: 1933-1934.
Remarks: 165 and 169 combined.

Serial No: 1369. Not Listed.

Serial No: 1370.
Title: Knights at Arms.
Pieces in box: ?
Issued: 1933-1934.
Remarks: No details known.

Serial No: 1371-1378. Not Listed.

Serial No: 1379.
Title: Belgian Cavalry.
Pieces in box: 5 Mtd.
Issued: 1933-1934.
Remarks: In Service Dress with
officer.

Serial No: 1380.
Title: Belgian Cavalry.
Pieces in box: 5 Mtd.
Issued: 1933-1934.
Remarks: In Service Dress with
officer.

Serial No: 1381.
Title Belgian Cavalry.
Pieces in box: 15 Mtd.
Issued: 1933-1934.
Remarks: Service Dress with
officer. See also 1379, 1381 and
1390.

Serial No: 1382.
Title: Belgian Cavalry and
Infantry.
Pieces in box: 18.
Issued: 1933-1934.
Remarks: Service Dress with
officer. See also 1379, 1381 and
1390.

Serial No: **1383** 00.
Title: Belgian Infantry.
Pieces in box: 14.
Issued: 1933-1934.
Remarks: Service Dress with steel
helmets, 3 positions firing, and
machine-gun.
See also 1384 and 1389.

Serial No: 1384.
Title: Belgian Infantry.
Pieces in box: 21.
Issued: 1933-1934.
Remarks: Details as for 1383 but
with more pieces. See also 1389.

Serial No: 1385.
Title: French Cavalry.
Pieces in box: 10.
Issued: 1935-1939.
Remarks: 139 and 140 combined.
See also 138.

Serial No: 1386.
Title: French Cavalry.
Pieces in box: 15.
Isued: 1935-1939.
Remarks: 138-140 combined,
plus Cuirassiers.

Serial No: 1387.
Title: French Infanterie de Ligne.
Pieces in box: 21.
Issued: 1935-1939.
Remarks: In Service Dress; in
action with machine-guns.

Serial No: 1388.
Title: French Infanterie de Ligne,
Turcos, and Dragons.
Pieces in box: 21.
Issued: 1935-1939.
Remarks: See 140, 191 and 1387.

Serial No: **1389** *00*.
Title: Belgian Infantry.
Pieces in box: 8.
Issued: 1933-1934.
Remarks: Service Dress with steel
helmets marching at the slope.

Serial No: 1390.
Title: Belgian Cavalry and
Infantry.
Pieces in box: 18.
Issued: 1933-1934.
Remarks: Active service dress
with officer.

Serial No: 1391.
Title: Fort.
Issued: 1935-1936.
Remarks: Printed cardboard.

Serial No: 1392.
Title: Cierva C30 Autogyro.
Pieces in box: 2.
Issued: 1935-1936.
Remarks: British Army
co-operation Autogyro with pilot.
To run down string cable. See also
1431 and 1894.

Serial No: 1393.
Title: 'Bluebird' Car.
Pieces in box: 1.
Issued: 1935-1936.
Remarks: Without chassis. See
also 1400.

Serial No: 1394.
Title: Display box.
Pieces in box: 16.
Issued: 1935-1936.
Remarks: With Fort, West
Surreys, and Fusiliers.

Serial No: 1395.
Title: King's Own Scottish
Borderers.
Pieces in box: 8.
Issued: 1935-1936.
Remarks: Marching at the slope in
Review Order.

Serial No: 1396. Not Listed.

Serial No: 1397.
Title: Model Fort, with Infantry of
the Line. 'A' Series.
Pieces in box: 18.
Issued: 1936.
Remarks: Infantry standing,
kneeling and prone firing. Fort as
1391.

Serial No: 1398.
Title: Sport Tourer Car.
Pieces in box: 1.
Issued: 1936.
Remarks: See also 1656 and LV
601-602.

Serial No: 1399.
Title: Two-Seater Coupé Car.
Pieces in box: 1.
Issued: 1936.
Remarks: See also 1656.

Serial No: 1400.
Title: 'Bluebird' Racing Car.
Pieces in box:
Issued: 1936.
Remarks: See also 1393.

Serial No: 1401-1406. Not Listed.

Serial No: 1407.
Title: Modern Army Presentation Box.
Pieces in box: 72.
Issued: 1936.
Remarks: Included 94, 159, 160, 194, 195, 298, 1290 and officers.

Serial No: 1408-1412. Not Listed.

Serial No: 1413.
Title: Mobile Police Car.
Pieces in box: 3.
Issued: 1936.
Remarks: Crew of two cast in one piece. Included in box 1430. See also 239, 319, 621, 659, 775, 808, 1413, 1430, 1477, 1443, 1511, 1792, 1491 and LB550.

Serial No: 1414-1422. Not Listed.

Serial No: 1423.
Title: Railway Station Staff and Passengers.
Pieces in box: 9.
Issued: 1936-1937.
Remarks: Numbered individually 800-816 when sold separately.

Serial No: 1424.
Title: Abyssinian Royal Bodyguards.
Pieces in box: 8.
Issued: 1936-37.
Remarks: At attention.
Combined with 1425 in box 1434 during 1936-37.

Serial No: 1425 00.
Title: Abyssinian Tribesmen.
Pieces in box: 8.
Issued: 1936-1937.
Remarks: Marching at the slope over left shoulder. One piece moulding with fixed arms. Combined with 142 in box 1434 during 1936-37.

Serial No: 1426 00.
Title: St John Ambulance First Aid Section.
Pieces in box: 8.
Issued: 1936-1937.
Remarks: Motor Ambulance with officer, NCO, nurse, stretcher bearers and injured man on stretcher. See also 1512-1514.

Serial No: 1427.
Title: Road Signs Set.
Pieces in box: 8.
Issued: 1936-1937.
Remarks: 4 Road Signs, 1 Belisha Beacon, 2 Traffic Lights, 1 Large Sign.

Serial No: 1428.
Title: Road Signs Set.
Pieces in box: 16.
Issued: 1936-1947.
Remarks: 8 Road Signs, 2 Belisha Beacons, 2 Large Signs, 1 Lamp Post, 2 Traffic Lights, 1 Policeman.

Serial No: 1429.
Title: Road Signs Set.
Pieces in box: 24.
Issued: 1936-1937.
Remarks: 15 Road Signs, 2 Large Signs, 2 Belisha Beacons, 2 Lamp Posts, 2 Traffic Lights, 1 Policeman. See boxes 346Bu-350Bu, 377Bu, 239, 621, 1427-28, 1430.

Serial No: 1430.
Title: Traffic Display.
Pieces in box: ?
Issued: 1936-1937.
Remarks: Box comprised printed
pedestrian crossing and
background with items from 239,
501, 521, 523, 524, 562, 586, 652,
659, 672, 925-927, 1413,
1427-28.

Serial No: 1431.
Title: Cierva C30 Autogyro.
Pieces in box: 2.
Issued: 1936-1937.
Remarks: As 1392 but with
different painting.
See also 1899.

Serial No: **1432** *00*.
Title: Army Tender.
Pieces in box: 1.
Issued: 1936-1937.
Remarks: 10 wheeled with driver.
See also 1334, 1335, 1724, 1832,
1833, 6IF and 92F.

Serial No: **1433** *00*.
Title: Half-tracked Army Tender.
Pieces in box: 1.
Issued: 1936-1937.
Remarks: With covered tipper
body and driver. Changed to
modern cab post-war. Final
version had streamlined cab and
fenders, and tinplate tilt. Driver in
beret. See also 1333, 1335, 1462
and 1727.

Serial No: **1434** *00*.
Title: Abyssinian Royal
Bodyguard and Tribesmen.
Pieces in box: 16.
Issued: 1936-1937.
Remarks: Combination of boxes
1424-25.

Serial No: **1435** *00*.
Title: Italian Infantry.
Pieces in box: 8.
Issued: 1936-1937.
Remarks: Marching at the slope.
In Service Dress and steel
helmets. Figure with baggy
trousers.

Serial No: **1436** *00*.
Title: Italian Infantry.
Pieces in box: 8.
Issued: 1936-1937.
Remarks: Marching at the slope in
Colonial Service Dress. See also
166, 1368, 1437-1438. As 1435
but in sun helmets.

Serial No: 1437.
Title: Italian Carabinieri Infantry.
Pieces in box: 8.
Issued: 1936-1937.
Remarks: Marching at the slope in
Review Order with officer. See
also 166, 1368, 1435, 1436 and
1438.

Serial No: 1438.
Title: Italian Infantry.
Pieces in box: 16.
Issued: 1936-1937.
Remarks: In Colonial Service
Dress wearing active service order
and steel helmets. See also 166,
1368, 1435-1437.

Serial No: 1439.
Title: Fair Roundabout.
Pieces in box: ?
Issued: 1936-1937.
Remarks: See also 1539 and
2056.

Serial No: 1440.
Title: Royal Artillery.
Pieces in box: 9.
Issued: 1936-1937.
Remarks: Team at walk with gun
No. 1201 and detachment in steel
helmets.

Serial No: 1441.
Title: Flying Trapeze.
Pieces in box: ?
Issued: 1936-1937.
Remarks: See also 2054.

Serial No: 1442.
Title: Circus Selection.
Pieces in box: 6.
Issued: 1936-1937.
Remarks: With
351Bulk-353Bulk, 355Bulk,
357Bulk and 358Bulk. See also
1539.

Serial No: 1443.
Title: Circus Selection.
Pieces in box: 10.
Issued: 1936-1937.
Remarks: 2 × 351Bulk, 2 ×
352Bulk, 2 × 353Bulk, 354Bulk,
355Bulk, 357Bulk and 358Bulk.
See also 1539.

Serial No: 1444.
Title: Circus Selection.
Pieces in box: 14.
Issued: 1936-1937.
Remarks: With 2 × 351Bulk, 2 ×
352Bulk, 2 × 353Bulk,
354Bulk-357Bulk, 2 × 358Bulk,
359Bulk and 446Bulk. See also
1539.

Serial No: 1445.
Title: 'Huntsmen'.
Pieces in box: 11.
Issued: 1936-1937.
Remarks: Mounted and
dismounted with fox and pack of
hounds. See 608, 610, 612, 616.

Serial No: 1446. (9650)
Title: 'The Meet'.
Pieces in box: 11.
Issued: 1936-1937.
Remarks: Mounted and on foot
with hounds. As 608, 2 × 613, 4 ×
614.

Serial No: 1447 (9651)
Title: 'Full Cry'.
Pieces in box: 11.
Issued: 1936-1937.
Remarks: With Huntsmen, pack
of hounds and fox.

Serial No: **1448** 00.
Title: British Army Staff Car.
Pieces in box: 2.
Issued: 1936-1937.
Remarks: Crew of two cast in one
piece.
See also 1413, 1430 and 1909.

Serial No: 1449. Not Known.

Serial No: 1450.
Title: R.A.M.C. Ambulance
Waggon.
Pieces in box: 7.
Issued: 1936-1937.
Remarks: As 145 Service Dress
version but with steel helmeted
crew.

Serial No: 1451-1457. Not Listed.

Serial No: 1458.
Title: Band of the Line.
Pieces in box: ?
Issued: 1936-1937.
Remarks: No details known.

Serial No: 1459. Not Listed.

Serial No: 1460.
Title: Royal Army Service Corps
General Service Waggon.
Pieces in box: 5.
Issued: 1936-1937.
Remarks: In Active Service
Dress. See also 145, 146,
1329-1331 and 1893.

Serial No: 1461. Not Listed.

Serial No: **1462** *00*.
Title: Covered Lorry with Gun
1201 and Limber 1479.
Pieces in box:
Issued: 1936-1937.
Remarks: Complete with short
pole ammunition limber 1479.

Serial No: 1463.
Title: Racing Colours.
Pieces in box: 12.
Issued: 1936-1937.
Remarks: 1 each of 1486-1491.

Serial No: 1464.
Title: Racing Colours.
Pieces in box: ?
Issued: 1936-1937.
Remarks: See also 237 and 1463.

Serial No: 1465.
Title: Racing Colours.
Pieces in box: ?
Issued: 1936-1937.
Remarks: See also 237, 1463 and
1464.

Serial No: 1466.
Title: Racing Colours.
Pieces in box: ?
Issued: 1936-1937.
Remarks: See also 237,
1463-1465.

Serial No: 1467.
Title: Racing Colours.
Pieces in box: ?
Issued: 1936-1937.
Remarks: See also 237,
1463-1466.

Serial No: 1468.
Title: Racing Colours.
Pieces in box: ?
Issued: 1936-1937.
Remarks: See also 237, 1463-67.

Serial No: 1469.
Title: Racing Colours.
Pieces in box: ?
Issued: 1936-1937.
Remarks: See also 237,
1463-1468.

Serial No: 1470. (9401)
Title: Coronation State Coach.
Pieces in box: 11.
Issued: 1936-1937.
1st change: 1937.
2nd change: 1953-1956.
Remarks: State Coach of England
complete with Royal passengers
and outriders. It was later issued
with King George VI and the
Queen and later with Queen
Elizabeth II and Prince Philip. See
also 1476, 1478 and 2094.

Serial No: 1471.
Title: King Edward VIII.
Pieces in box: 1.
Issued: 1936-1937.
Remarks: In copper finish and in
Coronation robes. See also 1470,
1472, 1473, 1476 and 1477.

Serial No: 1472.
Title: King Edward VIII.
Pieces in box; 1.
Issued: 1936-1937.
Remarks: Gilt finish and in
Coronation robes. See also 1470,
1471, 1476 and 1477.

Serial No: 1473.
Title: King Edward VIII.
Pieces in box: 1.
Issued: 1936-1937.
Remarks: Painted figure. See also
1470-1472, 1476 and 1477.

92   88   141   174   27

16   16 (Officer)   16   36   130
(Special painting
for the Boer War)

76   37   27   76   27
(2nd version)

21st Lancer (X list)
32
(NB X list was
forerunner of
Crown range)

33 (1st version)   94 (4th version)

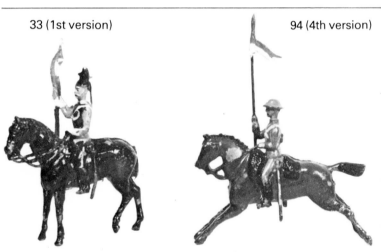

106 (with one eared horse)

31   And
Life Guards
(06 series)
(06 model was
from British
encampment set)

108   43

99 (early)   99 (late)

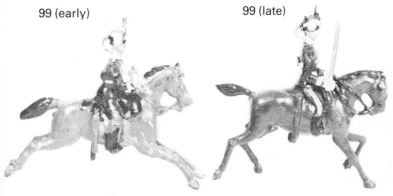

(R.A. Officers)   144   39 (with collar harness)
144, 39, 316, 73

39 (1st version)   39 (2nd version)

11B   10B   22B

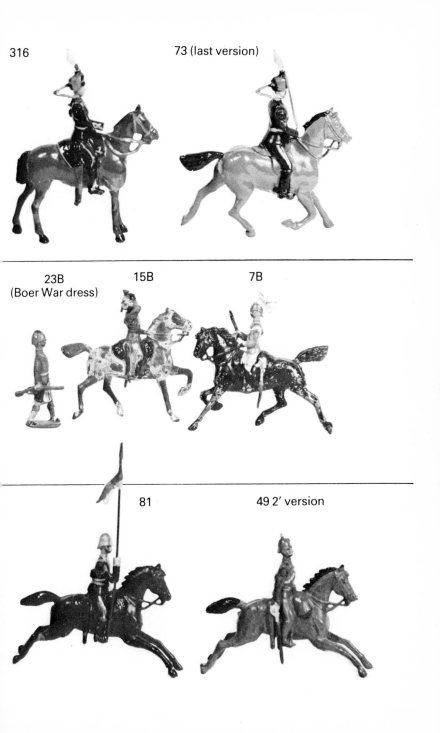

316

73 (last version)

23B
(Boer War dress)

15B

7B

81

49 2' version

39
(Service dress)

2077
(last version
post 1918
RHA at walk)

39 (set incomplete:
Should have two men
on the gun)

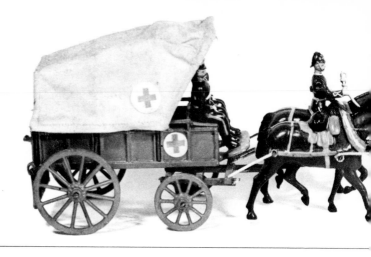

203

C.I.V
G.S. Waggon
    (larger wheels)

145 (early version –
   last version had
   larger wheels

146A

461B 845B

Indian Infantry 83
(unidentified)

(Special Paint models,
6d extra in customer's choice
of colours)

205   206   137   97

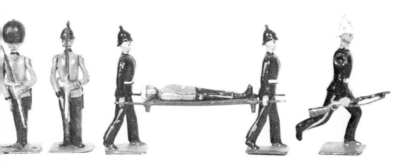

330

34   36   50   102

113 (2nd version)　　113 (3rd version)　　77 (pre 1940

213　　　213　　　212　　　212　　35 (2nd version

908　　　　　　　　　　　931

7 (post 1940)   75   11   1021B   1610

rd version) 35 (4th version) 35 (white helmet) 35 (no gaiters) 1619

915   921   918

147   147

758   647

188 960

901 596

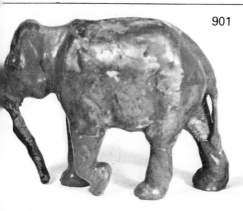

513
5F (and 505)
576

4F

20F

| 645 | 594 | 595 | 561 (on 568) | 554 |

532   531   555   556

503   557   504   577   593

598   745   744

2042
(part of set
combined
with 2034)

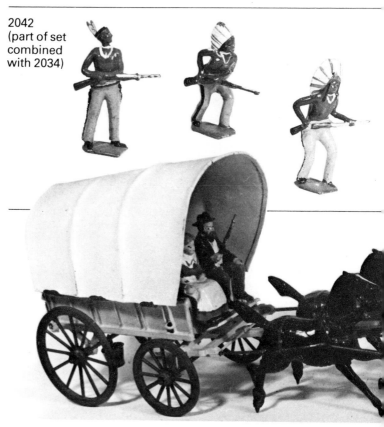

609   608

| 563 | 747 | 745 (late) | 501 |

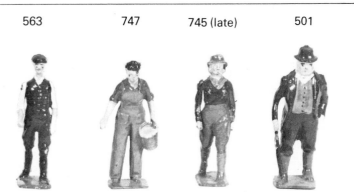

2034 (Prairie Schooner)   2070 (part of set)

2042 (part of set combined with 2034)

2059 (part of set)   1361B   2059

2070 (part of set) – also 2059, 2060, 2055, 2056, etc.

228
(early versions had
blue-tipped cap)

1253

36N

92P

1904

2117

2117

299

2021

2027

227 (officer)

1603 (officer)

2110

2110

2051 (officer)

2051

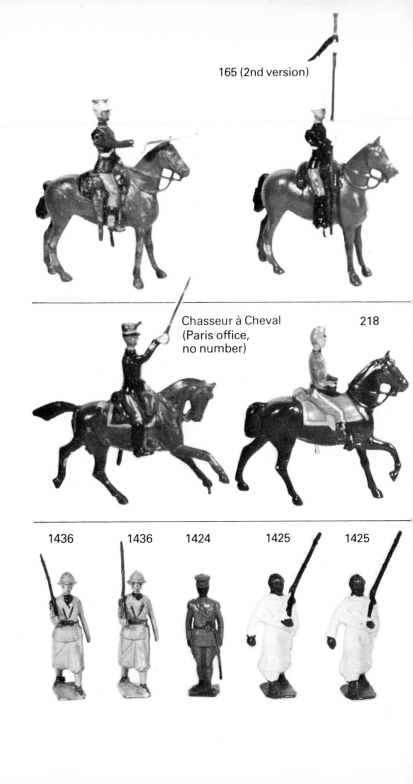

165 (2nd version)

Chasseur à Cheval
(Paris office,
no number)

218

1436   1436   1424   1425   1425

190 (officer)   190 (trooper)

St Cyr Officer
(Paris office,
no number)   2028 (officer)

1424   196 (pre 1946)   196 (post 1946)   1485

222   220   216

143   214   French Infantry   1900   1900
(Paris office,   (officer)
no number)

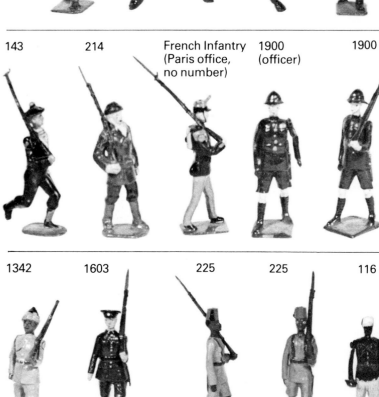

1342   1603   225   225   116

221
(1st version)

219

217

141
(officer)

2022

2022
(officer)

2022

2104

116

2031

2031

2095 (part)

2097 (part)

2009   2009 (officer)   1389   1383

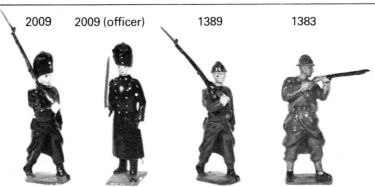

219   169   1437

PRAVACHOL™ pravastatin sodium 20 mg tablets

5188L

5270L

5193L

5289L

5292 KB39L

8813

8621 Hours USL

5187L

0541-204R

2172
2172
1329B

Note 2172 plug-armed

---

191   142   2095/2097

2046 or 2097 (part)

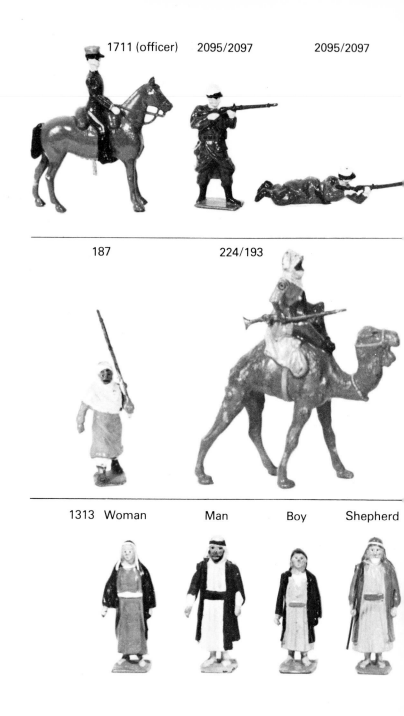

1711 (officer)   2095/2097   2095/2097

187   224/193

1313 Woman   Man   Boy   Shepherd

2095/2097   1711   1367B (officer)

164/2046

Note: 1313 castings also used as
Noah and Wife in Noah's Ark, 1550.

1856 (officer)   1856   136

225b   2019   2019   2035   2035 (officer)

149P   158/776   659   621

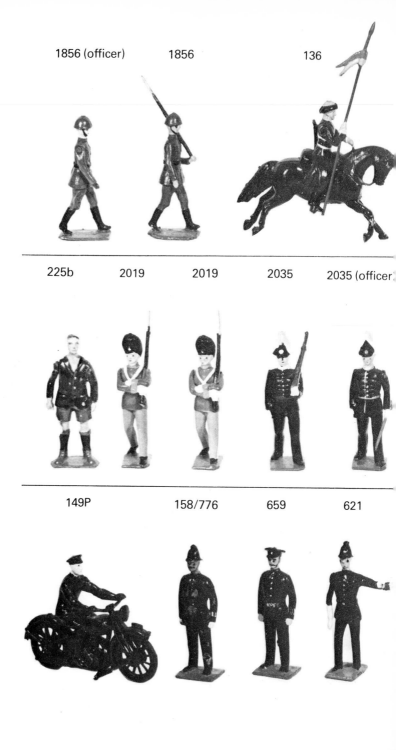

2032   2032   775

2018 (trumpeter)   2018

172b   562   254b   189b   173b

578 (A.A.)   578 (R.A.C.)   1426   1426

Below left
2054 (part)
Below right
1539 (part)

1426   1426 (St John's Ambulance set)

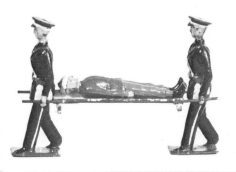

1654
(complete set)

2054 (part)

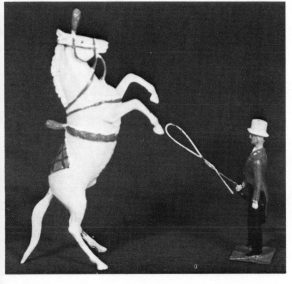

1539   2054

82 (1954 version)   2084 (earlier flag tin)   340B

71N   7N   28N   88N

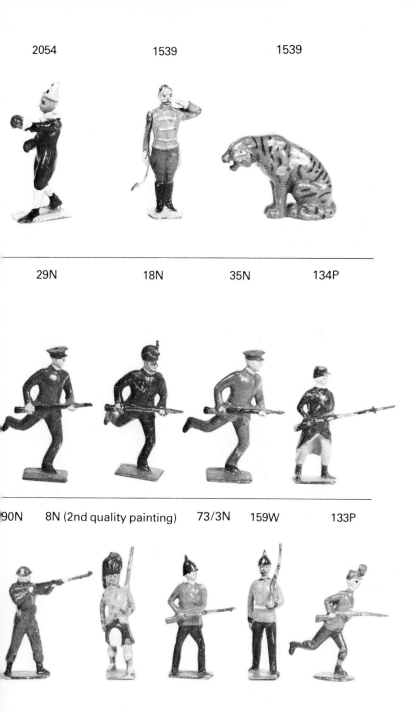

2054   1539   1539

29N   18N   35N   134P

90N   8N (2nd quality painting)   73/3N   159W   133P

1662

1258
Knight
Marshal

1664
(part of Knights
on Foot set)

1661 1663

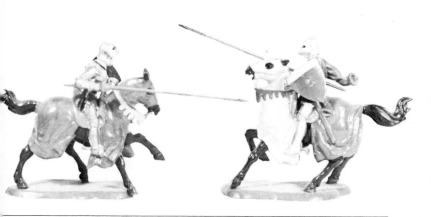

1258
Squire
Herald

1518 Sold as 89th or 49th   1518 (9160/9155)   1516 (sergeant)   1519
Foot with different
coloured facings

Lifeguard (possibly from 72 but probably a   101 (last version)
                          prototype – not
                          issued; made
                          when this pattern
                          helmet was
                          contemplated for
                          re-issue)

2075   315

2152 2152 2152

101 (Band Master) 151P

1343 400

2076   24

2075   50

1911   1911   1911   2080   207/51N
(midshipman)

1342B   182

1720 (1st version)   2074

417   78/79   151 (2nd version)   151 (1st version)

1322   1203   1322

1321

1331

434

1462

1876

1432

1614   194

1264   1859

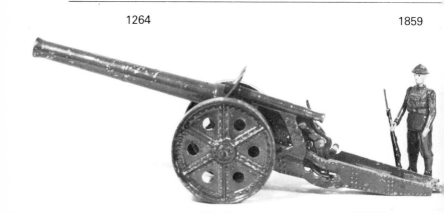

198 (with Maxim)   198 (with Vickers)   1318 (1954 issue)

1512

1448

1759 (A.R.P. set)   72N

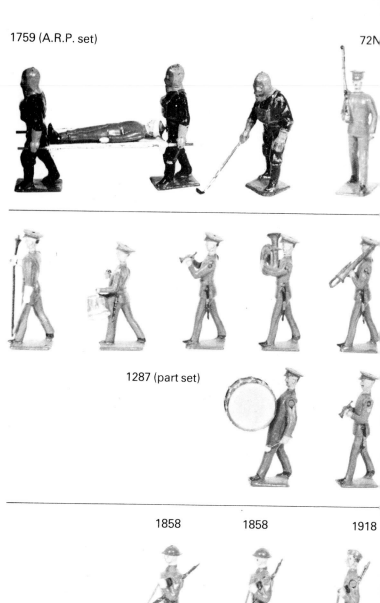

1287 (part set)

1858   1858   1918

1320 unknown 313 313 1320

1855

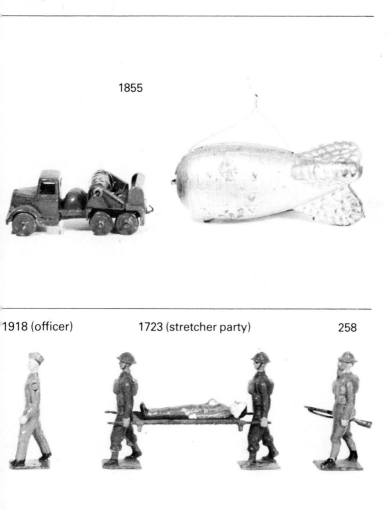

1918 (officer)   1723 (stretcher party)   258

1289   1730   1730

1641 (with balloon winch)

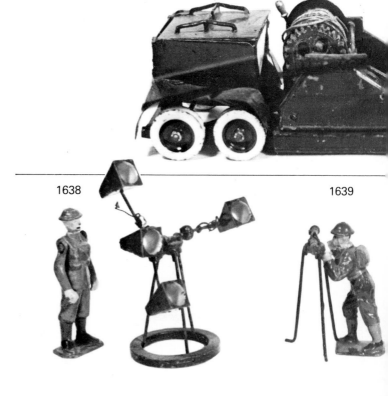

1638   1639

1522   1731   1289

1289

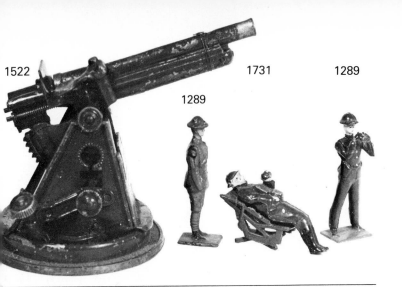

1729   1728

2115   2080   2011   2073
(from set) (officer)

1895   2011   2011   2011
(from set)

1725   1726

1510   116P   2011   2073

240   2011   1905   2011
      (from set)   (from set)

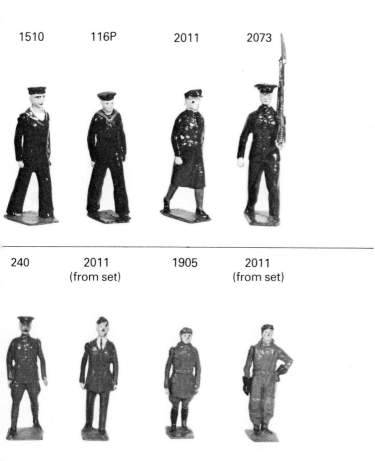

1877

2085
(LG)

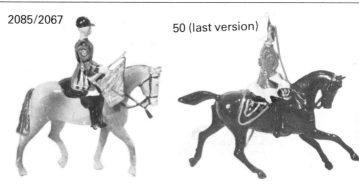

2085/2067

50 (last version)

2067 (LG)   2067 (LG)

2037

1325B   2067 (RHG)

1265

| 74 | 74 (officer) | 2113 | 17 (officer last version) | 2113 |

| 1603 | 2072 | 2072 (officer) | 1475 |

2109 (from set but painted as Gordon Highlanders by Britains)

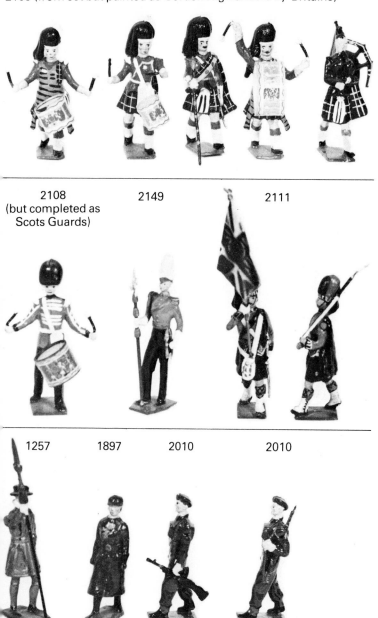

2108
(but completed as
Scots Guards)

2149

2111

1257   1897   2010   2010

1347B

838B

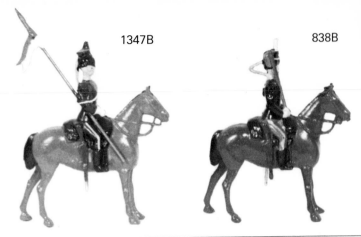

1345B

315

2029

1343 B
(officer)

1343B

2118 1339B

1337B 1338B

340B 329 2124 (officer) 2124

2184/2185/2186 (from sets)

1631   2066

202   2031   2096 (from complete sets)

2094

2087 (special figures for Lyons display)   2090   2090 (officer)   2089

2079 (officer)   2149   2065

1433 (last version)

2092   Special   2091   2088

2079   2079   2079

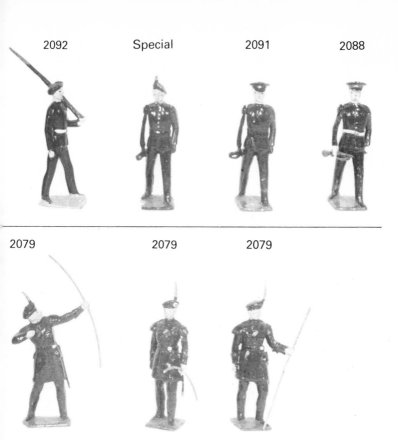

2102

160
(pre 1945 box)

2148 9154 2182 9154

9158
Final version
box from 1962

BRITAINS M

2148   9154   1633   9154

authentic handpainted metal toys

Officers from Set No. 28. L to R last version and 2nd version

Figures from set 28. L to R early mule and man, last man and

French General
Paris office

Cameronian Officer
Special painted set

Serial No: 1474.
Title: Coronation Chair.
Pieces in box: 2.
Issued 1936-1937.
Remarks: Chair of King Edward I
$3\frac{1}{4}''$ high with removable Stone of
Scone. See also 860.

Serial No: **1475** *00* (9404).
Title: Attendants to the State
Coach.
Pieces in box: 18.
Issued: 1936-1937.
Remarks: 'Historical Series'.
Figures to go with 1470 included
walking outriders, footmen of the
Royal Household and yeomen.

Serial No: 1476.
Title: State Coach and
Attendants.
Pieces in box: 29.
Issued: 1936-1937.
Remarks: 1470 and 1475
combined.

Serial No: 1477.
Title: Royal Presentation Box.
Pieces in box: 75.
Issued: 1936-1937.
Remarks: With coach, attendants,
foot guards, staff officers,
mounted and foot police.

Serial No: 1478.
Title: Coronation State Coach.
Issued: 1936-1937.
Remarks: $6\frac{1}{4}''$ long with 4 horse
team.

Serial No: 1479.
Title: Short Pole Limber.
Pieces in box: 1.
Issued: 1936-1937.
Remarks: Pole adapted for M.T.
towing. See also 1201, 1462 and
1831.

Serial No: 1480.
Title: Racing Colours, H.M. The
King.
Pieces in box: 2.
Issued: 1936-1937.
Remarks: Large Scale Race-horse
and separate Jockey. See also 237.

Serial No: 1481.
Title: Racing Colours, Lord
Derby.
Pieces in box: 2.
Issued: 1936-1937.
Remarks: See also 237.

Serial No: 1482.
Title: Racing Colours, Lord
Astor.
Pieces in box: 2.
Issued: 1936-1937.
Remarks: See also 237.

Serial No: 1483.
Title: Racing Colours, Major
Furlong.
Pieces in box: 2.
Issued: 1936-1937.
Remarks: See also 237.

Serial No: 1484.
Title: Racing Colours, Sir H.
Cunliffe-Owen.
Pieces in box: 2.
Issued: 1936-1937.
Remarks: See also 237.

Serial No: 1485.
Title: Racing Colours, Duke of
Portland.
Pieces in box: 2.
Issued: 1936-1937.
Remarks: See also 237.

Serial No: 1486.
Title: Racing Colours, H.H. The
Aga Khan.
Pieces in box: 2.
Issued: 1936-1937.
Remarks: See also 1463.

Serial No: 1487.
Title: Racing Colours, Lord
Glanely.
Pieces in box: 2.
Issued: 1936-1937.
Remarks: See also 1463.

Serial No: 1488.
Title: Racing Colours, Lord
Rosebery.
Pieces in box: 2.
Issued: 1936-1937.
Remarks: See also 1463.

Serial No: 1489.
Title: Racing Colours, Miss D.
Paget.
Pieces in box: 2.
Issued: 1936-1937.
Remarks: See also 1463.

Serial No: 1490.
Title: Racing Colours, Miss J. de
Selincourt.
Pieces in box: 2.
Issued: 1936-1937.
Remarks: See also 1463.

Serial No: 1491.
Title: Racing Colours, Lord
Mildmay of Flete.
Pieces in box: 2.
Issued: 1936-1937.
Remarks: See also 1463.

Serial No: 1492.
Title: Racing Colours, Mr A. de
Rothschild.
Pieces in box: 2.
Issued: 1936-1937.
Remarks: See also 237 and 1463.

Serial No: 1493-1494. Not
Known.

Serial No: 1495.
Title: Painters, with Ladder.
Pieces in box: 3.
Issued: 1937.
Remarks: See also 779-781.

Serial No: 1496-1501. Not Listed.

Serial No: 1502.
Title: Grenadier Guards.
Pieces in box:
Issued: 1937.
Remarks: Second quality figures.

Serial No: 1503.
Title: Miniature State Coach.
Pieces in box: 3.
Issued: 1937.
Remarks: 2 horse team. See also
1470, 1478 and 44D.

Serial No: 1504-1507. Not Listed.

Serial No: 1508.
Title: Texas Rangers.
Pieces in box: 5.
Issued: 1937.
Remarks: Cowboys on horseback.
All Blue painting.

Serial No: 1509. Not Listed.

Serial No: 1510.
Title: Royal Navy Sailors.
Pieces in box: 8.
Issued: 1936-1941.
Remarks: Marching in Regulation
Dress without weapons or
equipment. Revised figure.

Serial No: 1511.
Title: Mounted Police.
Pieces in box: 5.
Issued: 1937.
Remarks: At halt in peaked caps
as 775.

Serial No: **1512** *00*.
Title: Army Ambulance, Motor
Type.
Pieces in box: 4.
Issued: 1937.
Remarks: With driver and
wounded man on stretcher. See
also 1513, 1514, 1897, 1824 and
1909.

Serial No: 1513.
Title: Volunteer Corps
Ambulance.
Pieces in box: 2.
Issued: 1937.
Remarks: As 1512 painted blue.

Serial No: 1514.
Title: Corporation Type Motor
Ambulance.
Pieces in box: 2.
Issued: 1937.
Remarks: As 1512 painted cream.

Serial No: 1515. (9124)
Title: Coldstream Guards.
Pieces in box: 8.
Issued: 1937.
Remarks: Marching at the slope
with officer.

Serial No: **1516** *00*.
Title: Historical Series, Line
Infantry.
Pieces in box: 8.
Issued: 1937.
Remarks: Waterloo Period with
pikes at attention with officer.

Serial No: 1517.
Title: Historical Series,
Highlanders.
Pieces in box: 8.
Issued: 1937.
Remarks: Waterloo Period with
pikes at attention with officer.

Serial No: **1518** *00*.
Title: Historical Series, Line
Infantry.
Pieces in box: 8.
Issued: 1937.
Remarks: Line Infantry Waterloo
Period carrying muskets; shoulder
arms at attention with officer.

Serial No: 1519.
Title: Historical Series,
Highlanders.
Pieces in box: 8.
Issued: 1937.
Remarks: Waterloo Period
carrying muskets; shoulder arms
at attention with officer.

Serial No: 1520.
Title: Short Monoplane Flying
Boat.
Pieces in box: 2.
Issued: 1937.
Remarks: Working model with
launching wheels. Ran along a
wire and propellers turned.

Serial No: **1521** *00*.
Title: Biplane.
Pieces in box: 3.
Issued: 1937.
Remarks: With pilot and hangar
formed from box.

Serial No: 1522.
Title: 4.5 inch A.A. Gun.
Pieces in box: 1.
Issued: 1937.
Remarks: Model with
semi-automatic action and pinion
elevation and traverse.

Serial No: 1523.
Title: R.A.F. Band.
Pieces in box: 11.
Issued: 1937.
Remarks: See also 1523, 1527
and 2116.

Serial No: 1524.
Title R.A.F. Band.
Pieces in box: 21.
Issued: 1937.
Remarks: See also 1523, 1527
and 2116.

Serial No: **1525** *00*.
Title: U.S. Biplane.
Pieces in box: 3.
Issued: 1937.
Remarks: With Pilot and hangar
as 1521.

Serial No: 1526.
Title: All Metal Flower Holder.
Pieces in box: 1.
Issued: 1937.
Remarks: See also 426.

Serial No: 1527.
Title: R.A.F. Band.
Pieces in box: 12.
Issued: 1937.
Remarks: See also 1523, 1524.
Replaced by 2116 in 1950-54.

Serial No: 1528-29. Not Listed.

Serial No: 1530.
Title: Mediaeval Display.
Pieces in box: 19.
Issued: 1937.
Remarks: With Marshal, Knights,
Squires and Herald.

Serial No: 1531-36. Not Listed.

Serial No: 1537.
Title: Territorial Army.
Pieces in box: 8.
Issued: 1937.
Remarks: Marching at the slope in
Blue uniform with officer
(Coronation Dress).

Serial No: 1538.
Title: Territorial Army.
Pieces in box: 8.
Issued: 1937.
Remarks: As 1537 but in green.
At slope. Uniform for 1937
Coronation.

Serial No: **1539***00*.
Title: Circus Display.
Pieces in box: 23.
Issued: 1937.
Remarks: With Circus Ring, 4 ×
351Bulk, 2 × 352Bulk,
353Bulk-355Bulk, 357Bulk,
358Bulk, 2 × 359Bulk, 446Bulk,
2 × 447Bulk, 448Bulk, 2 ×
449Bulk, 2 × 450Bulk and
451Bulk. See also 1439,
1441-1444 and 2054.

Serial No: 1540.
Title: Territorial Army.
Pieces in box: 8.
Issued: 1937.
Remarks: At Present Arms in
blue uniforms as 1537.

Serial No: 1541.
Title: Territorial Army.
Pieces in box: 8.
Issued: 1937.
Remarks: As 1538 but at Present
Arms.

Serial No: 1542.
Title: New Zealand Infantry.
Pieces in box: 8.
Issued: 1937.
Remarks: Marching at the slope in
Service Dress.
See also 1543.

Serial No: 1543.
Title:New Zealand Infantry.
Pieces in box: 8.
Issued: 1937.
Remarks: At Present Arms in
Service Dress.

Serial No: 1544.
Title: Australian Infantry.
Pieces in box: 8.
Issued: 1937.
Remarks: In Service Dress
marching at the slope with officer.

Serial No: 1545.
Title: Australian Infantry.
Pieces in box: 8.
Issued: 1937.
Remarks: In Service Dress at present arms with officer.

Serial No: 1546-49. Not Listed.

Serial No: **1550** *00*.
Title: Noah's Ark.
Pieces in box: 25.
Issued: 1937-1938.
Remarks: Noah and Wife (from 1313) with Wooden Ark and one each of 910, 911, 966, 967, two each of 901, 903, 908, 923, 934, 946, 950 and 955.

Serial No: 1551. Not Listed.

Serial No: 1552.
Title: Royal Mail Van.
Pieces in box: 2.
Issued: 1937-1938.
Remarks: As Ambulance 1512, etc, but painted in G.P.O. colours. See also LV619.

Serial No: 1553. Not Known.

Serial No: 1554. (9156)
Title: Royal Canadian Mounted Police.
Pieces in box: 8.
Issued: 1937-1938.
Remarks: In Summer Full Dress, marching.

Serial No: 1555. (9424)
Title: Changing of the Guard at Buckingham Palace.
Pieces in box: 83.
Issued: 1937-1938.
Remarks: Scots Guards as 75 and Coldstream Guards as 205 with Officers, Colours, full band and sentry boxes as 329.

British Army Regiments Parade Series Nos 1556-1602.

Serial No: 1556.
Title: Lincolnshire Regt.
Pieces in box: ?
Issued: 1937-1938.
Remarks: Marching at the slope in Review Order.

Serial No: 1557.
Title: East Yorkshire Regt.
Pieces in box: 8.
Issued: 1937-1938.
Remarks: Marching at the slope in Review Order. See also 113.

Serial No: 1558.
Title: Bedfordshire and Hertfordshire Regiment.
Pieces in box: 8.
Issued: 1936-1941.
Remarks: Marching at the slope.

Serial No: 1559.
Title: Lancashire Fusiliers.
Pieces in box: 8.
Issued: 1937-1938.
Remarks: Marching at the slope in Review Order. See also 86 and 17B.

Serial No: 1560.
Title: East Lancs. Regt.
Pieces in box: 8.
Issued: 1937-1938.
Remarks: Marching at the slope in Review Order.

Serial No: 1561.
Title: East Surrey Regt.
Pieces in box: 8.
Issued: 1937-1938.
Remarks: Marching at the slope in Review Order.

Serial No: 1562.
Title: South Staffs Regt.
Pieces in box: 8.
Issued: 1937-1938.
Remarks: Marching at the slope in
Review Order.

Serial No: 1563.
Title: The Welsh Regt.
Pieces in box: 8.
Issued: 1937-1941.
Remarks: Marching at the slope in
Review Order.

Serial No: 1564.
Title: Loyal North Lancs.
Pieces in box:
Issued: 1937-1938.
Remarks: Marching at the slope in
Review Order.

Serial No: 1565.
Title: The Manchester Regt.
Pieces in box: 8.
Issued: 1937-1938.
Remarks: Marching at the slope in
Review Order.
See also 20B and 151W.

Serial No: 1566.
Title: North Staffordshire Regt.
Pieces in box: 8.
Issued: 1939.
Remarks: Marching at the slope.

Serial No: 1567.
Title: York and Lancaster Regt.
Pieces in box: 8.
Issued: 1939.
Remarks: Marching at the slope in
Review Order.
See also 96.

Serial No: 1568.
Title: The Essex Regt.
Pieces in box: 8.
Issued: 1939.
Remarks: Marching at the slope in
Review Order.

Serial No: 1569.
Title: Duke of Cornwall's Light
Infantry.
Pieces in box: 8.
Issued: 1937-1938.
Remarks: Marching at the slope in
Review Order. See also 2088.

Serial No: 1570.
Title: Oxon and Bucks Light
Infantry.
Pieces in box: 8.
Issued: 1937-1938.
Remarks: Marching at the slope in
Review Order.

Serial No: 1571.
Title: Queen's Royal West Surrey
Regt.
Pieces in box: 8.
Issued: 1937-1938.
Remarks: Marching at the slope in
Review Order. See also 29, 121,
447 and 2086.

Serial No: 1572.
Title: King's Own Royal
Lancaster Regt.
Pieces in box: 8.
Issued: 1937-1938.
Remarks: Marching at the slope in
Review Order. See also 148 and
149.

Serial No: 1573.
Title: Royal Warwickshire Regt.
Pieces in box: 8.
Issued: 1936-1941.
Remarks: Marching at the slope in
Review Order. See also 206.

Serial No: 1574.
Title: King's (Liverpool) Regt.
Pieces in box:
Issued: 1937-1938.
Remarks: Marching at the slope in
Review Order.

Serial No: 1575.
Title: Royal Sussex Regt.
Pieces in box: 8.
Issued: 1937-1938.
Remarks: Marching at the slope in
Review Order.

Serial No: 1576.
Title: Royal Berkshire Regt.
Pieces in box: 8.
Issued: 1937-1938.
Remarks: Marching at the slope in
Review Order. See also 2093.

Serial No: 1577.
Title: Queen's Own Royal West
Kent Regiment.
Pieces in box: 8.
Issued: 1937-1938.
Remarks: Marching at the slope in
Review Order. See also 726A.

Serial No: 1578.
Title: Somerset Light Infantry.
Pieces in box: 8.
Issued: 1937-1938.
Remarks: Marching at the slope in
Review Order. See also 17 and 40.

Serial No: 1579.
Title: King's Own Yorkshire Light
Infantry.
Pieces in box: 8.
Issued: 1937-1938.
Remarks: Marching at the slope in
Review Order.

Serial No: 1580.
Title: King's Own Shropshire
Light Infantry.
Pieces in box:
Issued: 1937-1938.
Remarks: Marching at the slope in
Review Order.

Serial No: 1581.
Title: Royal Irish Fusiliers.
Pieces in box: 8.
Issued: 1937-1941.
Remarks: Marching at the slope in
Review Order. See also 2090.

Serial No: 1582.
Title: East Kent Regt (The Buffs).
Pieces in box: 8.
Issued: 1937-1938.
Remarks: Marching at the slope in
Review Order. See also 16.

Serial No: 1583.
Title: West Yorkshire Regt.
Pieces in box: 8.
Issued: 1937-1938.
Remarks: Marching at the slope in
Review Order.

Serial No: 1584.
Title: Cheshire Regt.
Pieces in box: 8.
Issued: 1937-1938.
Remarks: Marching at the slope in
Review Order.

Serial No: 1585.
Title: Prince of Wales's (South
Lancs.) Volunteers.
Pieces in box: 8.
Issued: 1937-1938.
Remarks: Marching at the slope in
Review Order. See also 1798.

Serial No: 1586.
Title: Northamptonshire Regt.
Pieces in box: 8.
Issued: 1937-1938.
Remarks: Marching at the slope in
Review Order.

Serial No: 1587.
Title: Wiltshire Regt.
Pieces in box: 8.
Issued: 1937-1938.
Remarks: Marching at the slope in
Review Order.

Serial No: 1588.
Title: Royal Norfolk Regt.
Pieces in box: 8.
Issued: 1937-1938.
Remarks: Marching at the slope in
Review Order.

Serial No: 1589.
Title: Suffolk Regt.
Pieces in box: 8.
Issued: 1937-1938.
Remarks: Marching at the slope in
Review Order.

Serial No: 1590.
Title: The Border Regt.
Pieces in box: 8.
Issued: 1936-1941.
Remarks: Marching at the slope in
Review Order.

Serial No: 1591.
Title: Hampshire Regt.
Pieces in box:
Issued: 1937-1938.
Remarks: Marching at the slope in
Review Order.

Serial No: 1592.
Title: Gloucestershire Regt.
Pieces in box: 8.
Issued: 1937-1938.
Remarks: Marching at the slope in
Review Order. See also 119 and
2089.

Serial No: 1593.
Title: Devonshire Regt.
Pieces in box:
Issued: 1937-1938.
Remarks: Marching at the slope in
Review Order. See also 110.

Serial No: 1594.
Title: Sherwood Foresters.
Pieces in box: 8.
Issued: 1937-1938.
Remarks: Marching at the slope in
Review Order.

Serial No: 1595.
Title: Green Howards.
Pieces in box: 8.
Issued: 1937-1938.
Remarks: Marching at the slope in
Review Order. See also 255.

Serial No: 1596.
Title: South Wales Borderers.
Pieces in box: 8.
Issued: 1937-1938.
Remarks: Marching at the slope in
Review Order.

Serial No: 1597.
Title: Dorset Regt.
Pieces in box: 8.
Issued: 1937-1938.
Remarks: Marching at the slope in
Review Order.

Serial No: 1598.
Title: Worcestershire Regt.
Pieces in box:
Issued: 1937-1938.
Remarks: In Review Order
marching at the slope. See also 18,
22 and 131.

Serial No: 1599.
Title: Royal Northumberland
Fusiliers.
Pieces in box: 8.
Issued: 1937-1938.
Remarks: Marching at the slope in
Review Order. See also 85 and
21B.

Serial No: 1600.
Title: Durham Light Infantry.
Pieces in box: 8.
Issued: 1937-1938.
Remarks: Marching at the slope in
Review Order.

Serial No: 1601.
Title: Leicestershire Regt.
Pieces in box: 8.
Issued: 1937-1938.
Remarks: Marching at the slope in
Review Order.

Serial No: 1602.
Title: Duke of Wellington's Regt.
Pieces in box:
Issued: 1937-1938.
Remarks: Marching at the slope in
Review Order: Last known set of
the British Army Parade Series –
issued in the 1937-1938 period.

Serial No: **1603** *00*.
Title: Republic of Ireland
Infantry.
Pieces in box: 8.
Issued: 1937-1938.
Remarks: Marching at the slope in
peaked caps and Service Dress
with officer. Figure similar to
Mounties but with head change.

Serial No: 1604-06. Not Listed.

Serial No: 1607.
Title: Display Box.
Pieces in box: 45.
Issued: 1937-1938.
Remarks: With Royal Scots
Greys, Scots Guards, Scots
Guards Band and sentry boxes.
See also 32, 329, 1722.

Serial No: 1608.
Title: Modern Army Presentation
Box.
Pieces in box: 43.
Issued: 1937-41.
Remarks: Contained Service
Dress Infantry, and Cavalry, plus
Dispatch Riders and
Machine-gunners.

Serial No: 1609. Not Listed.

Serial No: **1610** *00*.
Title: Royal Marines.
Pieces in box: 8.
Issued: 1937.
Remarks: At Present Arms with
officer.

Serial No: 1611.
Title: British Infantry.
Pieces in box: 8.
Issued: 1937-1938.
Remarks: 7 men in prone position
with fixed bayonets, steel helmets
and gasmasks. Officer standing in
helmet and gasmask with sword
and pistol.

Serial No: 1612.
Title: British Infantry.
Pieces in box: 8.
Issued: 1937-1938.
Remarks: In steel helmets and
gasmasks throwing grenades;
Officer with sword and pistol.

Serial No: 1613. (9146)
Title: British Infantry.
Pieces in box: 7.
Issued: 1937-1938.
Remarks: Charging with fixed
bayonets in gasmasks and steel
helmets; Officer with drawn
sword and pistol.

Serial No: **1614** *00*. (9346)
Title: British Infantry.
Pieces in box: 24.
Issued: 1937-1938.
Remarks: Figures as 1612-13 with
digging and lying
machine-gunners and
infantryman marching at the trail.

Serial No: 1615.
Title: British Infantry.
Pieces in box: 15.
Issued: 1937-1938.
Remarks: Smaller version of 1614
without the lying
machine-gunners.

Serial No: 1616.
Title: British Infantry.
Pieces in box: 15.
Issued: 1937-1938.
Remarks: Smaller version of
1614.

Serial No: 1617.
Title: Line Regiments.
Pieces in box: 8.
Issued: 1937-1938.
Remarks: Regular and Territorial
Army in Blue Walking Out Dress
with officer. See also 1537 and
1546.

Serial No: 1618.
Title: Rifle Regiments.
Pieces in box: 8.
Issued: 1937-1938.
Remarks: Walking Out Dress
with Green peaked caps. Officer
included. See also 9 and 2091.

Serial No: **1619** 00.
Title: Royal Marines.
Pieces in box: 8.
Issued: 1936-1941.
Remarks: In Tropical dress
marching at the slope with officer.
Same figure as 35, final version,
but with khaki tunic.

Serial No: 1620.
Title: Royal Marine Light
Infantry.
Pieces in box: 8.
Issued: 1939.
Remarks: At the slope with
officer. See also 35.

Serial No: 1621.
Title: 3/12th (Sikh) Frontier
Force Regt.
Pieces in box: 8.
Issued: 1939.
Remarks: In khaki marching at
the slope.

Serial No: 1622.
Title: Band of the Royal Marine
Light Infantry.
Pieces in box: 21.
Issued: 1939.
Remarks: 20 instrumentalists and
drum major.

Serial No: 1623.
Title: U.S. Infantry.
Pieces in box: 8.
Issued: 1939.
Remarks: In Service Dress
crawling prone in gas masks with
standing officer as 1611.

Serial No: 1624.
Title: U.S. Infantry.
Pieces in box: 8.
Issued: 1939.
Remarks: In Service Dress and
gas masks throwing grenades with
officer all as 1612. See also 1623.

Serial No: 1625.
Title: U.S. Infantry.
Pieces in box: 7.
Issued: 1939.
Remarks: As 1613.

Serial No: 1626.
Title: U.S. Infantry Display.
Pieces in box: 24.
Issued: 1939.
Remarks: As 1614. See also 359
amd 1623-1625.

Serial No: 1627.
Title: U.S. Infantry Display.
Pieces in box: 15.
Issued: 1939.
Remarks: As 1615. See also
1623-1626.

Serial No: 1628.
Title: U.S. Infantry Display.
Pieces in box: 15.
Issued: 1939.
Remarks: As 1616. See also
1623-1627.

Serial No: 1629.
Title: Lord Strathcona's Horse.
Pieces in box: 5.
Issued: 1939.
Remarks: In Review Order with
officer, similar figure to 31. See
also 1635.

Serial No: 1630.
Title: Royal Canadian Dragoons.
Pieces in box: 5.
Issued: 1939.
Remarks: As 127. See also 1636.

Serial No: 1631*00*. (9257)
Title: Governor General's Horse
Guards of Canada.
Pieces in box: 5. Mtd.
Issued: 1939.
Remarks: As 127. See also 1637
and 2133.

Serial No: 1632.
Title: Royal Canadian Regt.
Pieces in box: 8.
Issued: 1939.
Remarks: Marching at the slope in
Review Order with officer.
See also 1633 and 1635. Similar
hat and tunic to 1633.

Serial No: **1633** *00*. (9157)
Title: Princess Patricia's Canadian
Light Infantry.
Pieces in box: 8.
Issued: 1939.
Remarks: As 1632 with different
painting. See also 1636.

Serial No: 1634. (9159)
Title: Governor General's Foot
Guards of Canada.
Pieces in box: 8.
Issued: 1939.
Remarks: Similar to British Foot
Guards; marching at the slope in
Review Order.

Serial No: 1635.
Title: Lord Strathcona's Horse
and the Royal Canadian Regt.
Pieces in box: 13.
Issued: 1939.
Remarks: Combination at 1629
and 1632.

Serial No: 1636.
Title: Princess Patricia's Canadian
Light Infantry and the Royal
Canadian Dragoons.
Pieces in box: 13.
Issued: 1939.
Remarks: Combination of 1630
and 1633.

Serial No: 1637. (9356)
Title: Governor General's Horse
and Foot Guards of Canada.
Pieces in box: 13.
Issued: 1939.
Remarks: Combination of 1631
and 1634. See also 2133.

Serial No: **1638** *00*.
Title: Sound Locator.
Pieces in box: 2.
Issued: 1939.
Remarks: With operator. See also
1639, 1724, 1728, 1729, 1731,
2052 and 2188.

Serial No: **1639** *00*.
Title: Range Finder.
Pieces in box: 2.
Issued: 1939.
Remarks: With operator. See also
1638, 1728, 1729, 1731, 2052 and
2188.

Serial No: 1640.
Title: Search light.
Pieces in box: 1.
Issued: 1939.
Remarks: Battery powered in
base. See also 1642, 1718, 1724
and 1833.

Serial No: **1641** *00*.
Title: Heavy Duty Underslung
Army Lorry.
Pieces in box: 2.
Issued: 1939.
Remarks: 18 Wheeled with
driver. Last production version
(1941) had all-metal wheels due
to rubber shortage. See also 1642,
1643, 1757, LV603 and LV614.

Serial No: 1642.
Title: Heavy Duty Underslung
Army Lorry with Searchlight.
Pieces in box: 3.
Issued: 1939.
Remarks: Combination of 1640
and 1641. Carried battery in front
compartment of trailer.

Serial No: 1643.
Title: Heavy Duty Underslung
Army Lorry with Heavy A.A.
Gun.
Pieces in box: 3.
Issued: 1939.
Remarks: As 1641. Carried 4.5
inch gun (No. 1522).

Serial No: 1644.
Title: Mickey Mouse at the
Cinema.
Pieces in box: ?
Remarks: No details known.
See also 1645 and 1654.

Serial No: 1645.
Title: Micky Mouse Set.
Pieces in box: 6.
Issued: 1939-1941.
Remarks: Included Micky,
Minnie, Donald Duck, Pluto,
Clarabelle and Goofy. All had
moveable heads.
See also 1644 and 1654. Also sold
separately as 16H, 17H, 19H,
18H, 20H, and 21H respectively.

Serial No: 1646-7. Not Listed.

Serial No: 1648.
Title: Royal Navy Display Box.
Pieces in box: 51.
Issued: 1936-1941.
Remarks: Included the Landing
Party, Officers and Blue and
Whitejackets in various positions.

Serial No: 1649-1653. Not Listed.

Serial No: 165400.
Title: Snow White and the Seven
Dwarfs.
Pieces in box: 8.
Issued: 1939-1941.
Remarks: Each figure
recognisable dwarf. Also sold
separately as 541B Sleepy, 542B
Happy, 543B Sneezy, 544B
Bashful, 545B Grumpy, 546B
Doc, 547B Dopey, 548B Snow
White.

Serial No: 1655. Not Listed.

Serial No: 1656.
Title: John Cobb's 'Railton
Wonder Car'.
Pieces in box: 1.
Issued: 1939.
Remarks: See also 1400 and
1658.

Serial No: 1657. Not Listed.

Serial No: 1658.
Title: John Cobb's 'Railton
Wonder Car'.
Pieces in box: 1.
Issued: 1939.
Remarks: Chromium plated.
See also 1400 and 1656.

Serial No: 1659. (9492)
Title: Knight with Mace.
Pieces in box: 1.
Issued: 1939-1941.
Remarks: 'Agincourt Series'.
See also 1660, 1664 and 2161.

Serial No: 1660. (9493)
Title: Knight with Sword.
Pieces in box: 1.
Issued: 1939-1941.
Remarks: 'Agincourt Series'.
See also 1669, 1664 and 2161.

Serial No: **1661** *00*. (9494)
Title: Knight with Lance.
Pieces in box: 1.
Issued: 1939-1941.
Remarks: 'Agincourt Series' with
visor open on charging horse. See
also 1307, 1308, 1662, 1663 and
2161.

Serial No: 1662. (9495)
Title: Knight with Standard.
Pieces in box: 1.
Issued: 1939-1941.
Remarks: 'Agincourt series'. With
visor on reined in horse. See also
1661, 1663 and 2161.

Serial No: **1663** *00*. (9496)
Title: Knight with Lance.
Pieces in box: 1.
Issued: 1939-1941.
Remarks: 'Agincourt Series'.
With closed visor on rearing
horse. See also 1307, 1308, 1661,
1662 and 2161.

Serial No: 1664.
Title: Knights on Foot.
Pieces in box: 5.
Issued: 1939-1941.
Remarks: Carrying Lance, Sword,
Battleaxe and Mace.
See also 1307, 1308, 1659 and
1660.

Serial No: 1665-1710. Not Listed.

Serial No: **1711** *00*. (9167)
Title: French Foreign Legion.
Pieces in box: 7.
Issued: 1939.
Remarks: Figures from box 141
with mounted officer.
See also 2136, 561B and 1035B.

Serial No: **1712** *00*.
Title: French Foreign Legion.
Pieces in box: 15.
Issued: 1939.
Remarks: Larger version of 1711.

Serial No: 1713-1714. Not Listed.

Serial No: 1715. (9706)
Title: 2 Pdr. (40 mm) Light A.A.
Gun.
Pieces in box: 1.
Issued: 1939.
Remarks: See also 1715-1718,
1832, 1866 and 2052.

Serial No: 1716.
Title: Chassis.
Pieces in box: 1.
Issued: 1939.
Remarks: 4 wheeled chassis with
extendible stays and screw jacks to
take 1640 or 1715.

Serial No: 1717. (9735)
Title: 2 pdr (40 mm) A.A. on
chassis (Mobile Unit).
Pieces in box: 2.
Issued: 1939.
Remarks: 1715 and 1716 combined.

Serial No: 1718. (9765)
Title: Searchlight on chassis.
Pieces in box: 2.
Issued: 1939.
Remarks: 1642 combined with
1716.

Serial No: 1719.
Title: Stretcher Party of the
R.A.M.C.
Pieces in box: 3.
Issued: 1939.
Remarks: Figures as 1426 painted
khaki in peaked cap. Also steel
helmeted version. See also 1896
and 2132.

Serial No: **1720** *00*. (9312)
Title: Band of the Royal Scots
Greys (2nd Dragoons).
Pieces in box: 7.
Issued: 1939.
Remarks: 1st version drum's ,
embossed and drummer's arms
apart. Later versions had the arms
joined at the sticks. See also 1721
and 1344B.

Serial No: 1721.
Title: Band of the Royal Scots
Greys (2nd Dragoons).
Pieces in box: 12.
Issued: 1939.
Remarks: Full band with kettle
drummer on walking horses. See
also 1720 and 1344B.

Serial No: 1722.
Title: Pipe Band of the Scots
Guards.
Pieces in box: 21.
Issued: 1939.
Remarks: See also 69, 75 and 130.

Serial No: 1723 00.
Title: R.A.M.C. Unit.
Pieces in box: 8.
Issued: 1939.
Remarks: 2 Nurses with bearers.
First version in service dress, later
in Battle Dress. Men in steel
helmets.

Serial No: 1724.
Title: A.A. Unit.
Pieces in box: 15.
Issued: 1939.
Remarks: With 1432, 1640, 1638,
2 × 1731. Six man searchlight
operating detachment and tent.
With spotters.

Serial No: 1725. (9725)
Title: 4.5 inch Howitzer.
Pieces in box: 1.
Issued: 1939.
Remarks: Modern type on rubber
tyres. See also 1265, 1266, 1726,
1727, 1824, 1861, 1863, 2008,
2106 and 2107.

Serial No: 1726 00.
Title: Regulation Limber.
Pieces in box: 1.
Issued: 1939.
Remarks: Modern type with
rubber tyres. See also 1725, 1727
and 2008.

Serial No: 1727.
Title: Complete Mobile Howitzer
Unit.
Pieces in box: 3.
Issued: 1939.
Remarks: With 1725, 1726 and
1462. See also 1265, 1266, 1433,
2008, 2106 and 2107.

Serial No: 1728 00.
Title: Predictor.
Pieces in box: 2.
Issued: 1939.
Remarks: With operator. See also
1638, 1639, 1729, 1731 and 2052.

Serial No: 1729 00.
Title: Height finder.
Pieces in box: 2.
Issued: 1939.
Remarks: With operator. See also
1638, 1639, 1728, 1731, 2052 and
2188.

Serial No: 1730 00. (9148)
Title: Modern Army Team of
Gunners.
Pieces in box: 7.
Issued: 1939.
1st change: 1940-1945.
Remarks: 4 kneeling and 3
standing figures in Service Dress
and steel helmets carrying shells.
Officer with binoculars added
1940, and some figures no longer
held shells.

Serial No: 1731 00.
Title: Spotting Chair.
Pieces in box: 2.
Issued: 1939.
Remarks: Swivelling, with officer
in Service Dress with binoculars.
See also 1638, 1639, 1724, 1728,
1729 and 2052.

Serial No: 1732 00.
Title: Standard Type Army Hut.
Pieces in box: 2.
Issued: 1939.
Remarks: Plywood construction.

Serial No: 1733.
Title: Nissen Type Army Hut.
Pieces in box: 1.
Issued: 1939.
Remarks: Wood and cardboard
construction.

Serial No: 1734.
Title: Guard Room.
Pieces in box: 2.
Issued: 1939.
Remarks: With detachable roof.
See also 1748.

Serial No: 1735.
Title: Gun Shed.
Pieces in box: 1.
Issued: 1939.
Remarks: Fitted with roller doors
to take 1647 or 1717. See also
1736. Could also be combined
with 1740 for use as a gun
platform.

Serial No: 1736.
Title: Gun Shed.
Pieces in box: 1.
Issued: 1939.
Remarks: With roller and shutter
doors to house three guns and
limbers. Could also be combined
with 1739 and 1740.

Serial No: 1737.
Title: Army Transport Shed.
Pieces in box: 1.
Issued: 1939.
Remarks: To hold three vehicles.

Serial No: 1738.
Title: Army Stable.
Pieces in box: 2.
Issued: 1939.
Remarks: To hold six horses. Had
a detachable roof.

Serial No: 1739.
Title: Gunners' Quarters.
Pieces in box: 2.
Issued: 1939.
Remarks: With detachable roof.
Could be used with 1736 and
1740.

Serial No: 1740.
Title: Flight of Steps.
Pieces in box: 1.
Issued: 1939.
Remarks: To fit 1735, 1736 or
1747.

Serial No: 1741. Not Listed.

Serial No: 1742.
Title: Field Gun Emplacement.
Pieces in box: 1.
Issued: 1939.
Remarks: Concrete type.

Serial No: 1743.
Title: Field Gun Emplacement.
Pieces in box: 1.
Issued: 1939.
Remarks: Open type of banked
earth.

Serial No: 1744.
Title: Machine-gun
Emplacement.
Pieces in box: 1.
Issued: 1939.
Remarks: Sandbagged sides with
corrugated iron roof. See also
1860.

Serial No: 1745.
Title: Machine-gun
Emplacement.
Pieces in box: 1.
Issued: 1939.
Remarks: Twin sandbagged type.
Can be used with 1746 to make a
continuous defence line. See also
1860 and 1864.

Serial No: 1746.
Title: Gun Emplacement.
Pieces in box: 1.
Issued: 1939.
Remarks: Sandbagged trench
type for machine-guns or small
field guns. See also 1860.

Serial No: 1747.
Title: Barrack Buildings with
Parade Ground.
Pieces in box: 3.
Issued: 1939.
Remarks: With detachable roof
used to mount AA guns and
searchlights when 1740 is fitted.

Serial No: 1748.
Title: Barrack Buildings with
Guard Huts.
Pieces in box: 2.
Issued: 1939.
Remarks: Different types to
1732-1734.

Serial No: 1749.
Title: Balloon with Winch.
Pieces in box: 2.
Issued: 1939.
Remarks: For use with 1641. See
also 1757, 1760 and 1855.

Serial No: 1750-1756. Not Listed.

Serial No: **1757** *00*.
Title: Balloon Barage Unit.
Pieces in box: 4.
Issued: 1939.
Remarks: Combination of 1641
and 1749.

Serial No: 1758.
Title: R.A.F. Fire Fighters.
Pieces in box: 8.
Issued: 1939.
Remarks: Figures in Asbestos
suits. See also 1906 and 587B.

Serial No: **1759** *00*.
Title: (A.R.P.)
(National Service).
Pieces in box: 9.
Issued: 1936-1941.
Remarks: Stretcher Party Squad
with 2 stretcher teams, 2 casualties
and 1 man with a gas detector
stick. Warden figures were in
anti-gas suits and wearing
respirators.

Serial No: 1760.
Title: Barrage Balloon.
Pieces in box: 1.
Issued: 1939.
Remarks: Rubber compound
mould. See also 1749, 1757, 1855
and 1879.

Serial No: 1761.
Title: Hiking or Boy Scout Tent.
Pieces in box: 1.
Issued: 1939.
Remarks: See also 161-163, 180,
181, 289, 293, 423N.

Serial No: 1762-1790. Not Listed.

Serial No: 1791. (9153)
Title: Dispatch Rider Motor
Cyclist Royal Corps of Signals.
Pieces in box: 4.
Issued: 1939.
Remarks: On Norton motorcycle
with revolving wheels. See also
200, 323, 1608, 1791-1792, 1907,
2011, 148P and 149P.

Serial No: **1792** *00*.
Title: Mobile Traffic Police.
Pieces in box: 4.
Issued: 1939.
Remarks: On motor cycles.
See also 239, 319, 621, 654, 659,
775, 776, 808, 824, 1413, 1430,
1477, 1511, 149P and LB550.

Serial No: 1793.
Title: Machine Gun Corps.
Pieces in box: 2.
Issued: 1939.
Remarks: New version of 199
with revolving wheels.

Serial No: 1794.
Title: Detachment of Infantry.
Pieces in box: 8.
Issued: 1939.
Remarks: For use with
Searchlight 1718. Men standing
and kneeling in Service Dress with
steel helmets.

Serial No: 1795-1797. Not Listed.
Remarks: Numbers 1795-1797
are believed to be export boxes
containing 6 or 12 figures.

Serial No: 1798.
Title: Prince of Wales's (South
Lancs.) Volunteers.
Pieces in box: 8.
Issued: 1940.
Remarks: Marching at the slope.
See also 1585.

Serial No: 1799-1823. Not Listed.

Serial No: 1824.
Title: Large Display Box.
Pieces in box: 36.
Issued: 1939.
Remarks: Contained A.A.
personnel, Motor Ambulance, 4.5
inch howitzer, Nurses, Stretcher
Bearers. As 1512, 1639, 1717,
1718, 1723, 1727, 1728, 1729,
1731.

Serial No: 1825-1826. Not Listed.

Serial No: 1828.
Title: Large Display Box.
Pieces in box: ?
Issued: 1939.
Remarks: Contents as 1824 but
with fewer figures.

Serial No: 1829.
Title: Racing Colours, American
Owners.
Pieces in box: 12.
Issued: 1939.
Remarks: Colours of Marshall
Field, J. E. Widener, H. Maxwell,
J. H. Lonchiem, Wheatley
Stables, C. V. Whiting.

Serial No: 1830.
Title: Racing Colours, American
Owners.
Pieces in box: 12.
Issued: 1939.
Remarks: Colours of E. R.
Bradley, John H. Whitney, Bing
Crosby Stables, Greentree
Stables, Mrs E. Benemark,
August Belmont.

Serial No: 1831.
Title: R.A. Gun with Short Pole
Limber.
Pieces in box: 2.
Issued: 1939-1940.
Remarks: Gun No. 1201 and
limber as used in R.H.A. sets.

Serial No: 1832.
Title: Army Tender and 2 pdr
A.A. Gun on chassis.
Pieces in box: 3.
Issued: 1939.
Remarks: As 1432, 1715 and
1716.

Serial No: 1833.
Title: Army Tender.
Issued: 1939-1940.
Remarks: 1432 and 1718
combined. See also 1724.

Serial No: 1834. Not Listed.

Serial No: 1835.
Title: Argentina Cadettes
Navales.
Pieces in box: 8.
Remarks: Same casting as U.S.
Marine figure.

Serial No: 1836.
Title: Argentine Cadettes
Militares.
Pieces in box: 8.
Issued: 1940.
Remarks: Same casting as U.S.
Marine figure.

Serial No: 1837-1849. Not Listed.

Serial No: 1850.
Title: Netherland Infantry.
Pieces in box: 8.
Issued: 1940.
Remarks: Marching at the slope
with officer in Service Dress.
Figures from 1856 used with
different painting detail: light
khaki.

Serial No: 1851-1853. Not Listed.

Serial No: 1854.
Title: Militia Men.
Pieces in box: 8.
Issued: 1939.
1st change: 1940.
Remarks: Marching at the slope in
Battle Dress and SD caps. Officer
figure had coloured cap. Later
title changed to LDV. See also
1918.

Serial No: **1855** *00*.
Title: Balloon unit.
Pieces in box: 4.
Issued: 1939.
Remarks: 'OO' gauge model with
balloon made of hollow lead. See
also 1749, 1757, 1760 and 1879.
Last listed 'New Line' in 1939
catalogue.

Serial No: **1856** *00*.
Title: Polish Infantry.
Pieces in box: 8.
Issued: 1940.
Remarks: Marching at the slope in
Service Dress with officer. These
figures were also used for set
1850.

Serial No: 1857. Not Listed.

Serial No: **1858** *00*.
Title: British Infantry.
Pieces in box: 8.
Issued: 1940-1941.
Remarks: Full Battle Dress with
slung rifles. Later edition has Bren
Gunner.

Serial No: **1859** *00*.
Title: Sentry Box with Sentry.
Pieces in box: 2.
Issued: 1940-1941.
Remarks: Sentry similar to
Predictor Man box 1728. See also
329 and 1607.

Serial No: 1860,
Title: Sand Bags.
Pieces in box: 1.
Issued: 1940.
Remarks: Can be added to
1744-1746.

Serial No: 1861.
Title: Camouflaged Netted Field
Emplacement.
Pieces in box: 2.
Issued: 1940.

Serial No: 1862.
Title: Camouflaged Emplacement
Machine-gun.
Pieces in box: 1.
Issued: 1940.

Serial No: 1863.
Title: Concrete Pill Box.
Pieces in box: 2.
Issued: 1940.
Remarks: For heavy artillery.
With detachable roof.

Serial No: 1864.
Title: Concrete Pill Box.
Pieces in box: 3.
Issued: 1940.
Remarks: With detachable
machine-gun positions similar to
1745.

Serial No: 1865.
Title: Bayonet Practice Frame.
Pieces in box: 4.
Issued: 1940.
Remarks: With three hanging sandbags.

Serial No: 1866.
Title: Circular Sand Bag Emplacement.
Pieces in box: 1.
Issued: 1940.
Remarks: For AA guns and searchlights.

Serial No: 1867.
Title: Open Type Field Shelter.
Pieces in box: 1.
Issued: 1940.
Remarks: With camouflaged corrugated iron roof.

Serial No: 1868.
Title: Air Raid Wardens Post.
Pieces in box: 1.
Issued: 1940.
Remarks: 'with gas detector platform', like bird table, painted lime green.

Serial No: 1869.
Title: R.A.M.C. Casualty Clearing Station.
Issued: 1940.
Remarks: With thatched barn and open cartshed.
See also 1867.

Serial No: 1870-1875. Not Listed.

Serial No: **1876** *00*.
Title: Bren Gun Carrier.
Pieces in box: 4.
Issued: 1940.
Remarks: With crew of 3. All half figures as in 1448. See also 1203 and 1321.

Serial No: **1877** *00*.
Title: 15 cwt Beetle Lorry.
Pieces in box: 2.
Issued: 1940.
Remarks: With driver and canvas side screens. Originally lacked a towing hook which was added about 1952. Model of Guy Beetle platoon truck. See also 1909 and 2048.

Serial No: 1878. Not Listed.

Serial No: 1879.
Title: 'OO' Gauge Lorry and Trailer.
Pieces in box: 4.
Issued: 1940.
Remarks: Carrying detachable Hydrogen cylinders for use with 1855. See also 1749, 1757, 1760, 1855, LV612, LV613 and LV616.

Serial No: 1880-1891. Not Listed.

Serial No: 1892.
Title: Indian Infantry.
Pieces in box: 8.
Issued: 1940.
Remarks: In Service Dress at trail arms with British officer in Battle Dress carrying cane. See also 64, 252, 1342 and 1621.

Serial No: 1893.
Title: Royal Indian Army Service Corps.
Pieces in box: 7.
Issued: 1940.
Remarks: With mule, Sepoys at Trail Arms and British officer in Battle Dress with cane as 1892.

Serial No: 1894.
Title: R.A.F. Pilots & W.A.A.F.'s.
Pieces in box: 8.
Issued: 1940-1941.
Remarks: 6 walking pilots in full flying kit and 2 WAAFs. See also 1395, 1897, 1906, 66B, 1054B, 150P.

Serial No: **1895** *00*.
Title: Pilots of the Luftwaffe.
Pieces in box: 8.
Issued: 1940-1941.
Remarks: In full flying kit. Same
figure as RAF pilot 1894, 66B,
1054B and 150P.

Serial No: 1896.
Title: R.A.M.C. Stretcher Party.
Pieces in box: 8.
Issued: 1940-1941.
Remarks: In Battle Dress with
steel helmets. See also 1719 and
1897.

Serial No: **1897** *00*.
Title: R.A.M.C. Unit.
Pieces in box: 18.
Issued: 1940-1941.
1st change: 1941.
Remarks: 1512, 1896 plus Battle
Dress steel helmet figure for the
Doctor and Orderlies were as
W.A.A.F. in 1894. Later a special
figure was introduced; Battle
Dress Nurse.

Serial No: 1898 (9147)
Title: British Infantry.
Pieces in box: 8.
Issued: 1940-1941.
Remarks: In steel helmets; 1
officer as 87N, 4 men 'On Guard'
position with rifle as 89N, 3 men
with Thompson SMGs as 93N.

Serial No: 1899.
Title: U.S. Army Air Corps.
Pieces in box: 2.
Issued: 1940-1941.
Remarks: Autogiro and pilot. See
also 1392 and 1431.

Serial No: **1900** *00*.
Title: Regiment Lou Wepener.
Pieces in box: 8.
Issued: 1940-1941.
Remarks: Marching at the slope in
shorts and 'Topee' with officer.
See also 38, 1901, 1902 and 1293.

Serial No: 1901.
Title: Cape Town Highlanders.
Pieces in box: 8.
Issued: 1940-1941.
Remarks: In Service Dress with
officer. At slope with modern sun
helmet.

Serial No: 1902.
Title: Infantry of the Union of
South Africa Defence Forces.
Pieces in box: 8.
Issued: 1940-1941.
Remarks: Marching at the slope in
steel helmets and Service Dress
with officer as 434. See also 38,
1900, 1901 and 1293.

Serial No: 1903.
Title: Mountain Battery with
Gun.
Pieces in box: 12.
Issued: 1940-1941.
Remarks: Sepoy figure in Service
Dress with mules, gun and
mounted officer.

Serial No: **1904** *00*.
Title: U.S. Army Air Corps.
Pieces in box: 8.
Issued: 1940-1941.
Remarks: With Pilots, Officers
and men.

Serial No: 1905.
Title: U.S. Army Air Corps.
Pieces in box: 16.
Issued: 1940-1941.
Remarks: With Pilots, Officers
and men.

Serial No: 1906.
Title: R.A.F. Set.
Pieces in box: 16.
Issued: 1940-1941.
Remarks: With figures from 240,
1758 and walking pilots from
1894.

Serial No: 1907.
Title: General Staff Officers.
Pieces in box: 5.
Issued: 1940.
Remarks: All in Service Dress
with figures from 1791, 1918 (the
officer), a horse as 182. Officer
with binoculars similar to 72N and
a mounted General. See also 201
and 1908.

Serial No: 1908.
Title: Officers of the General
Staff.
Pieces in box: 8.
Issued: 1940-1941.
Remarks: Guards, Line Infantry,
Fusiliers, and Rifles officers using
the Medical officer figure from
1910.

Serial No: 1909.
Title: R.A.M.C. Unit.
Pieces in box: 28.
Issued: 1940-1941.
Remarks: Contained Officers,
Nurses, Orderlies, Tent,
Ambulance, Car and Lorry. As
1448, 1512, 1877, 1896, 1897 and
2005.

Serial No: 1910.
Title: R.A.M.C. Field Hospital
Staff and wounded.
Pieces in box: 24.
Issued: 1940-1941.
Remarks: Battle Dress figures.
See also 1723, 1896 and 1897.

Serial No: 1911.
Title: Officers and Petty Officers
of the Royal Navy.
Pieces in box: 7.
Issued: 1940-1941.
Remarks: In blue and white
uniforms.

Serial No: 1912-13. Not Listed.

Serial No: 1914.
Title: A.R.P. Wardens.
Pieces in box: 8.
Issued: 1940-1941.
Remarks: In regulation dress with
steel helmets, as 1723.

Serial No: 1915-1917. Not Listed.

Serial No: **1918** *00*.
Title: The Home Guard.
Pieces in box: 8.
Issued: 1940-1941.
Remarks: Marching with slung
rifles in Battle Dress and SD caps.
Officer figure as men but with
plain moveable arm. See also
1854.

Serial No: 1919. Not Listed.

Serial No: 1920.
Title: Chess Set.
Pieces in box: 25.
Issued: 1941.
Remarks: White metal figures.
Last item officially listed till the
end of the war. Also listed as 1990
in 1945.

Serial No: 1921-2001. Not Listed.

Serial No: 2002-2007
Single items also issued with larger
sets under different numbers.

Serial No: 2002.
Title: Bell Tent.
Issued: 1946.

Serial No: 2003.
Title: Bell Tent.
Issued: 1946.
Remarks: See also 2005.

Serial No: 2004.
Title: Bell Tent.
Issued: 1946.
Remarks: See also 2002.

Serial No: 2005.
Title: Marquee.
Issued: 1946.
Remarks: See also 2002.

Serial No: 2006.
Title: Marquee.
Issued: 1946.
Remarks: See also 2005.

Serial No: 2007.
Title: Marquee.
Issued: 1946.
Remarks: See also 2002 and
2005.

Serial No: 2008.
Title: 4.5 inch Howitzer and
Limber.
Pieces in box: 2.
Issued: 1946-1947.
Remarks: As 1725 and 1726 but
packed together.

Serial No: 2009.
Title: Belgium: Regiment des
Grenadiers.
Pieces in box: 8.
Issued: 1946-1947.
Remarks: Review Order in great
coats at the slope. French infantry
figure with British fusilier heads.

Serial No:2010.
Title: Airborne Infantry.
Pieces in box: 8.
Issued: 1946-1947.
Remarks: All with Red Berets; 1
officer, 1 man carrying Bren gun,
6 men with slung rifles. See also
2092.

Serial No: **2011** *00*.
Title: R.A.F. Display Set.
Pieces in box: 22.
Issued: 1946-1947.
Remarks: With figures from 1758,
1791, 1894 and 2073, and R.A.F.
Regiment similar to 2010.

Serial No: 2012-2013.
Title: Not Known.

Serial No: 2014.
Title:Band of the U.S. Marine
Corps.
Pieces in box: 21.
Issued: 1946-1947.
Remarks: Review Order in red
coats, white trousers with officer.
Later sets had a Sousaphone
added. See also 2112.

Serial No: 2015-2016. Not Listed.

Serial No: **2017** *00*.
Title: Ski Troops.
Pieces in box: 4.
Issued: 1946-1947.
Remarks: Plug in rifle on back.
See also 2037.

Serial No: 2018.
Title: Denmark: Garde Hussar
Regt.
Pieces in box: 8.
Issued: 1948.
Remarks: In Review Order with
officer and trumpeter. Similar
figures to 153 without carbine on
the horse.

Serial No: 2019.
Title: Denmark: Livgarde.
Pieces in box: 7.
Issued: 1948.
Remarks: In Review Order in
bearskins with officer. Rifle held
in crossed arms in front of the
body.

Serial No: 2020. Not Listed.

Serial No: 2021. (9183)
Title: U.S. Military Police.
Pieces in box: 8.
Issued: 1948.
Remarks: Marching in Service
Dress; sub titled 'Snowdrops',
their popular nickname.

Serial No: 2022. (9371)
Title: Papal State Swiss Guards.
Pieces in box: 9.
Issued: 1948.
Remarks: In Review Order with
pikes and officer. See also 2181.

Serial No: 2023. Not Listed.

Serial No: 2024.
Title: Light Goods Van.
Pieces in box: 2.
Issued: 1948.
Remarks: With driver. Completed
in various colour schemes
including Britain's Ltd on side.
See also 2045.

Serial No: 2025. (9334)
Title: Queen's Own Cameron
Highlanders.
Pieces in box: 18.
Issued: 1948.
Remarks: 3 positions firing, 2
officers, 1 piper all in Tropical
helmets.

Serial No: 2026. (9705)
Title: 25 pdr Gun.
Pieces in box: 1.
Issued: 1947-1948.
Remarks: With rubber tyres. See
also 2048 and 71S.

Serial No: **2027** *00*.
Title: Red Army Guards.
Pieces in box: 8.
Issued: 1950.
Remarks: Russian Guards
standing in great coats with
peaked caps and slung rifles.
Officer in Service Dress and
peaked cap.

Serial No: **2028** *00*.
Title: Red Army Cavalry.
Pieces in box: 5.
Issued: 1950-1954.
Remarks: With officer. All at halt
in Parade Dress with drawn swords.

Serial No: **2029** *00*. (9105)
Title: Life Guard Sentries.
Pieces in box: 6.
Issued: 1950.
Remarks: Mounted at halt and
dismounted. See also 1, 52, 101,
400, 2067, 2118 and 1198B.

Serial No: 2030.
Title: Royal Australian Regt.
Pieces in box: 8.
Issued: 1950-1954.
Remarks: In blue Coronation
uniform and white shirt. Marching
at the slope with officer.

Serial No: **2031** *00*.
Title: Australian Infantry.
Pieces in box: 8.
Issued: 1950.
Remarks: In Battle Dress with
Bush hat, marching at the slope.
Officer had Service Dress peaked
cap. See also 49, 1544, 1545 and
2030.

Serial No: **2032** *00*.
Title: Red Army Infantry.
Pieces in box: 8.
Issued: 1950.
Remarks: In Summer Dress with
steel helmet marching 'On Guard'
position. Arms are as for the British
gasmask charging figure 1613.

Serial No: 2033. (9180)
Title: U.S. Infantry.
Pieces in box: 8.
Issued: 1953.
Remarks: Marching at the slope in
Service Dress. Same figure as
2021.

Serial No: **2034** *00*.
Title: 'Prairie Schooner'.
Pieces in box: 7.
Issued: 1950-1954.
Remarks: With 4 galloping horses
and pioneer with rifle (555 with
new arm) and wife as 561.
Waggon was as last version of
1329.

Serial No: **2035** *00*.
Title: Sweden: Svea Hvgarde.
Pieces in box: 8.
Issued: 1950.
Remarks: Marching at the slope
with officer.

Serial No: 2036. (9311)
Title: Display Set.
Pieces in box: 19.
Issued: 1950.
Remarks: Guards marching at the
slope. Royal Scots Greys and
Black Watch charging.

Serial No: **2037** *00*.
Title: Ski Trooper.
Pieces in box: 1.
Issued: 1950.
Remarks: Figure as 2017.

Serial No: 2038-2040. Not Listed.

Serial No: 2041.
Title: Clockwork Trailer.
Pieces in box: 1.
Issued: 1950.
Remarks: To drive various
vehicles. Was attached to vehicles
to drive them forward.

Serial No: **2042** *00*.
Title: Covered Wagon Set.
Pieces in box: 13.
Issued: 1950-1954.
Remarks: As 2034 plus attacking
Indians and Cowboy outriders.

Serial No: 2043.
Title: Wild West Rodeo Set.
Pieces in box: 12.
Issued: 1950-1956.
Remarks: With stockade,
Cowboys, bucking bronco, steers
and wild horse as 756. Also new
seated cowboy. See also 2145 and
1219B.

Serial No: 2044. (9179)
Title: U.S. Air Corps.
Pieces in box: 8.
Issued: 1950.
Remarks: In 1949 pattern blue
uniforms marching with slung
rifles and officer. All figures as
2030.

Serial No: 2045.
Title: Clockwork Light Goods
Work Van.
Pieces in box: 3.
Issued: 1950-1954.
Remarks: As 2024 with
clockwork motor in back.

Serial No: **2046** *00*. (9301)
Title: Arabs of the Desert.
Pieces in box: 12.
Issued: 1950-1954.
Remarks: Running with either
spear, scimitar or rifle on new
casting. Walking and mounted
figures as box 164 and 187.

Serial No: 2047. Not Listed.

Serial No: 2048.
Title: Clockwork Army Set.
Pieces in box: 3.
Issued: 1950-1954.
Remarks: 1877, 2026 and 2041
combined.

Serial No: 2049-2050. Not Listed.

Serial No: **2051** *00*.
Title: Uruguayan Military School Cadets.
Pieces in box: 8.
Issued: 1950-1954.
Remarks: Marching at the slope with officer. See also 221.

Serial No: 2052. (9448)
Title: A.A. Unit.
Pieces in box: 15.
Issued: 1950-1954.
Remarks: With gun, searchlight, ranging equipment, gun crew and operators.

Serial No: 2053. Not Listed.

Serial No: **2054** *00*.
Title: Circus Display.
Pieces in box: 12.
Issued: 1950.
Remarks: See also 1539.

Serial No: **2055** *00*. (9286)
Title: U.S. Civil War Confederate Cavalry, 1862.
Pieces in box: 5.
Issued: 1950-1954.
Remarks: On trotting horse with carbines carried in right hand. Officer from Indian cavalry set. See also 2088, 2070 and 2141.

Serial No: **2056** *00*. (9287)
Title: U.S. Civil War Union Cavalry, 1862.
Pieces in box: 5.
Issued: 1950-1954.
Remarks: All as 2055 with different painting detail. See also 2069, 2070 and 2140.

Serial No: **2057** *00*. (9481)
Title: U.S. Civil War Union Artillery.
Pieces in box: 3.
Issued: 1950-1954.
Remarks: 2 Gunners and Gun similar to 2189. See also 2070.

Serial No: **2058** *00*. (9486)
Title: U.S. Civil War Confederate Artillery.
Pieces in box: 3.
Issued: 1950-1954.
Remarks: As 2057 with different painting detail. See also 2070.

Serial No: **2059** *00*. (9187)
Title: U.S. Civil War Union Infantry.
Pieces in box: 7.
Issued: 1950-1956.
Remarks: With Colour Bearer and 2 officers, Bugler and 4 men. See also 2069, 2070 and 2142.

Serial No: **2060** *00*. (9186)
Title: U.S. Civil War Confederate Infantry.
Pieces in box: 7.
Issued: 1950-1954.
Remarks: All as 2059. See also 2068, 2070 and 2143.

Serial No: 2061.
Title: Wild West Display.
Pieces in box: 54.
Issued: 1950-1954.
Remarks: See also 185.

Serial No: 2062. (9332)
Title: Seaforth Highlanders.
Pieces in box: 17.
Issued: 1950.
Remarks: Charging figures with mounted officer and two pipers.

Serial No: 2063. (9133)
Title: Argyll & Sutherland Highlanders.
Pieces in box: 6.
Issued: 1950.
Remarks: 5 firing, 1 officer.

Serial No: 2064. (9745)
Title: U.S. 155mm. Gun M.1.
Pieces in box: 1.
Issued: 1950-1954.
Remarks: With detachable rubber wheels. See also 2164.

Serial No: **2065** *00*. (9400)
Title: H.M. Queen Elizabeth II.
Pieces in box: 1.
Remarks: Riding side saddle in
the uniform of Colonel-in-Chief,
Grenadier Guards.

Serial No: **2066** *00*.
Title: R.C.M.P. Officer.
Pieces in box: 1.
Issued: 1950-1954.
Remarks: Turned in saddle,
similar to officer in box 24 but on a
different horse. See also 214,
1369 2158 and 1267B.

Serial No: **2067** *00*. (9307)
Title: Sovereign Standard of the
Life Guards and Escort.
Pieces in box: 7.
Issued: 1953.
Remarks: 2 Farriers, 3 Troopers,
Trumpeter and Standard.

Serial No: **2068** *00*. (9386)
Title: U.S. Civil War Confederate
Cavalry and Infantry.
Pieces in box: 12. Tptr/Bugler.
Issued: 1950-1954.
Remarks: Combination of 2055
and 2060. See also 36s and 46s.

Serial No: **2069** *00*. (9387)
Title: U.S. Civil War Union
Cavalry and Infantry.
Pieces in box: 12.
Issued: 1950-1954.
Remarks: Combination of 2056
and 2059. See also 36s and 46s.

Serial No: **2070** *00*. (9485)
Title: U.S. Civil War Union and
Confederate Cavalry, Infantry
and Artillery.
Pieces in box: 30.
Issued: 1950-1954.
Remarks: Combination of
2055-2060.

Serial No: 2071.
Title: Royal Marines.
Pieces in box: 7.
Issued: 1953.
Remarks: At Present Arms with
officer.

Serial No: 2072.
Title: King's Royal Rifle Corps.
Pieces in box: 8.
Issued: 1953.
Remarks: Marching at the trail in
Review Order with officer. See
also 98 and 18N.

Serial No: 2073.
Title: R.A.F. Regt.
Pieces in box: 8.
Issued: 1953.
Remarks: Marching at the slope
with officer.

Serial No: **2074** *00*. (9212)
Title: 1st King's Dragoon Guards.
Pieces in box: 5.
Issued: 1953.
Remarks: At the trot with officer
distinguished by a gold belt.

Serial No: **2075** *00*. (9214)
Title: 7th Queen's Own Hussars.
Pieces in box: 5.
Issued: 1953.
Remarks: Officer on trotting
horse.

Serial No: **2076** *00*. (9217)
Title: 12th (Prince of Wales's)
Royal Lancers.
Pieces in box: 5.
Issued: 1953.
Remarks: On trotting horses.

Serial No: 2077.
Title: King's Troop R.H.A.
Pieces in box: 8.
Issued: 1953.
Remarks: Team at the walk in
Review Order. Officer included
only in larger display set 131.

Serial No: 2078.
Title: Irish Guards.
Pieces in box: 7.
Issued: 1953.
Remarks: At Present Arms with officer.

Serial No: **2079** *00*. (9301)
Title: The Royal Company of Archers.
Pieces in box: 13.
Issued: 1953.
Remarks: Sub-titled The Queen's Scottish Body Guard. Included 1 officer in cocked hat and archers in three positions.

Serial No: **2080** *00*.
Title: Royal Navy Sailors.
Pieces in box: 8.
Issued: 1953.
Remarks: Marching at the slope with fixed bayonets and white gaiters. Officer with drawn sword in gaiters and boots.

Serial No: 2081. Not Listed.

Serial No: 2082. (9125)
Title: Coldstream Guards.
Pieces in box: 8.
Issued: 1953.
Remarks: At attention with officer.

Serial No: 2083. (9127)
Title: Welsh Guards.
Pieces in box: 7.
Issued: 1953.
Remarks: 'At Ease' position with fixed arm mounted officer on walking horse.

Serial No: **2084** *00*.
Title: Colour party of the Scots Guards.
Pieces in box: 6.
Issued: 1952-1960.
Remarks: With 4 Sergeants and 2 Colour bearers. See also 82 and 460.

Serial No: 2085. (9405)
Title: Household Cavalry Musical Ride.
Pieces in box: 23.
Issued: 1953.
Remarks: 4 Trumpeters, 9 Troopers from each regiment and a Drum Horse. Troopers all carried lances.

Serial No: 2086. (9339)
Title: Queen's Royal West Surrey Regt.
Pieces in box: 16.
Issued: 1953.
Remarks: 3 positions firing with officer holding binoculars.

Serial No: **2087** *00*.
Title: 5th Inniskilling Dragoon Guards.
Pieces in box: 8.
Issued: 1953.
Remarks: New dismounted figures with drawn swords and peaked caps. Officer included. See also 3.

Serial No: **2088** *00*.
Title: Duke of Cornwall's Light Infantry.
Pieces in box: 8.
Issued: 1953.
Remarks: In No. 1 Dress marching at the trail in peaked caps with officer. See also 1569.

Serial No: **2089** *00*.
Title: Gloucestershire Regiment.
Pieces in box: 8.
Issued: 1953.
Remarks: Marching at the slope with officer. All in No. 1 Dress with Presidential Unit Citation from Korea on sleeve. See also 119, 1592 and 2158.

Serial No: **2090** *00*.
Title: Royal Irish Fusiliers.
Pieces in box: 8.
Issued: 1953.
Remarks: No. 1 Dress with
'Caubeen' head: at attention.
Officer with sash and sheathed
sword. See also 1581.

Serial No: **2091** *00*.
Title: The Rifle Brigade.
Pieces in box: 8.
Issued: 1953.
Remarks: In No. 1 Dress with
peaked caps. Marching at the trail
with officer. See also 9 and 1618.

Serial No: **2092** *00*.
Title: The Parachute Regt.
Pieces in box: 8.
Issued: 1953.
Remarks: Marching at the slope
with officer, all in No. 1 Dress with
berets. See also 2010.

Serial No: 2093.
Title: Band of the Royal
Berkshire Regt.
Pieces in box: 25.
Issued: 1953.
Remarks: No. 1 Dress with
bandmaster.

Serial No: **2094** *00*. (9402)
Title: State Landau.
Pieces in box: 9.
Issued: 1953.
Remarks: With H.M. Queen
Elizabeth II and Prince Philip in
Admiral's uniform. Outriders
were detachable from their
horses. See also 1470.

Serial No: 2095. (9366)
Title: French Foreign Legion.
Pieces in box: 14.
Issued: 1953.
Remarks: Charging, 3 positions
firing, machine-gunners and
officer kneeling with binoculars.

Serial No: **2096** *00*. (9428)
Title: Pipe band of the Irish
Guards.
Pieces in box: 12.
Issued: 1952-1960.
Remarks: With 6 Pipers, 3 Side,
Bass drummers, Drum Major, and
Cymbal Player.

Serial No: **2097** *00*.
Title: French Foreign Legion and
Arabs.
Pieces in box: 26.
Issued: 1953.
Remarks: As 2095 with 12 Arabs
from box 2046.

Serial No: 2098.
Title: Venezuela Cadets.
Pieces in box: 7.
Issued: 1954.
Remarks: Marching at the slope in
Review Order with Colour
Bearer. Similar to No 228 with
different painting.

Serial No: 2099.
Title: Venezuela Military School
Cadets.
Pieces in box: 15.
Issued: 1954.
Remarks: Marching at the slope in
Review Order with colour bearer.
As 2098 with additional figures
and officer. See also 2100.

Serial No: 2100. (9375)
Title: Venezuela Military School
Cadets, Infantry and Sailors.
Pieces in box: 23.
Issued: 1954.
Remarks: With Cadet officer,
Naval officer, Colour Bearer.
Navy and Infantry figures,
American sailors and 'Snowdrop'.

Serial No: 2101. (9482)
Title: Colour Guard U.S.
Marines.
Pieces in box: 4.
Issued: 1956.
Remarks: With officer. See also
228, 261, 265, 399 and 1157B.

Serial No: **2102** *00*. (9760)
Title: Austin 'Champ'.
Pieces in box: 1.
Issued: 1956.
Remarks: See also 2174 and
LV609.

Serial No: 2103.
Title: Venezuela Infantry.
Pieces in box: 15.
Remarks: Larger version of 2104.

Serial No: 2104.
Title: Venezuela Infantry.
Pieces in box: 7.
Issued: 195 .
Remarks: Repainted 'Snowdrop'
figure marching at the slope with
Colour Bearer. See also 2100 and
2105.

Serial No: 2105.
Venezuela Infantry.
Pieces in box: 15.
Issued: 195 .
Remarks: In Service Dress with
officer and Colour Bearer
carrying National Standard. See
also 2100 and 2104.

Serial No: 2106.
Title: Heavy 18 inch Howitzer No.
1.
Pieces in box: 1.
Issued: 1955.
Remarks: Garrison Mounting as
1265 with new shells and loader.
See also 1265, 1266, 1725, 1726,
2008 and 2107.

Serial No: 2107. (9740)
Title: Heavy 18 inch Howitzer No.
2.
Pieces in box: 1.
Issued: 1955.
Remarks: On Field Carriage with
tractor wheels as 1266 with new
shells and loader. See also 1265,
1725, 1726, 1861, 1863, 2008 and
2106.

Serial No: **2108** *00*.
Title: Drums and Fifes of the
Welsh Guards.
Pieces in box: 12.
Issued: 1956.
Remarks: Included 1 tenor drum,
5 fifes, 3 side drums, 1 bass drum,
9 cymbals and Drum Major.

Serial No: **2109** *00*. (9435)
Title: Highland Pipe Band of the
Black Watch (Royal Highlanders).
Pieces in box: 20.
Issued: 1956.
Remarks: New drums of plastic
with printed surrounds and new
Highland bandsmen.

Serial No: **2100** *00*. (9478)
Title: U.S. Military Band.
Pieces in box: 25.
Issued: 1956.
Remarks: In Full Dress yellow
uniform. With sousaphones and
bandmaster. See also 1301, 1302
and 2117.

Serial No: **2111** *00*.
Title: Colour Party of the Black
Watch (Royal Highlanders).
Pieces in box: 6.
Issued: 1956.
Remarks: New arm on Sergeant
with plaid attached.

Serial No: 2112.
Title: U.S. Marine Corps Band.
Pieces in box: 25.
Issued: 1956.
Remarks: Full band in Summer
Dress with officer, replacing 2014.
Saxophone and French Horns
introduced as in 2113.

Serial No: **2113** *00*.
Title: Band of the Grenadier
Guards.
Pieces in box: 25.
Issued: 1956.
Remarks: Contained Drum Major
in State Dress and Bandmaster.
Similar to No 37 with Drum Major
in Review Order, not State Dress.

Serial No: 2114.
Title; Band of the Line.
Pieces in box: 12.
Issued: 1956.
Remarks: Review Order
replacing 27. See also 1287, 1290
and 1458.

Serial No: **2115** *00*.
Title: Drums and Bugles of the
Royal Marines.
Pieces in box: 12.
Issued: 1956.
Remarks: Replaced 1291
included Tenor Drummer etc.

Serial No: 2116.
Title: R.A.F. Band.
Pieces in box: 12.
Issued: 1956.
Remarks: Replaced 1527. See
also 1523 and 1524.

Serial No: **2117** *00*.
Title: U.S. Army Band.
Pieces in box: 12.
Issued: 1956.
Remarks: In steel helmets,
replacing 2110.
See also 130 and 1302.

Serial No: 2118.
Title: 1st Life Guards.
Peices in box: 3.
Issued: 1957.
Remarks: New line series in
smaller boxes. Mounted and
dismounted figures.

Serial No: 2119.
Title: The Royal Scots Greys (2nd
Dragoons).
Pieces in box: 3.
Issued: 1957.
Remarks: New mounted and
dismounted figures.

Serial No: 2120.
Title: 3rd Hussars.
Pieces in box: 3.
Issued: 1957.
Remarks: Mounted and
dismounted figures.

Serial No: 2121.
Title: Grenadier Guards.
Pieces in box: 4.
Issued: 1957.
Remarks: 3 positions firing. See
also 34.

Serial No: 2122.
Title: Scots Guards.
Pieces in box: 4.
Issued: 1952-1960.
Remarks: With officer and Colour
Bearer.

Serial No: 2123.
Title: Irish Guards.
Pieces in box: 4.
Issued: 1957.
Remarks: Marching at the slope
with officer and piper.

Serial No: 2124.
Title: Royal Welch Fusiliers.
Pieces in box: 4.
Issued: 1957.
Remarks: At attention; officer
with sword and Goat mascot.

Serial No: 2125.
Title: The Loyal Regiment.
Pieces in box: 4.
Issued: 1957.
Remarks: 'On Guard' positions
with officer holding field glasses.

Serial No: 2126.
Title: The Black Watch (Royal
Highlanders).
Pieces in box: 3.
Issued: 1957.
Remarks: Charging figures with
officer.

Serial No: **2127** *00*.
Title: Royal Marines.
Pieces in box: 4.
Issued: 1950-1954.
Remarks: Two men at Present
Arms. Officer and Bugler at
Attention.

Serial No: 2128.
Title: Display Set.
Pieces in box: 3.
Issued: 1952-1960.
Remarks: Life Guards and Scots
Guards in Winter Dress similar to
400 and 431.

Serial No: 2129.
Title: Royal Artillery
Detachment.
Pieces in box: 4.
Issued: 1957.
Remarks; Men standing and
kneeling with shells. Set included
officer.

Serial No: 2130.
Title: British Infantry.
Pieces in box: 4.
Issued: 1950-1954.
Remarks: All in Battle Dress with
1 officer, 1 marching Bren Gunner
and 2 men.

Serial No: 2131.
Title: British Army Machine-gun
Section.
Pieces in box: 3.
Issued: 1957.
Remarks: Lying and sitting
positions. Figures in Battle Dress
and new rimless steel helmet.

Serial No: 2132.
Title: R.A.M.C. Stretcher Party.
Pieces in box: 4.
Issued: 1957.
Remarks: With 1 nurse.
See also 1896.

Serial No: 2133.
Title: Governor General's Horse
and Foot Guards of Canada.
Pieces in box: 3. Mtd.
Issued: 1952-1960.
Remarks: See also 1631, 1634
and 1637.

Serial No: 2134 Royal
Canadian Mtd. Police.
Pieces in box: 3.
Remarks: Mtd Officer with
one figure at attention
one marching.

Serial No: 2135.
Title: Danish Hussars and Life
Guards.
Pieces in box: 3.
Issued: 1957.
Remarks: Figures from 2018 and
2019.

Serial No: 2136.
Title: French Foreign Legion.
Pieces in box: 3.
Issued: 1957.
Remarks: Marching at slope with
mounted officer.
See also 1711 and 1035.

Serial No: 2137.
Title: French Foreign Legion.
Pieces in box: 4.
Issued: 1957.
Remarks: With charging, standing
and lying firing figures and officer
kneeling with binoculars.

Serial No: 2138.
Title: French Tirailleurs.
Pieces in box: 3.
Issued: 1957.
Remarks: With mounted officer.
See also 141.

Serial No: 2139.
Title: U.S. Cavalry and Infantry.
Pieces in box: 3.
Issued: 1957.
Remarks: With Infantry Colour
Bearer. See also 2033 and 229.

Serial No: 2140.
Title: U.S. Civil War Union
Cavalry.
Pieces in box: 3.
Issued: 1957.
Remarks: 2 mounted troopers and
dismounted officer.

Serial No: 2141.
Title: U.S. Civil War Confederate
Cavalry.
Pieces in box: 3.
Issued: 1957.
Remarks: As 2140 with different
painting.

Serial No: 2142.
Title: U.S. Civil War Union
Infantry.
Pieces in box: 4.
Issued: 1957.
Remarks: With bugler, officer and
2 men.

Serial No: 2143.
Title: U.S. Civil War Confederate
Infantry.
Pieces in box: 4.
Issued: 1957.
Remarks: Figures as 2142.

Serial No: 2144.
Title: Russian Infantry and
Cavalry.
Pieces in box: 3.
Issued: 1958.
Remarks: With officer. Mounted
man and two infantrymen
advancing.

Serial No: 2145.
Title: Cowboys.
Pieces in box: 3.
Issued: 1950-1956.
Remarks: Mounted and on foot
with Bronco figure from 2043.
See also 1219B.

Serial No: 2146.
Title: North American Indians.
Pieces in box: 3.
Issued: 1956-1957.
Remarks: Mounted and on foot.

Serial No: 2147.
Title: Arabs.
Pieces in box: 3.
Issued: 1956-1957.
Remarks: Mounted and on foot.

Serial No: 2148. (9158)
Title: Fort Henry Guard.
Pieces in box: 7.
Issued: 1958.
Remarks: With officer and Goat.
Figures in the dress of the 1800s
similar to 1516 and 1518.

Serial No: 2149.
Title: Gentlemen at Arms.
Pieces in box: 9.
Issued: 1958.
Remarks: Included officers and
Gentlemen standing with
halberds.

Serial No: 2150. (9770)
Title: Centurion Tank.
Pieces in box: 1.
Issued: 1958-1960.
Remarks: See also 1203, 2154
and 2175.

Serial No: 2151.
Title: Kettle Drummer of the Life
Guards.
Pieces in box: 1.
Issued: 1958-1960.
Remarks: Specially painted.

Serial No: 2152 00. (9499)
Title: Waterloo Period Gunners
and gun.
Pieces in box: 3.
Issued: 1958-1960.
Remarks: Figures as 1518 but
with sword and rammer and
painted as artillery men. See also
2189.

Serial No: 2153.
Title: Band of the Royal Marines.
Pieces in box: 12.
Issued: 1958-1960.
Remarks: With Tenor drummer.
Replacement for 1291.

Serial No: 2154.
Title: Centurion Tank.
Pieces in box: 1.
Issued: 1958-1960.
Remarks: As 2150 but in sand
colour. See also 1203 and 2175.

Serial No: 2155.
Title: United Nations Infantry.
Pieces in box: 8.
Issued: 1958-1960.
Remarks: With U.S. pattern
helmet painted blue, Battle Dress,
and including Bren gunners.
Based on marching British
Infantry figures. See also 2089.

Serial No: 2156.
Title: H.M. Queen Elizabeth II.
Pieces in box: 1.
Issued: 1958-1960.
Remarks: Special box marked
with 'Souvenir of London'. In
uniform of Colonel of the
Grenadier Guards.

Serial No: 2157.
Title: Life Guards Drummer.
Pieces in box: 1.
Issued: 1958-1960.
Remarks: Special Souvenir box,
marked as 2156.

Serial No: 2158.
Title: Royal Canadian Mounted
Police Officer.
Pieces in box: 1.
Issued: 1958-1960.
Remarks: As 2066. See also 214,
1349 and 1267B.

Serial No: 2159.
Title: Fort Henry Guard Sentry
and Box.
Pieces in box: 2.
Issued: 1950-1960.
Remarks: See also 2148, 2160,
2182, 9155 and 9158.

Serial No: 2160.
Title: Fort Henry Guard.
Pieces in box: ?
Issued: 1958-1960.
Remarks: Export box only. See
also 2148 and 9158.

Serial No: 2161. (9392)
Title: Knights of Agincourt.
Pieces in box: 5.
Issued: 1958-1960.
'Remarks: See also 1659-1664.

Serial No: 2162-2163.
Title: Assorted Soldiers, Cowboys
and Indians.
Pieces in box: ?
Ossied: 1958-1960.
Remarks: Special lead free paint
figures for export to Australia.
From boxes 150, 179 etc.

Serial No: 2164.
Title: 155mm Gun.
Pieces in box: 1.
Issued: 1950-1954.
Remarks: See also 2064.

Serial No: 2165-2167.
Title: Australian Export
Assortments.
Pieces in box: ?
Issued: 1950-1954.
Remarks: As 2162-2163.

Serial No: 2168.
Title: Officer of the Gordon
Highlanders.
Pieces in box: 1. Mtd.
Issued: 1958.
Remarks: Special Souvenir. See
also 437, 60B, 292B, 461B, 845B.

Serial No: 2169.
Title: 12th (Prince of Wales's)
Royal Lancers Officer.
Pieces in box: 1.
Issued: 1958.
Remarks: Special souvenir of
London. At the halt, turned in the
saddle.

Serial No: 2170.
Title: Life Guards Trumpeter.
Pieces in box: 1. Mtd.
Issued: 1958.
Remarks: Special Souvenir box.

Serial No: 2171.
Title: R.A.F. Colour Party.
Pieces in box: 4.
Issued: 1958-1960.
Remarks: See also 2073.

Serial No: 2172 00.
Title: Algerian Spahis.
Pieces in box: 5.
Issued: 1958-1960.
Remarks: One of the last new
figures produced. All were plug
armed like the first issue in the
1880s. Set had five figures on
galloping horses; four troopers
with rifles and one standard
bearer.

Serial No: 2173. (9720)
Title: B.A.T. 120mm Gun.
Pieces in box: 1.
Issued: 1958-1960.
Remarks: Modern Anti-tank gun.
See also 2174.

Serial No: 2174. (9750)
Title: B.A.T. gun and towing
vehicle.
Pieces in box: 2.
Issued: 1958-1960.
Remarks: Champ was without
driver. See also 2102, 2173 and
LV 609.

Serial No: 2175. (9748)
Title: 155 mm Mobile Gun.
Pieces in box: 1.
Issued: 1958-1960.
Remarks; Mounted on Centurion
chassis as set 2150 and 2154. See
also LV 611.

Serial No: 2176.
Title: Greek Evzones.
Pieces in box: 4.
Issued: 1958-1960.
Remarks: Marching at the slope in
Review Order. See also 170, 171
and 196.

Serial No: **2177** *00*.
Title: Fort Henry Guard Band.
Pieces in box: 5.
Issued: 1958-1960.
Remarks: See also 2178, 2180
and 9154.

Serial No: 2178.
Title: Fort Henry Guard Drums
and Fifes.
Pieces in box: 5.
Issued: 1958-1960.
Remarks: See also 2148, 2177,
2180, 2182 and 9154.

Serial No: 2179.
Title: Pipe Band of the Black
Watch (Royal Highlanders).
Pieces in box: 9.
Issued: 1958-1960.
Remarks: Smaller version of
2109.

Serial No: **2180** *00*.
Title: Fort Henry Guard Band.
Pieces in box: ?
Issued: 1958-1960.
Remarks: With Drum Major. See
also 2177, 2178 and 9154.

Serial No: 2181.
Title: The Papal Guard.
Pieces in box: ?
Issued: 1958-1960.
Remarks: In Review Order. See
also 2022. Export box.

Serial No: 2182.
Title: Fort Henry Guard Pioneer.
Pieces in box: 1.
Issued: 1958-1960.
Remarks: see also 2148. Standing
at ease. Export box.

Serial No: 2183.
Title: Fort Henry Guard Cannon.
Pieces in box: 1.
Issued: 1958-1960.
Remarks: Export box.

Serial No: 2184/2185/2186.
Title: Bahamas Police Band.
Pieces in box: ?
Issued: 1958-1960.
Remarks: 3 boxes of differing
sizes. All included an officer.
Export boxes.

Serial No: 2187. (9174)
Title: Red Army Guards Infantry.
Pieces in box: 6.
Issued: 1958-1960.
Remarks: In greatcoat and
summer dress with mounted
officer.

Serial No: 2188.
Title: A.A. Personnel.
Pieces in box: 6.
Issued: 1958-1960.
Remarks: With 1639, 1728 and
1729. See also 1724 and 2052.

Serial No: 2189. (9721)
Title: 18th Century Cannon.
Pieces in box: 7.
Issued: 1961.
Remarks: Issued with six cannon
balls. Brightly plated barrel and
plastic carriage.

Serial No: 9154.
Title: Fort Henry Guard Band.
Pieces in box: 5.
Issued: 1963-1965.
Remarks: Export box only. See
also 2160, 2177, 2178 and 2180.
In new 9000 series post-1962.

Serial No: 9155.
Title: Fort Henry Guard 49th Foot.
Pieces in box: ?
Issued: 1963-1965.
Remarks: In Waterloo Dress. See
also 1516, 1518, 2148 and 9160.
In new 9000 series post-1962.

Serial No: 9158.
Title: Fort Henry Guard.
Pieces in box: 7.
Issued: 1963-1965.
Remarks: With Goat. See also
2148, 2160 and 2182. In 9000
series post-1962.

Serial No: 9160.
Title: 89th Regt.
Pieces in box: 7.
Issued: 1963-1965.
Remarks: Waterloo period figure.
See also 72, 1516-1519, 2148,
2152 and 9155. In 9000 series
post-1962.

Picture Packs

Single painted figures in
individual boxes first issued as
such in 1955 although items that
were later included in this range
were available in earlier years.

Serial No: 14B.
Title: Scots Guards Piper.
Issued: 1955.
Remarks: See also 75.

Serial No: 20B.
Title: U.S. Marine.
Issued: 1955.
Remarks: At slope.

Serial No: 22B.
Title: North American Indian
Chief.
Issued: 1955.
Remarks: With knife in moving
arm.

Serial No: 23B.
Title: North American Indian
Chief.
Issued: 1955.
Remarks: With tomahawk in
moving arm.
See also 24B, 99P.

Serial No: 24B.
Title: North American Indian
Chief.
Issued: 1955.
Remarks: Fixed Arm figure with
tomahawk. See also 23B.

Serial No: 25B.
Title: Cowboy.
Issued: 1955.
Remarks: Walking with rifle.
See also 183.

Serial No: 28B.
Title: Guardsman.
Issued: 1955.
Remarks: Marching at the slope.

Serial No: 29B.
Title: Gordon Highlander.
Issued: 1955.
Remarks: Marching at the slope in
Review Order. See also 73, 77,
441 and 482.

Serial No: 31B.
Title: U.S. Cavalry.
Issued: 1955.
Remarks: Mounted.
See also 229.

Serial No: 32B.
Title: North American Indian.
Remarks: Mounted with
tomahawk. See also 152, 117P.

Serial No: 33B.
Title: North American Indian.
Issued: 1955.
Remarks: With rifle.
See also 17N and 51P.

Serial No: 34B.
Title: Cowboy.
Issued:
Remarks: Mounted with pistol.
See also 118P.

Serial No: 35B.
Title: Cowboy.
Issued:
Remarks: Mounted with lassoo.

Serial No: 37B.
Title: 1st Life Guards.
Issued: 1955.
Remarks: Full Dress on walking
horse.

Serial No: 39B.
Title: U.S. Cavalry.
Issued: 1955.
Remarks: Mounted. See also 276.

Serial No: 40B.
Title: Arab.
Issued: 1955.
Remarks: Mounted with Scimitar.

Serial No: 41B.
Title: Royal Scots Greys (2nd
Dragoons) Trooper.
Issued: 1955.
Remarks: On trotting horse. See
also 32, 695A and 668A.

Serial No: 48B.
Title: 11th (Prince Albert's Own)
Hussars Trooper.
Issued: 1955.
Remarks: Dismounted figure as
182.

Serial No: 52B.
Title: Royal Canadian Mounted
Police.
Issued: 1955.
Remarks: As 214.

Serial No: 53B.
Remarks: Arab marching with
rifle.
Issued: 1955.

Serial No: 55B.
Title: Cowboy.
Issued: 1955.
Remarks: Standing with pistol in
moving arm.

Serial No: 60B.
Title: Gordon Highlander Officer.
Issued: 1955.
Remarks: Kneeling with
binoculars.
See also 89, 118, 437, 2168, 292B
and 461B.

Serial No: 61B.
Title: Gordon Highlander.
Issued: 1955.
Remarks: Standing firing. See also
157, 1325, 62B and 63B.

Serial No: 62B.
Title: Gordon Highlander.
Issued: 1955.
Remarks: Kneeling firing. See
also 157, 1325, 62B and 63B.

Serial No: 63B.
Title: Gordon Highlander.
Issued: 1955.
Remarks: Lying firing.
See also 118, 157, 1325, 61B,
62B.

Serial No: 66B.
Title; R.A.F. Pilot.
Issued: 1955.
Remarks: In Sidcot Suit with
moving arm. See also 1894.

Serial No: 67B.
Title: Royal Marine.
Issued: 1955.
Remarks: Marching at the slope.

Serial No: 74B.
Title: North American Indian.
Issued: 1955.
Remarks: Standing with rifle 'at the ready'. See also 150.

Serial No: 107B.
Title: U.S. West Point Cadet.
Issued: 1955.
Remarks: See also 226.

Serial No: 116B.
Title: 1st Life Guard Trooper.
Issued: 1955.
Remarks: Mounted; In cloak. See also 400.

Serial No: 143B.
Title: North American Indian.
Issued: 1955.
Remarks: With knife and tomahawk. See also 711A, 52P.

Serial No: 219B.
Title: Yeomen of the Guard, Officer.
Issued: 1955.
Remarks: See also 1257, 1475-76 and 1138B.

Serial No: 239B.
Title: Scots Guards, Queen's Colour Bearer.
Issued: 1955.
Remarks: See also 2122.

Serial No: 240B.
Title: Scots Guards, Regimental Colour Bearer.
Issued: 1955.
Remarks: See also 2122.

Serial No: 271B.
Title: Royal Canadian Mounted Police.
Issued: 1955.
Remarks: As 1349.

Serial No: 274B.
Title: Cowboy.
Issued: 1955.
Remarks: Kneeling with pistol. See also 1252 707A, 80P.

Serial No: 275B.
Title: Cowboy.
Issued: 1955.
Remarks: Standing firing pistol. See also 1252.

Serial No; 281B.
Title: Royal Horse Guards (The Blues) Officer.
Issued: 1955.
Remarks: On rearing horse as box 2.

Serial No: 292B.
Title: Gordon Highlander Officer.
Issued: 1955.
Remarks: Standing holding binoculars. See also 89, 437, 2168, 60B, 461B.

Serial No: 327B.
Title: Gordon Highlander, Piper.
Issued: 1955.
Remarks: See also 73 and 77.

Serial No: 339B.
Title: Scots Guard Pioneer.
Issued: 1955.
Remarks: See also 8L.

Serial No: 340B-00.
Title: Scots Guards Queen's Colour Bearer.
Issued: 1955.
Remarks: Marching with Colour at slope furled. See also 239B.

Serial No: 356B.
Title: Cowboy.
Issued: 1955.
Remarks: Standing with lassoo.

Serial No: 429B.
Title: Bluejacket.
Issued: 1955.
Remarks: Marching in Bell
Bottoms. See also 1510, 709A,
731A, 1081A, 116P, 156W and
162W.

Serial No: 461B.
Title: Gordon Highlanders
Officer.
Issued: 1955.
Remarks: Marching in Full Dress.
See also 437, 2168, 60B, 292B.

Serial No: 488B.
Title: Royal Marine.
Issued:
Remarks: At Present Arms.

Serial No: 561B.
Title: French Foreign
Legionnaire.
Issued: 1955.
Remarks: Marching at the slope.
See also 1711.

Serial No: 587B.
Title: R.A.F. Firefighter.
Issued: 1955.
Remarks: See also 1758 and
1906.

Serial No: 591B.
Title: Royal Canadian MounteD
Police.
Issued: 1955.
Remarks: Marching in Regulation
Summer Dress. See also 214, 52B,
1374B and 57S.

Serial No: 645B.
Title: 1st Life Guard Officer.
Issued: 1955.
Remarks: On trotting horse. See
also 844B.

Serial No: 647B.
Title: 11th (Prince Albert's Own)
Hussars Officer.
Issued: 1955.
Remarks: On prancing horse with
sword at the carry. See also 12.

Serial No: 666B.
Title: Scots Guards Officer.
Issued: 1955.
Remarks: Marching without
sword.

Serial No: 477B.
Title: Life Guard.
Remarks: Drummer State Dress.
See also 2157.

Serial No: 668B.
Title: The Royal Scots Greys (2nd
Dragoons) Officer.
Issued: 1955.
Remarks: On trotting horse. See
also 59, 51B.

Serial No: 768B.
Title: Scots Guards Side
Drummer.
Issued: 1955.
Remarks: See also 1607.

Serial No: 778B.
Title: Scots Guardsman.
Issued: 1955.
Remarks: At attention.

Serial No: 829B.
Title: Mounted Arab with rifle.
Issued: 1955.
Remarks: Figure as in set 164.

Serial No: 844B.
Title: 1st Life Guards Officer.
Issued: 1955.
Remarks: In cloak with sword.
See also 400 and 645B.

Serial No: 845B.
Title: Gordon Highlander Officer.
Issued: 1955.
Remarks: Mounted figure. See
also 437 and 2168.

Serial No: 883B.
Title: 11th (Prince Albert's Own)
Hussars Trooper.
Remarks: At the halt with sword.
See also 270.

Serial No: 898B.
Title: Scots Guardsman.
Issued: 1955.
Remarks: Marching at the slope in
Greatcoat.

Serial No: 899B.
Title: Scots Guards Officer.
Issued: 1955.
Remarks: In Greatcoat with
drawn sword. See also 915B,
1006B and 1350B.

Serial No: 906B.
Title: Scots Guardsman.
Issued: 1955.
Remarks: Standing 'at Ease' to go
with 339.

Serial No: 914B.
Title: Scots Guards Colour
Sergeant.
Issued: 1955.
Remarks: Marching at the slope.
See also 2122.

Serial No: 915B.
Title: Scots Guards Officer.
Issued: 1955.
Remarks: Marching with drawn
sword. See also 899B, 1006B and
1350B.

Serial No: 1005B.
Title: Scots Guardsman.
Issued: 1955.
Remarks: At the 'Present'.

Serial No: 1006B.
Title: Scots Guards Officer.
Issued: 1955.
Remarks: At half salute with
sword.

Serial No: 1021B.
Title: Royal Marine Officer.
Issued: 1955.
Remarks: At half salute with
sword.

Serial No: 1035B.
Title: French Foreign Legion
Officer.
Issued: 1955.
Remarks: Mounted figure at the
halt. See also 1711, 1712 and
2136.

Serial No: 1054B.
Title: R.A.F. Pilot.
Issued: 1955.
Remarks: In full flying kit.

Serial No: 1055B.
Title: W.R.A.F.
Issued: 1955.
Remarks: See also 1894, 1897
and 2011.

Serial No: 1081B.
Title: R.A.F. Air Commodore.
Issued: 1955.
Remarks: See also 817 and 2011.
Carrying coat over arm.

Serial No: 1138B.
Title: Yeoman of the Guard.
Issued: 1955.
Remarks: See also 1257, 1475-76
and 219B.

Serial No: 1149B.
Title: R.A.F. Regt. Officer.
Issued: 1955.
Remarks: Carrying stick. See also
2073 and 2171.

Serial No: 1150B.
Title: R.A.F. Regt. Airman.
Issued: 1955.
Remarks: Marching with slung
rifle and beret. See also 2073.

Serial No: 1151B.
Title: R.A.F. Regt. Bren Gunner.
Issued: 1955.
Remarks: Marching with Bren
gun at the carry. See also 2073.

Serial No: 1157B.
Title: U.S. Marine Corps Officer.
Issued: 1155.
Remarks: Marching.

Serial No: 1179B.
Title: North American Indian.
Issued: 1955.
Remarks: Crawling with knife.
See also 703A.

Serial No: 1180B.
Title: Cowboy.
Issued: 1955.
Remarks: With rifle.

Serial No: 1190B.
Title: U.S. Military Policeman.
Issued: 1955.
Remarks: See also 428 and 2021.

Serial No: 1198B.
Title: 1st Life Guards Trooper.
Issued: 1955.
Remarks: Dismounted sentry.

Serial No: 1204B.
Title: U.S. Infantry.
Issued: 1955.
Remarks: M.P. figure as 428,
2021. See also 2033.

Serial No: 1205B.
Title: U.S. Infantry Officer.
Issued: 1955.
Remarks: M.P. figure as
428/2021. See also 2033.

Serial No: 1206B.
Title: U.S. Infantry Colour
Bearer.
Issued: 1955.
Remarks: See also 2101.

Serial No: 1216B.
Title: North American Indian
Chief.
Issued: 1955.
Remarks: With rifle.

Serial No: 1217B.
Title: North American Indian.
Issued: 1955.
Remarks: With rifle.
See also 150.

Serial No: 1219B.
Title: Cowboy.
Issued: 1955.
Remarks: Mounted on bucking
bronco. See also 2043, 2145.

Serial No: 1226B.
Title: U.S. Air Corps.
Issued: 1955.
Remarks: In peaked cap. Slung
rifle.

Serial No: 1229B.
Title: Arab running with scimitar.
Issued: 1955.
Remarks: Same figure as in set
2046, etc.

Serial No: 1231B.
Title: Arab running with rifle.
Issued: 1955.
Remarks: Same figure as in set
2046, etc.

Serial No: 1232B.
Title: Arab mounted with spear.
Issued: 1955.
Remarks: Same figure as in set
2046, etc.

Serial No: 1237B.
Title: U.S. Civil War Confederate
Officer.
Issued: 1955.
Remarks: See also 2060.

Serial No: 1238B.
Title: U.S. Civil War Confederate
Colour Bearer.
Issued: 1955.
Remarks: See also 2060.

Serial No: 1239B.
Title: U.S. Civil War Confederate
Bugler.
Issued: 1955.
Remarks: See also 2060.

Serial No: 1240B.
Title: U.S. Civil War Confederate
Infantryman.
Issued: 1955.
Remarks: Standing on Guard in
Slouch Hat. See also 2060 and
2143.

Serial No: 1241B.
Title: U.S. Civil War Confederate
Infantryman.
Issued: 1955.
Remarks: Standing firing. See also
2060 and 2143.

Serial No: 1242B.
Title: U.S. Civil War Confederate
Infantryman.
Issued: 1955.
Remarks: Kneeling: On Guard.
See also 2060 and 2143.

Serial No: 1243B.
Title: U.S. Civil War Confederate
Infantryman.
Issued: 1955.
Remarks: Kneeling firing. See
also 2060 and 2143.

Serial No: 1249.
Title: U.S. Civil War Union
Officer.
Issued: 1955.
Remarks: See also 2059 and
2142.

Serial No: 1250B.
Title: U.S. Civil War Union
Infantry Standard Bearer.
Issued: 1955.
Remarks: See also 2054 and
2142.

Serial No: 1251B.
Title: U.S. Civil War Union
Infantry Bugler.
Issued: 1955.
Remarks: See also 2054 and
2142.

Serial No: 1252B.
Title: U.S. Civil War Union
Infantryman.
Issued: 1955.
Remarks: Standing 'On Guard' in
Kepi. See also 2054 and 2142.

Serial No: 1253B.
Title: U.S. Civil War Union
Infantryman.
Issued: 1955.
Remarks: Standing firing.
See also 2054 and 2142.

Serial No: 1254B.
Title: U.S. Civil War Union
Infantryman.
Issued: 1955.
Remarks: Kneeling to receive
cavalry.

Serial No: 1255B.
Title: U.S. Civil War Union
Infantryman.
Issued: 1955.
Remarks: Kneeling firing. See
also 2054 and 2142.

Serial No: 1267B.
Title: Royal Canadian Mounted
Police Officer.
Remarks: As 2066 and 2158.

Serial No: 1268B.
Title: Life Guards
Corporal-Major with Standard.
Issued: 1955.
Remarks: On walking horse. See
also 2067 and 1268B.

Serial No: 1269B.
Title: Life Guard Trumpeter.
Issued: 1955.
Remarks: State Dress.

Serial No: 1270B.
Title: Lift Guards Farrier.
Issued: 1955.
Remarks: On walking horse. See
also 2067.

Serial No: 1276B.
Title: R.A.F. Officer.
Issued: 1955.
Remarks: In No 1 Dress in peaked
cap and carrying sword. See also
2073.

Serial No: 1277B.
Title: R.A.F. Airman.
Issued: 1955.
Remarks: Marching at the slope in
peaked cap. See also 2073.

Serial No: 1278B.
Title: 1st King's Dragoon Guards
Officer.

Issued: 1955.
Remarks: On trotting horse. See
also 57 and 2074.

Serial No: 1279B.
Title: 1st King's Dragoon Guards
Tropper.
Issued: 1955.
Remarks: On trotting horse. See
also 57 and 2074.

Serial No: 1289B.
Title: Royal Navy Bluejacket.
Issued: 1955.
Remarks: Marching at the slope.
See also 2080, 22B, 24B.

Serial No: 1290B.
Title: Royal Navy Officer.
Issued: 1955.
Remarks: Marching in gaiters
with drawn sword. See also 2080.

Serial No: 1325B.
Title: Life Guards Trumpeter.
Issued: 1955.
Remarks: Mounted figure in
Regimental Dress. Scarlet coat.

Serial No: 1329B-00.
Title: French Foreign Legion
Officer.
Issued: 1955.
Remarks: On trotting horse with
sword extended. See also 1035B.

Serial No: 1333B.
Title: Life Guards Trumpeter.
Issued: 1955.
Remarks: Mounted figure in
Regimental Dress in cloak.

Serial No: 1334B.
Title: Life Guards Farrier.
Issued: 1955.
Remarks: In cloak. See also 400
and 2067.

Serial No: 1335B.
Title: Lifeguards Corporal-Major
with Standard.
Issued: 1955.
Remarks: In cloak. See also 400
and 2067.

Serial No: 1336B.
Title: Royal Horse Guard (The
Blues) Trooper.
Issued: 1955.
Remarks: Mounted figure at the
halt.

Serial No: 1337B.
Title: Royal Horse Guards (The
Blues) Trumpeter.
Issued: 1955.
Remarks: Mounted figure in
Regimental Dress at the halt. See
also 2, 103 and 2085.

Serial No: 1338B.
Title: Royal Horse Guard Farrier.
Issued: 1955.
Remarks: Mounted figure at the
halt.

Serial No: 1339B.
Royal Horse Guards (The Blues)
Corporal Major with Standard.
Issued: 1955.
Remarks: At halt.

Serial No: 1340B.
Title: Royal Horse Guards (The
Blues) Trooper.
Issued: 1955.
Remarks: Dismounted figure.

Serial No: 1341B.
Title: 1st King's Dragoon Guards
Trumpeter.
Issued: 1955.
Remarks: On walking horse.

Serial No: 1342B.
Title: 1st King's Dragoon Guards
Standard Bearer.
Issued: 1955.
Remarks: On trotting horse. See
also 2074.

Serial No: 1343B.
Title: 1st King's Dragoon Guards.
Remarks: Dismounted Trooper.
See also 182 and 1279B.

Serial No: 1344B.
Title: The Royal Scots Greys (2nd
Dragoons) Trumpeter.
Issued: 1955.
Remarks: On walking horse.

Serial No: 1345B.
Title: 11th (Prince Albert's Own)
Hussars Trumpeter.
Issued: 1955.
Remarks: Mounted figure at the
halt.

Serial No: 1346B.
Title: 12th (Prince of Wales's)
Royal Lancers Trooper.
Issued: 1955.
Remarks: At halt with lance at
carry.

Serial No: 1347B.
Title: 12th (Prince of Wales's)
Royal Lancers Trooper.
Issued: 1955.
Remarks: At halt with lance slung.

Serial No: 1348B.
Title: 12th (Prince of Wales's)
Royal Lancers Trumpeter.
Issued: 1955.
Remarks: At halt. See also 128.

Serial No: 1349B.
Title: 12th (Prince of Wales's)
Royal Lancers Officer.
Issued: 1955.
Remarks: At halt, figure turned in
saddle. See also 2168.

Serial No: 1350B.
Title: Scots Guards Officer.
Issued: 1955.
Remarks: At Attention.

Serial No: 1351B.
Title: Scots Guards Bugler.
Issued: 1955.
Remarks: See also 130.

Serial No: 1352B.
Title: Gordon Highlander.
Issued: 1955.
Remarks: In Full Dress charging
with bayonet.

Serial No: 1353B.
Title: Royal Marines Officer.
Issued: 1955.
Remarks: Marching with sword.

Serial No: 1354B.
Title: Royal Marines Officer.
Issued: 1955.
Remarks: With Regimental
Colour furled over the shoulder.

Serial No: 1355B.
Title: Royal Marine Officer.
Issued: 1955.
Remarks: With Regimental
Colour carried over the shoulder.

Serial No: 1356B.
Title: Royal Marine.
Issued: 1955.
Remarks: At Ease.

Serial No: 1357B.
Title: Royal Marine.
Issued: 1955.
Remarks: At Attention.

Serial No: 1358B.
Title: U.S. Civil War Union
Cavalry Officer.
Issued: 1955.
Remarks: At the halt with sword
extended.

Serial No: 1359B.
Title: U.S. Civil War Union
Cavalry Trumpeter.
Issued: 1955.
Remarks: At the halt. See also
2056 and 2140.

Serial No: 1360B.
Title: U.S. Civil War Union
Cavalry Trooper.
Issued: 1955.
Remarks: At the halt wearing
slouch hat with carbine in hand.
See also 2056 and 2140.

Serial No: 1361B.
Title: U.S. Civil War Union
Infantry Officer.
Issued: 1955.
Remarks: Kneeling with field
glasses. See also 2059 and 2142.

Serial No: 1362B.
Title: U.S. Civil War Union
Infantry Zouave.
Issued: 1955.
Remarks: Charging figure. See
also 2069.

Serial No: 1363B.
Title: U.S. Civil War Confederate
Cavalry Officer.
Issued: 1955.
Remarks: As 1358B. See also
2055 and 2141.

Serial No: 1364B.
Title: U.S. Civil War Confederate
Cavalry Trumpeter.
Issued: 1955.
Remarks: As 1359B. See also
2055 and 2141.

Serial No: 1365B.
Title: U.S. Civil War Confederate
Cavalry Trooper.
Issued: 1955.
Remarks: As 1360B. See also
2055 and 2141.

Serial No: 1366B.
Title: U.S. Civil War Confederate
Infantry Officer.
Issued: 1955.
Remarks: As 1361B.
See also 2060 and 2143.

Serial No: 1367B.
Title: French Foreign Legion
Officer.
Issued: 1955.
Remarks: Marching with sword.
See also 141.

Serial No: 1368B.
Title: French Foreign
Legionnaire.
Issued: 1955.
Remarks: Charging figure. See
also 2095 and 2137.

Serial No: 1369B.
Title: French Foreign
Legionnaire.
Issued: 1955.
Remarks: Standing firing. See also
2095 and 2137.

Serial No: 1370B.
Title: French Foreign
Legionnaire.
Issued: 1955.
Remarks: Kneeling firing. See
also 2095.

Serial No: 1371B.
Title: French Foreign
Legionnaire.
Issued: 1955.
Remarks: Lying firing. See also
2095B and 2137.

Serial No: 1372B.
Title: French Foreign Legion
Machine Gunner.
Pieces in box: 2.
Issued: 1955.
Remarks: See also 2095.

Serial No: 1373B.
Title: Royal Canadian Mounted
Police.
Issued: 1955.
Remarks: With lance. See also
1349.

Serial No: 1374B.
Title: Royal Canadian Mounted
Police.
Issued: 1955.
Remarks: In Regulation Dress at
attention. See also 591B.

Animal Picture Packs

Serial No: 5001.
Title: Shire Horse.
Pieces in box: 1.
Issued: 1955.
Remarks: See also 506 and 507.

Serial No: 5002.
Title: Cart Horse.
Pieces in box: 1.
Issued: 1955.
Remarks: See also 541.

Serial No: 5004.
Title: Bull.
Pieces in box: 1.
Issued: 1955.
Remarks: See also 573, 758 and 78

Serial No: 5005.
Title: Cow Lying, Exmoor Horn
Sheep and Lamb.
Pieces in box: 3.
Issued: 1955.
Remarks: See also 536, 538 and 59

Serial No: 5006.
Title: Shepherd, Sheep Lyin with
lamb, Sheep walking, Feeding.
Pieces in box: 5.
Issued: 1955.
Remarks: See also 510, 511, 536
and 577.

Serial No: 5007.
Title: Cob and Foal.
Pieces in box: 2.
Issued: 1955.
Remarks: Both standing. See also
550 and 602.

Serial No: 5008.
Title: Milkmaid, Cow and Calf.
Pieces in box: 3.
Issued: 1955.
Remarks: See also 508, 509 and
537.

Serial No: 5009.
Title: Sheep Walking and
Feeding, 2 Lambs and Hurdles.
Pieces in box: 10.
Issued: 1955.
Remarks: See also 510-512 and
527.

Serial No: 5010.
Title: Farmer, Wife, Goose,
Gander and Pig.
Pices in box: 5.
Issued: 1955.
Remarks: See also 501, 502, 514,
519 and 520.

Serial No: 5011.
Title: 2 Pigs, 2 Piglets, 1 Trough
and Hurdles.
Pieces in box: 11.
Issued: 1955.
Remarks: See also 514, 527-529
and 546.

Serial No: 5012.
Title: Milkmaid, Jersey Cow and
Calf.
Pieces in box: 3.
Issued: 1955.
Remarks: See also 509, 532 and
599.

Serial No: 5013.
Title: Field Hurdles.
Pieces in box: 6.
Issued: 1955.
Remarks: See also 527.

Serial No: 5014.
Title: Highland Cattle.
Pieces in box: 1.
Issued: 1955.
Remarks: See also 647.

Serial No: 5015.
Title: Kennel and Sitting Dog.
Pieces in box: 2.
Issued:
Remarks: See also 569, 570 and
572.

Serial No: 5016.
Title: Farmer, Sheep, Pig and
Dog.
Pieces in box: 4.
Issued:
Remarks: See also 501, 510, 513
and 514.

Serial No: 5017.
Title: Lying Cow and 2 Calves.
Pieces in box: 3.
Issued:
Remarks: See also 509, 534 and
538.

Serial No: 5018.
Title: Shepherd, Dog, Sheep
walking and feeding and 2 Lambs.
Pieces in box: 6.
Issued:
Remarks: See also 510-513 and
577.

Serial No: 5019.
Title: Cow.
Pieces in box: 1.
Issued:
Remarks: Walking. See also 508.

Serial No: 5020.
Title: Jersey Cow.
Pieces in box: 1.
Issued:
Remarks: See also 599.

Serial No: 5021.
Title: Cow.
Pieces in box: 1.
Issued:
Remarks: Feeding. See also 539.

Serial No: 5022.
Title: Man & Wheel Barrow.
Pieces in box: 2.
Issued: 1956.
Remarks: See also 547.

Serial No: 5023.
Title: Horse Feeding and Trough.
Pieces in box: 2.
Issued: 1956.
Remarks: See also 528 or 529 and 543.

Serial No: 5024.
Title: 1 Pig, 2 Piglets, 1 Berkshire Pig and a trough.
Pieces in box: 5.
Issued: 1956.
Remarks: See also 514, 528 or 529, 546 and 596.

Serial No: 5025.
Title: Berkshire Pig.
Pieces in box: 1.
Issued: 1956.
Remarks: See also 596, 746 and 5024.

Serial No: 5026.
Title: Old Man and Woman on Log Seat.
Pieces in box: 3.
Issued: 1956.
Remarks: See also 555, 556 and 567.

Serial No: 5027.
Title: Calf, Lamb and 2 Goslings.
Pieces in box: 4.
Issued: 1956.
Remarks: See also 509, 512 and 565.

Serial No: 5028.
Title: Farmer and Dog.
Pieces in box: 2.
Issued: 1956.
Remarks: See also 501 and 513.

Serial No: 5029.
Title: Farmers Wife and 3 Fowls.
Pieces in box: 4.
Issued: 1956.
Remarks: See also 502 and 516 etc.

Serial No: 5030.
Title: 1 Pig, 2 Piglets and a Trough.
Pieces in box: 4.
Issued: 1956.
Remarks: See also 514, 528 or 529 and 546.

Serial No: 5031.
Title: Sheep and Lamb.
Pieces in box: 2.
Issued: 1956.
Remarks: See also 510 and 512.

Serial No: 5032.
Title: Man with Garden Roller.
Pieces in box: 2.
Issued: 1956.
Remarks: See also 715.

Serial No: 5033.
Title: Assorted Cocks, Hens,
Ducks and Drakes.
Pieces in box: 6.
Issued: 1956.
Remarks: See also 516 etc and
533.

Serial No: 5034.
Title: Man with Swing Water
Barrow.
Pieces in box: 2.
Issued: 1956.
Remarks: See also 564.

Serial No: 5035.
Title: Assorted Dogs.
Pieces in box: 6.
Issued: 1956.
Remarks: See also 513, 571, 572,
576, 605, 606 and 637.

Serial No: 5036.
Title: Blacksmith with Anvil and
Horse.
Pieces in box: 3.
Issued: 1956.
Remarks: See also 589, 650 and
506 etc.

Serial No: 5037.
Title: Girl with Cock and Hen
feeding.
Pieces in box: 3.
Issued: 1956.
Remarks: See also 660 and 747.

Serial No: 5038.
Title: Huntsman standing with
hound.
Pieces in box: 2.
Issued: 1956.
Remarks: See also 612 and 614.

Serial No: 5039.
Title: Huntswoman standing with
Hound.
Pieces in box: 2.
Issued: 1956.
Remarks: See also 613 and 614.

Zoo Series, Picture Packs

Serial No: 9001.
Title: Young and Baby Indian
Elephants.
Pieces in box: 2.
Issued: 1954.
Remarks: As 944 and 952.

Serial No: 9002.
Title: Wild Boar, Young and Baby
Rhino.
Pieces in box: 3.
Issued: 1954.
Remarks: As 942, 951, 960.

Serial No: 9003.
Title: Young and Baby
Hippopotamus.
Pieces in box: 2.
Issued: 1954.
Remarks: As 940 and 959.

Serial No: 9004.
Title: Kangaroo and Two Babies.
Pieces in box: 3.
Issued: 1954.
Remarks: As 902 and 950.

Serial No: 9005.
Title: Brown Bear and Cubs.
Pieces in box: 3.
Issued: 1954.
Remarks: As 934 and 936.

Serial No: 9006.
Title: Baby Camel and Malay
Tapir.
Pieces in box: 2.
Issued: 1954.
Remarks: As 943 and 949.

Serial No: 9007.
Title: Penguin and Polar Bears.
Pieces in box: 3.
Issued: 1954.
Remarks: As 903, 966 and 967.

Serial No: 9008.
Title: Zebra and Gazelle.
Pieces in box: 2.
Issued: 1954.
Remarks: As 907 and 963.

Serial No: 9009.
Title: Eland Bull and Stork.
Pieces in box: 2.
Issued: 1954.
Remarks: As 933 and 946.

Serial No: 9010.
Title: Lion, Lioness and Cub.
Pieces in box: 3.
Issued: 1954.
Remarks: As 910, 911 and 962.

Serial No: 9011.
Title: Giant Panda and Babies.
Pieces in box: 3.
Issued: 1954.
Remarks: As 969-971.

Serial No: 9012.
Title: Gorilla, Guenon Monkey,
Chimpanzee and Baby.
Pieces in box: 3.
Issued: 1955.
Remarks: As 906, 915, 921 and
978.

Serial No: 9013.
Title: Pelicans and Flamingos.
Pieces in box: 4.
Issued: 1955.
Remarks: As 909, 913 and 2 ×
947.

Serial No: 9014.
Title: Penguin, King Penguin,
Walrus and Sea Lion.
Pieces in box: 4.
Issued: 1955.
Remarks: As 903, 916, 956 and
964.

Serial No: 9015.
Title: Tigers.
Pieces in box: 2.
Issued: 1955.
Remarks: As 941, 992 and
449Bulk.

Zoo Series (Extra)

"Z" series. Items not in main Zoo
List. Issued 1950-1954.

Serial No: 1Z.
Title: Assortment of Zoo
Animals.
Pieces in box: 10.
Remarks: Contained 903, 904,
906, 907, 909-911, 913, 916 and
954.

Serial No: 2Z.
Title: Assortment of Zoo
Animals.
Pieces in box: 15.
Remarks: Contained 902-904,
907, 909-911, 913, 914, 916 and
918.

Serial No: 3Z.
Title: Assortment of Zoo
Animals.
Pieces in box: 16.
Remarks: Contained 902-904,
906, 907, 909, 910, 911, 913-915,
918-920 and 954.

Serial No: 4Z.
Title: Assortment of Zoo
Animals.
Pieces in box: 24.
Remarks: Contained 901-920,
922, 923 and 954.

Serial No: 6Z.
Title: Assortment of Zoo
Animals.
Pieces in box: 10.
Remarks: Contained 904, 915,
921-923, 933-936.

Serial No: 11Z.
Title: Assortment of Zoo
Animals.
Pieces in box: 11.
Remarks: Contained 903, 905,
907, 912, 921-923, 945, 952, 956.

Serial No: 17Z.
Title: Assortment of Zoo
Animals.
Pieces in box: 9.
Remarks: Contained 922, 937,
942, 945, 946, 954, 955, 958 and
966.

Serial No: 18Z.
Title: Mammal House.
Pieces in box: 6.
Remarks: With three
compartments, opening gates and
sliding doors at back. Animals
were 2 × 907, 908, 933 and 968.

Serial No: 19Z.
Title: Polar Bear Pool with Cave.
Pieces in box: 4.
Remarks: With 914, 966 and 967.

Serial No: 20Z.
Title: Large Pool Enclosure.
Pieces in box: 13.
Remarks: With 903, 916, 937,
956 and 964.

Serial No: 21Z.
Title: Monkey Hill.
Pieces in box: 9.
Remarks: With 904, 915, 921 and
954.

Serial No: 22Z.
Title: Animal House with
Enclosure.
Pieces in box: 3.
Remarks: Supplied with 2 × 942
or 2 × 948 or 2 ×949.

Serial No: 23Z.
Title: Rock Pool with Tree
Surround.
Pieces in box: 6.
Remarks: With 909, 913, 2 × 946
and 2 × 947.

Serial No: 24Z.
Title: Large Double Display Box.
Pieces in box: 55.
Remarks: Included 25Z, 918,
943, 923, 907, 933, 941, 948, 942,
937, 969, 970, 994, 993, 920.

Serial No: 25Z.
Title: Elephant with Keeper,
Howdah and two Children.
Pieces in box: 5.
Remarks: As 901, 932, 938 and
939.

Serial No: 26Z.
Title: Display Box.
Pieces in box: 9.
Remarks: Included 905, 908, 901,
961, 911, 907, 906, 933.

Serial No: 27Z.
Title: Display Box.
Pieces in box: 17.
Remarks: With lift-out tray
containing 901 and 905. No other
details known.

Serial No: 28Z.
Title: Display Box.
Pieces in box: 17.
Remarks: Included elephant,
hippo, zebra, crocodile, leopard,
baby elephant, and others.

Farm Series (Extra)

Serial No: 1F.
Title: Model Home Farm.
Pieces in box: 23.
Remarks: Included 506, 508, 509, 513, 514, 516-519, 520 and 577.

Serial No: 2F.
Title: Model Home Farm.
Pieces in box: 19.
Remarks: Included 506-508, 510-512, 514, 516-520, 523, 524, 527 and 577.

Serial No: 3F.
Title: Model Home Farm.
Pieces in box: 73.
Remarks: Included 506-510, 513, 514, 516-525, 527, 546 and 577.

Serial No: 4F. (9505)
Title: Tumbrel Cart.
Pieces in box: 3.
Remarks: Two wheeled. Driver with whip.

Serial No: 5F.
Title: Farm Wagon.
Pieces in box: 4.
Remarks: So-called Suffolk or Sussex wagon. Two horses, and walking driver with whip.

Serial No: 6F.
Title: General Purpose Plough.
Pieces in box: 4.
Remarks: With Farm Hand. Two horses.

Serial No: 7F.
Title: Tree and Gate.
Pieces in box: 2.
Remarks: Tree without foliage.

Serial No: 8F. (9506)
Title: Horse and Rake.
Pieces in box: 3.
Remarks: With seated driver and single horse.

Serial No: 9F. (9504)
Title: Horse Roller.
Pieces in box: 3.
Remarks: With walking farm hand and one horse.

Serial No: 12F.
Title: Timber Carriage with Log.
Pieces in box: 5.
Remarks: See also 541, 563, 648 and 129F. Adjustable chassis and real log.

Serial No: 16F.
Title: Stable Display.
Pieces in box: ?
Remarks: See also 506, 507, 513 and 563.

Serial No: 17F.
Title: Farm Display.
Pieces in box: 13.
Remarks: Included Drover 514, 540, 546, 552, 558 and 573.

Serial No: 18F.
Title: Farm Display.
Pieces in box: ?
Remarks: Included 501, 502, 510, 512, 513, 528 or 529.

Serial No: 19F.
Title: Tree, Gate and Swing.
Pieces in box: 3.
Remarks: See also 619, 630 and 7F.

Serial No: **20F** *00*.
Title: Farmer's Gig.
Pieces in box: 3.
Remarks: With seated Farmer.

Serial No: 30F.
Title: Farm Fence Enclosure.
Pieces in box: 90.
Remarks: Designed to interlock with pins and complete with gate.

Serial No: 36F.
Title: Farmyard Display.
Pieces in box: 7.
Remarks: Included 508, 509, 513, 550, 563, 596 and 601.

Serial No: 38F.
Title: Farm Display.
Pieces in box: 14.
Remarks: Included Farm Hand, 508, 510, 513, 514, 516, 523, 543, 546, 573, 596, 601 and 640.

Serial No: 39F.
Title: Farm Yard Display.
Pieces in box: 26.
Remarks: With Farm Hand, 510-512, 514, 532, 539, 546, 550, 639 and 640.

Serial No: 40F. (9500)
Title: Farm Cart and Horse.
Pieces in box: 2.
Remarks: See also 649 and 96F.

Serial No: 44F.
Title: Country Cottage.
Pieces in box: 1.
Remarks: With imitation thatched roof. See also 97F, L8 and L9.

Serial No: 45F. (9501)
Title: Milk Float.
Pieces in box: 2.
Remarks: See also 588, 649, 652, 131F, L7 and LV 605.

Serial No: 52F.
Title: Presentation Box.
Pieces in box:
Remarks: Included 508, 510, 514, 657, 5F and 8F.

Serial No: 53F.
Title: Model Home Farm.
Pieces in box: 9.
Remarks: Included 501, 502, 510, 511, 516, 539 and 644.

Serial No: 54F.
Title: Model Home Farm.
Pieces in box: 7.
Remarks: With 514, 535, 552, 597 and 599.

Serial No: 55F.
Title: Model Home Farm.
Pieces in box: 10.
Remarks: With 506, 507, 523, 550, 566, 571, 602 and 640.

Serial No: 56F.
Title: Model Home Farm.
Pieces in box: 13.
Remarks: With 501, 502, 508, 539 and 640.

Serial No: 58F.
Title: Tree.
Pieces in box: 6.
Remarks: Branches fit into centre trunk.
See also 521-524, 72F, 73F, 77F and LB513.

Serial No: 59F.
Title: 4 Wheeled Farm Lorry.
Pieces in box: 2.
Remarks: Tip up truck with driver. Cab changed to modern type, post-war.

Serial No: 60F.
Title: 6 Wheeled Lorry.
Pieces in box: 2.
Remarks: Tipper with driver. As
1335 main list.
See also 91F. Cab changed to
modern type, post-war.

Serial No: 61F.
Title: Farm Lorry.
Pieces in box: 2.
Remarks: 10 wheeled with driver
as 1432.
See also 92F.

Serial No: 62F.
Title: Model Home Farm.
Pieces in box: 23.
Remarks: With 501, 502, 510,
514, 543, 546, 573, 597, 599, 601,
639 and 640.

Serial No: 63F.
Title: Model Home Farm.
Pieces in box: 24.
Remarks: With 506, 508, 510,
511, 513, 527, 531, 563, 639, 640
and 660.

Serial No: 66F.
Title: Farm House Scene.
Pieces in box: 1.
Remarks: Coloured background
in card with cottage and bridge as
stand out items, for use with farm
animals.

Serial No: 67F.
Title: Model Home Farm.
Pieces in box: 17.
Remarks: As 66F but with stock
and farm hands added.

Serial No: 69F.
Title: Farm Assortment.
Pieces in box:
Remarks: With 510, 514 any of
521-524, 539 and 642.

Serial No: 70F.
Title: Farm Assortment.
Pieces in box: 6.
Remarks: With 510, 511, any of
521-524, 530 and 599.

Serial No: 71F.
Title: Farm Assortment.
Pieces in box: 6
Remarks: With 509, 534, 543 and
642.

Serial No: 72F.
Title: Farm Assortment.
Pieces in box: 6.
Remarks: With 508, 510, 514,
534 and 58F.

Serial No: 73F.
Title: Farm Assortment.
Pieces in box: 6.
Remarks: With 510, 514, 550,
602 and 58F.

Serial No: 74F.
Title: Farm Assortment.
Pieces in box: 6.
Remarks: With 508, 509, 520,
540 and 58F.

Serial No: 77F.
Title: Farm Assortment.
Remarks: 506, 508, 510, 511,
537, 596, 602 and 58F.

Serial No: 90F.
Title: Builder's Lorry.
Pieces in box: 2.
Remarks: As 59F.

Serial No: 91F.
Title: Builder's Lorry.
Pieces in box: 2.
Remarks: As 60F.

Serial No: 92F.
Title: Builder's Lorry.
Pieces in box: 2.
Remarks: As 61F.

Serial No: 94F.
Title: Farm House.
Pieces in box: 1.
Remarks: With one sliding and
one opening door. See also 111F.

Serial No: 95F.
Title: Large Barn and Cart Shed.
Pieces in box: 1.
Remarks: Upper floor granary
drop door on chain. To
accommodate 4F and 5F. See also
L10.

Serial No: 96F.
Title: Stable.
Pieces in box: 1.
Issued: 1939.
Remarks: With half doors and lift
off roof. For any of 506, 507, 541,
543, 550, 602, 648, 649, 769, 782,
783 and 40F.

Serial No: 97F.
Title: Small Country Cottage.
Pieces in box: 1.
Issued: 1939.
Remarks: With removable roof
and opening door. See also 44F,
L8 and L9.

Serial No: 98F.
Title: Store Shed.
Pieces in box: 1.
Issued: 1939.
Remarks: Made of cardboard to
simulate corrugated iron to hold
any of 590, 667, 670, 673 or 676.

Serial No: 99F.
Title: Cowshed.
Pieces in box: 1.
Issued: 1939.
Remarks: For 508, 538, 539 and
599.

Serial No: 100F.
Title: Pig Sty.
Pieces in box: 2.
Issued: 1939.
Remarks: For 514, 546, 596 or
746.

Serial No: 101F.
Title: Rabbit Hutch.
Pieces in box: 1.
Issued: 1939.
Remarks: Wooden model for use
with 603 and 636.

Serial No: 102F.
Title: Chicken House and Run.
Pieces in box: 1.
Issued: 1939.
Remarks: For 515-518, 544, 545,
642-644 and 660.

Serial No: 103F.
Title: Barn.
Pieces in box: 1.
Issued: 1939.
Remarks: Mansard type with
large sliding door. See also 111F.

Serial No: 111F.
Title: Farm Yard Presentation
Box.
Pieces in box: 50.
Issued: 1939.
Remarks: Included 508, 509, 510,
512, 514, 519, 520, 526 or 639,
544, 546, 586, 657, 94F and 103F.

Serial No: 112F.
Title: Green House.
Pieces in box: 1.
Issued: 1939.
Remarks: Metal structure.
See also 675.

Serial No: 113F.
Title: Garden Shelter.
Pieces in box: 1.
Issued: 1939.

Serial No: 120F.
Title: Farm Yard Display.
Pieces in box: 14.
Remarks: Animals only. No
further details known.

Serial No: 121F.
Title: Farm Yard Display.
Pieces in box: 16.
Remarks: No details known.

Serial No: 122F.
Title: Farm Yard Display.
Pieces in box: 12.
Remarks: No details known.

Serial No: 123F.
Title: Farm Yard Display.
Pieces in box: 7.
Remarks: No details known.

Serial No: 125F.
Title: Farm Yard Display.
Pieces in box: 7.
Remarks: No details known.

Serial No: 126F. (9502)
Title: Horse Drawn Cart.
Pieces in box: 2.
Remarks: With Rubber Tyres.

Serial No: 127F.
Title: Fordson Tractor.
Pieces in box: 2.
Remarks: With metal spiked
wheels and driver.

Serial No: 128F.
Title: Fordson Tractor.
Pieces in box: 2.
Remarks: With rubber tyres and
driver.

Serial No: 129F.
Title: Timber Trailer.
Pieces in box: 1.
Remarks: With Log.

Serial No: 130F.
Title: Trailer.
Pieces in box: 1.
Remarks: With rubber tyres to be
pulled by tractor.

Serial No: 131F. (9503)
Title: Milk Float.
Pieces in box: 5.
Remarks: With 652 and 588. See
also 45F, L7 and LV605.

Serial No: 132F.
Title: Farm Yard Display.
Pieces in box: 23.
Remarks: Included 4F.

Serial No: 133F.
Title: Farm Yard Display.
Pieces in box: 7.
Remarks: No details known.

Serial No: 134F.
Title: Tractors and Implements.
Pieces in box: 9.
Remarks: 127F, 128F, 129F and
136F.

Serial No: 135F. (9534)
Title: Disc Harrow.
Pieces in box: 1.
Remarks: To be pulled by 127F or
128F.

Serial No: 136F. (9533)
Title: Roller.
Pieces in box: 1.
Remarks: For towing behind
127F or 128F. See also 146F.

Serial No: 137F.
Title: Farm Clockwork Set.
Pieces in box: 4.
Remarks: 127F or 128F with
2041 and Hay Cart.

Serial No: 138F.
Title: Four Farrow Tractor
Plough.
Pieces in box: 1.
Remarks: For tractor towing. See
also 145F and 146F.

Serial No: 139F.
Title: Clockwork Fordson Set.
Pieces in box: 3.
Remarks: 2041 with 127F or
128F.

Serial No: 142F.
Title: General Purpose Plough.
Pieces in box: 3.
Remarks: One horse with
ploughman. See also 6F.

Serial No: 144F.
Title: Haystack.
Pieces in box: 1.
Remarks: Made of Papier Mâché.
See also 542, 553 and 556.

Serial No: 145F.
Title: Tractor and Implements.
Pieces in box: 5.
Remarks: 127F or 128F, 130F,
135F and 138F.

Serial No: 146F.
Title: Tractor and Implements
Set.
Pieces in box: 10.
Remarks: 127F, 128F, 129F,
135F, 136F and 138F.

Serial No: 147F.
Title: Farm Yard Display.
Pieces in box: 5.
Remarks: Farm girl, cows, and
calves.

Serial No: 148F.
Title: Farm Yard Display.
Pieces in box: 6.
Remarks: Stable lad, dog, horse,
colt, and trough.

Serial No: 149F.
Title: Farm Yard Display.
Pieces in box: 9.
Remarks: Shepherd, sheep,
lambs, pigs and piglet.

Serial No: 150F.
Title: Farm Yard Display.
Pieces in box: 10.
Remarks: Shire horse, foal,
shepherd with lamb, sheep, lambs,
gander, donkey, and dogs.

Serial No: 151F.
Title: Farm Yard Display.
Pieces in box: 8.
Remarks: Cowman, bull, cows,
bullock, calves, and trough.

Serial No: 152F.
Title: Farm Yard Display.
Pieces in box: 10.
Remarks: Farmer, farmer's wife,
colt, Jersey cow, turkey, sheep,
lambs, pig, and piglet.

Serial No: 153F.
Title: Farm Yard Display.
Pieces in box: 11.
Remarks: Carter, land girl,
bullock, cows, calf, sheep, gander,
and elm tree.

Serial No: 154F.
Title: Farm Yard Display.
Pieces in box: 12.
Remarks: Shepherd, sheep, lamb,
farm girl, horses, cow, calf, pig, fir,
fir tree, and hedge.

Serial No: 155F.
Title: Farm Yard Display.
Pieces in box: 13.
Remarks: Farmer, farmer's wife,
dogs, cows, colt, horse, donkey,
pigs, gander, turkey, and fir tree.

Serial No: 156F.
Title: Farm Yard Display.
Pieces in box: 21.
Remarks: Mounted farmer, man sowing, boy, horse, cows, calves, sheep, lamb, pig, goat, turkey, hedges, and hurdles.

Serial No: 157F.
Title: Farm Yard Display.
Pieces in box: 21.
Remarks: Farmer, farmer's wife, dog, shire horse, foal, shepherd, sheep, lambs, pigs, piglet, turkey, gander, elm tree, fir tree, and small trees.

Lilliput Series

To match with1-10 Gauge Railways.

Serial No: L1.
Title: Land Girl and Assorted Farm Animals.
Pieces in box: 7.
Issued: 1954.
Remarks: See also 535.

Serial No: L2.
Title: Farmer and Wife with Animals.
Pieces in box: 6.
Issued: 1954.
Remarks: See also 501 and 502.

Serial No: L3.
Title: Land Girl and Stable Lad with Animals.
Pieces in box: 7.
Issued: 1954.
Remarks: See also 535 and 563.

Serial No: L4.
Title: Farmer, Stable Lad with Animals.
Pieces in box: 7.
Issued: 1954.
Remarks: See also 501 and 563.

Serial No: L5.
Title: Land Girl, Farmer, Wife and Animals.
Pieces in box: 6.
Issued: 1954.
Remarks: See also 501, 502 and 535.

Serial No: L6.
Title: Farm Animals.
Pieces in box: 8.
Issued: 1954.
Remarks: See also Farm Series.

Serial No: L7.
Title: Farm Display Box.
Pieces in box: 28.
Issued: 1955.
Remarks: Included 4F, 45F, 127F, 128F, LV602 and LV604.

Serial No: L8.
Title: Roadside Inn.
Pieces in box: 1.
Issued: 1955.
Remarks: See also 44F, 97F and L9.

Serial No: L9.
Title: Country Cottages.
Pieces in box: 2.
Issued: 1955.
Remarks: See also 44F, 97F and L8.

Serial No: L10.
Title: Barn and Cart Stable.
Pieces in box: 1.
Issued: 1955.
Remarks: See also 95F.

Serial No: L11.
Title: Railway Series Display.
Pieces in box: ?
Issued: 1956.
Remarks: Porters, Lorries,
Luggage etc.

Serial No: L51.
Title: Stable Lad, Land Girl and
Mixed Animals.
Pieces in box: 13.
Issued: 1954.
Remarks: See also 535 and 563.

Serial No: L52.
Title: Farmer with Dog and Mixed
Animals.
Pieces in box: 14.
Issued: 1954.
Remarks: See also 501 and 513.

Serial No: L53.
Title: Mixed Animals.
Pieces in box: 15.
Remarks: See also Farm Series.

Serial No: L101.
Title: Farm People and Animals.
Pieces in box: 22.
Issued: 1954.
Remarks: See also 657 and Farm
Series.

Serial No: L102.
Title: Farm People and Animals.
Pieces in box: 21.
Issued: 1954.
Remarks: See also 657 and Farm
Series.

Serial No: LP501.
Title: Sheep.
Pieces in box: 11.
Issued: 1955.
Remarks: See also 510-512, 530,
536, 597 and 601.

Serial No: LP502.
Title: Cows.
Pieces in box: 6.
Issued: 1955.
Remarks: See also 508, 583, 539,
599 and 785.

Serial No: LP503.
Title: Hurdles.
Pieces in box: 12.
Issued: 1955.
Remarks: See also 527.

Serial No: LP504.
Title: Cobs and Foals.
Pieces in box: 7.
Issued: 1955.
Remarks: See also 550 and 602.

Serial No: LP505.
Title: Land Girl, Geese and
Ducks.
Pieces in box: 11.
Issued: 1955.
Remarks: See also 519, 520, 533
and 535.

Serial No: LP506.
Title: Stable Lad, Dog and
Horses.
Pieces in box: 6.
Issued: 1955.
Remarks: See also 506 etc, 513
and 563.

Serial No: LP507.
Title: Cows and Calves.
Pieces in box: 7.
Issued: 1955.
Remarks: See also 508 and 509.

Serial No: LP508.
Title: Farmer, Dog and Pigs.
Pieces in box: 10.
Issued: 1955.
Remarks: See also 501, 513 and 514.

Serial No: LP509.
Title: Farm People and Dog.
Pieces in box: 7.
Issued: 1955.
Remarks: See also 513 and 657.

Serial No: LP510.
Title: Railway Staff.
Pieces in box: 6.
Issued: 1955.
Remarks: With barrow and News Vendor.

Serial No: LP511.
Title: Railway Passengers.
Pieces in box: 6.
Issued: 1955.
Remarks: 2 Ladies, 2 Men, Nurse and Child, Golfer.

Serial No: LP512.
Title: Railway Luggage.
Pieces in box: 10.
Issued: 1955.
Remarks: See also 155.

Serial No: LP513.
Title: Huntsman.
Pieces in box: 6.
Issued: 1955.
Remarks: See also 608-616.

'LB' Series. All issued in 1954.

Serial No: LB513.
Title: Tree.
Pieces in box: 1.
Remarks: See also 58F.

Serial No: LB514.
Title: Shire Horse.
Pieces in box: 1.
Remarks: See also 506 and 507.

Serial No: LB515.
Title: Farmer.
Pieces in box: 1.
Remarks: See also 501.

Serial No: LB 516.
Title: Farmer's Wife.
Pieces in box: 1.
Remarks: See also 502 and 503.

Serial No: LB517.
Title: Nurse and Child.
Pieces in box: 2.
Remarks: See also LP511.

Serial No: LB518.
Title: Foal.
Pieces in box: 1.
Remarks: See also 602.

Serial No: LB 519.
Title: Cob.
Pieces in box: 1.
Remarks: See also 550.

Serial No: LB520.
Title: Cow.
Pieces in box: 1.
Remarks: See also 508.

Serial No: LB521.
Title: Cow.
Pieces in box: 1.
Remarks: Feeding. See also 534.

Serial No: LB522.
Title: Calf.
Pieces in box: 1.
Remarks: Lying down. See also 534.

Serial No: LB523.
Title: Collie Dog.
Pieces in box: 1.
Remarks: See also 513.

Serial No: LB524.
Title: Goose.
Pieces in box: 1.
Remarks: See also 520.

Serial No: LB525.
Title: Sheep.
Pieces in box: 1.
Remarks: See also 510.

Serial No: LB526.
Title: Sheep.
Pieces in box: 1.
Remarks: Grazing. See also 511.

Serial No: LB527.
Title: Pig.
Pieces in box: 1.
Remarks: See also 514.

Serial No: LB528.
Title: Lamb.
Pieces in box: 1.
Remarks: See also 512.

Serial No: LB529.
Title: Ducks and Drakes.
Pieces in box: 2.
Remarks: See also 533.

Serial No: LB530.
Title: Hurdle.
Pieces in box: 1.
Remarks: See also 527.

Serial No: LB531.
Title: Stable Lad.
Pieces in box: 1.
Remarks: See also 563.

Serial No: LB532.
Title: Girl (with feeding bucket).
Pieces in box: 1.
Remarks: See also 747.

Serial No: LB533.
Title: Porter with Barrow.
Pieces in box: 2.
Remarks: See also 155.

Serial No: LB534.
Title: Guard with flag.
Pieces in box: 1.
Remarks: See also 155.

Serial No: LB535.
Title: Station Master.
Pieces in box: 1.
Remarks: See also 155.

Serial No: LB536.
Title: Civilian on Motor Cycle.
Pieces in box: 1.
Remarks: See also 653.

Serial No: LB538.
Title: News Vendor.
Pieces in box: 1.
Remarks: See also LP510.

Serial No: LB539.
Title: Lady with Case.
Pieces in box: 1.
Remarks: See also LP511.

Serial No: LB540.
Title: Man waiting with Book.
Pieces in box: 1.
Remarks: See also LP510.

Serial No: LB541.
Title: Man with Umbrella.
Pieces in box: 1.
Remarks: See also LP510.

Serial No: LB542.
Title: Lady with Hat Box.
Pieces in box: 1.
Remarks: See also LP510.

Serial No: LB543.
Title: Golfer.
Pieces in box: 1.
Remarks: See also 562.

Serial No: LB544.
Title: Barrel.
Pieces in box: 1.
Remarks: See also LP512.

Serial No: LB545.
Title: Hamper.
Pieces in box: 1.
Remarks:See also LP512.

Serial No: LB546.
Title: Large Packing Case.
Pieces in box: 1.
Remarks: See also LP512.

Serial No: LB547.
Title: Small Packing Case.
Pieces in box: 1.

Serial No: LB548.
Title: Telegraph Boy on Motor
Cycle.
Pieces in box: 2.
Remarks: See also 653 and
LB536.

Serial No: LB549.
Title: Electric Trolley.
Pieces in box: 2.
Remarks: See also LP512.

Serial No: LB550.
Title: Speed Cop.
Pieces in box: 1.
Remarks: On motor cycle.

Serial No: LB559.
Title: Huntsman.
Pieces in box: 1.
Remarks: On galloping horse. See
also 610.

Serial No: LB560.
Title: Huntswoman.
Pieces in box: 1.
Remarks: On galloping horse. See
also 611 and 623.

Serial No: LB561.
Title: Hound.
Pieces in box: 1.
Remarks: Running. See also 615
and LB562.

Serial No: LB562.
Title: Hound.
Pieces in box: 1.
Remarks: Running. See also 615
and LB561.

Serial No: LB563.
Title: Fox.
Pieces in box: 1.
Remarks: See also 616.

Serial No: LB564.
Title: Huntswoman.
Pieces in box: 1.
Remarks: In bowler hat on
standing horse. See also 609 and
623.

Serial No: LB565.
Title: Huntsman.
Pieces in box: 1.
Remarks: In cap on walking
horse. See also 608 and 598.

'LV' Series issued 1954-1956.

Serial No: LV601.
Title: Open Sports Car.
Pieces in box: 1.
Remarks: See also 1398 and
LV602.

Serial No: LV602.
Title: Saloon Car.
Pieces in box: 1.
Remarks: See also 1398, 1399, L7
and LV601.

Serial No: LV603.
Title: Articulated Lorry.
Pieces in box: 2.
Remarks: See also 1641 and
LV614.

Serial No: LV604.
Title: Fordson Tractor with
driver.
Pieces in box: 2.
Remarks: See also 127F and
128F.

Serial No: LV605.
Title: Milk Float.
Pieces in box: 3.
Remarks: With 588 and 652. See
also 45F and 131F.

Serial No: LV606.
Title: Tumbrel Cart.
Pieces in box: 3.
Remarks: See also 505, 541 and 4F.

Serial No: LV607.
Title: 3 ton Army Truck.
Pieces in box:
Remarks: See also LV612.

Serial No: LV608.
Title: 3 ton Farm Lorry.
Pieces in box: 1.
Remarks: See also LV616.

Serial No: LV609.
Title: Austin Champ.
Pieces in box: 2.
Remarks: See also 2102 and 2174.

Serial No: LV611.
Title: 'Sexton' Self Propelled Gun.
Pieces in box: 1.
Issued: 1956.
Remarks: See also 2175.

Serial No: LV612.
Title: 1½ ton Army Truck.
Pieces in box: 1.
Issued: 1956.
Remarks: See also 1879, LV613 and LV616.

Serial No: LV613.
Title: 1½ ton Army Truck.
Pieces in box: 1.
Issued: 1956.
Remarks: With cover.
See also 1879, LV612 and LV616.

Serial No: LV614.
Title: Articulated Truck.
Pieces in box: 2.
Issued: 1956.
Remarks: See also 1641 and LV603.

Serial No: LV615.
Title: 'Saracen' Armoured Personnel Carrier.
Pieces in box: 1.
Issued: 1956.
Remarks: See also 1203 and 1876.

Serial No: LV616.
Title: 1½ ton Farm Truck.
Pieces in box: 1.
Issued: 1956.
Remarks: See also LV608, LV612 and LV613.

Serial No: LV617.
Title: Local Authority Ambulance.
Pieces in box: 1.
Issued: 1956.
Remarks: See also 1514.

Serial No: LV618.
Title: Army Ambulance. Motor Type.
Pieces in box: 1.
Issued: 1956.
Remarks: See also 1512.

Serial No: LV619.
Title: Royal Mail Van.
Pieces in box: 2.
Issued: 1956.
Remarks: See also 1552.

'B' Series

'B' Series were half size figures pre
1914.
Infantry had all arms fixed.
Cavalry had moveable arms.
Usually boxes of 4–6.

Serial No: 1B.
Title: 1st Life Guards.
Pieces in box: 4.

Serial No: 2B.
Title: Royal Horse Guards (The
Blues).
Pieces in box: 4.

Serial No: 3B.
Titel: 5th Inniskillings Dragoon
Guards.

Serial No: 4B.
Title: Scots Guards.
Pieces in box: 7.

Serial No: 5B.
Title: 1st Dragoon Guards.
Pieces in box: 4.

Serial No: 6B.
Title: The Royal Scots Greys (2nd
Dragoons).
Pieces in box: 4.
Remarks: See also 32 and 695A.

Serial No: 7B.
Title: 2nd Life Guards.
Pieces in box: 4.
Remarks: On trotting horse with
carbine.

Serial No: 8B.
Title: 7th Royal Fusiliers.
Pieces in box: 7.
Remarks: Marching at the trail in
Review Order.
See also 7, 84, 251, 440, 448,
1323 and 1394.

Serial No: 9B.
Title: 13th Hussars.
Pieces in box: 4.
Remarks: At gallop.
Remarks: On 'rocking horse'. See
also 13, 87 and 99.

Serial No: 10B.
Title: 11th (Prince Albert's Own)
Hussars.
Pieces in box: 4.
Remarks: See also 12.

Serial No: 11B.
Title: Japanese Cavalry.
Pieces in box: 4.
Remarks: On trotting horse with
carbine.

Serial No: 12B.
Title: 16th Lancers.
Pieces in box: 4.
Remarks: At gallop, on active
service in sun helmets.

Serial No: 13B.
Title: 17th (Duke of Cambridge's
Own) Lancers.
Pieces in box: 4.

Serial No: 14B.
Title: Russian Cavalry.
Pieces in box: 4.
Remarks: Cossack figure.

Serial No: 15B.
Title: Mounted Infantry.
Pieces in box: 4.
Remarks: Scarlet coat, khaki
trousers.

Serial No: 16B.
Title: Coldstream Guards.
Pieces in box: 7.
Remarks: Marching at slope.

Serial No: 17B.
Title: Lancashire Fusiliers.
Pieces in box: 7.
Remarks: Marching at the trail.

Serial No: 18B.
Title: Grenadier Guards.
Pieces in box: 7.
Remarks: Running at the slope.

Serial No: 19B.
Title: Royal Dublin Fusiliers.
Pieces in box: 7.
Issued:
Remarks: Running at the trail in
Service Dress.

Serial No: 20B.
Title: The Manchester Regt.
Pieces in box: ?
Remarks: Marching at the slope in
Review Order.

Serial No: 21B.
Title: Northumberland Fusiliers.
Pieces in box: 7.
Remarks: Marching at the trail
arms in Tropical Helmet.

Serial No: 22B.
Title: Royal Navy Bluejackets.
Pieces in box: ? (Probably 7).
Remarks: Marching at the slope.
Round base figure.

Serial No: 23B.
Title: Queen's Own Cameron
Highlanders.
Pieces in box: 7.
Remarks: Marching at the trail in
Boer War Dress.

Serial No: 24B.
Title: Royal Navy Whitejackets.
Pieces in box: 7.
Remarks: Marching at the slope.
Round base figures.

Serial No: 25B.
Title: Japanese Infantry.
Pieces in box: 7.
Remarks: Running at the trail.

Serial No: 26B.
Title: Russian Infantry.
Pieces in box: 7.
Remarks: Marching at the trail.

Note: Other 'B' size figures
without the 'B' prefix are in the
early part of the Main List.

'W' Series

"W" or Woolworth Series.
Replaced 'B' size post-1918. All
with fixed arms. Sold in
Woolworth stores only.

Serial No: 145W.
Title: The Life Guards.
Pieces in box: 4.
Remarks: Walking horse.

Serial No: 146W.
Title: The Royal Scots Greys (2nd
Dragoons).
Pieces in box: 4.
Remarks: Walking horse.

Serial No: 147W.
Title: Modern Army British
Cavalry.
Pieces in box: 4.
Remarks: In Khaki with peaked
caps.

Serial No: 148W.
Title: Hussars.
Pieces in box: 4.
Remarks: At the walk in Review
Order.

Serial No: 149W.
Title: North American Indians.
Pieces in box: 5.
Remarks: Mounted and foot
figures.

Serial No: 150W.
Title: Cowboys.
Pieces in box: 5.
Remarks: Mounted and foot
figures.

Serial No: 151W.
Title: Infantry of the Line.
Pieces in box: 6.
Remarks: The Manchester Regt.
marching at the slope in Review
Order.

Serial No: 152W.
Title: Grenadier Guards.
Pieces in box: 6.
Remarks: Running.

Serial No: 153W.
Title: Highlanders.
Pieces in box: 6.
Remarks: Marching at the slope
arms in Review Order.

Serial No: 154W.
Title: North American Indian.
Pieces in box: 6.
Remarks: Foot figures.

Serial No: 155W.
Title: Cowboys.
Pieces in box: 6.
Remarks: Foot figures standing.

Serial No: 156W.
Title: British Bluejackets and
Whitejackets.
Pieces in box: 6.
Remarks: Marching in Regulation
Dress.

Serial No: 157W.
Title: U.S. Cavalry.
Pieces in box: 4.
Remarks: In peaked caps.

Serial No: 158W.
Title: U.S. Infantry.
Pieces in box: 6.
Remarks: Marching with dough boy hats.

Serial: 159W.
Title: Infantry of the Line.
Pieces in box: 10.
Remarks: Marching at the slope in Review Order.

Serial No: 160W.
Title: Highlanders.
Pieces in box: 10.
Remarks: Marching at the slope in Review Order.

Serial No: 161W.
Title: Grenadier Guards.
Pieces in box: 10.
Remarks: Review Order, running.

Serial No: 162W.
Title: British Bluejackets and Whitejackets.
Pieces in box: 10.
Remarks: Marching in Regulation Dress. See also 1570, 709A, 731A, 1081A, 429B, 116P and 156W.

Serial No: 163W.
Title: North American Indians.
Pieces in box: 10.
Remarks: On foot.

Serial No: 164W.
Title: Cowboys.
Pieces in box: 10.
Remarks: On foot.

Serial No: 165W.
Title: Life Guards and Infantry of the Line.
Pieces in box: 9.
Remarks: Life Guards at walk and Infantry at the slope, both in Review Order.

Serial No: 166W.
Title: The Royal Scots Greys (2nd Dragoons) and Highlanders.
Pieces in box: 9.
Remarks: All in Review Order.

Serial No: 167W.
Title: Hussars and Grenadier Guards.
Pieces in box: 9.
Remarks: Both in Review Order.

Serial No: 168W.
Title: Lancers and Infantry of the Line.
Pieces in box: 9.
Remarks: See also 698A and 165W.

Serial No: 169W.
Title: Cowboys and North American Indians.
Pieces in box: 9.
Remarks: See also 150 and 183.

Serial No: 170W.
Title: North American Indians.
Pieces in box: 9.
Remarks: Mounted and foot figures.

Serial No: 171W.
Title: Cowboys.
Pieces in box: 9.
Remarks: Mounted and foot figures.

Serial No: 172W.
Title: North American Indians and Cowboys.
Pieces in box: 9.
Remarks: Mounted and foot figures.

Serial No: 173W.
Title: U.S. Infantry.
Pieces in box: 10.
Remarks: See also 227.

Serial No: 174W.
Title: U.S. Cavalry and Infantry.
Pieces in box: 9.
Remarks: See also 223 and 229.

Serial No: 200W.
Title: Royal Horse Artillery.
Pieces in box: 13.
Remarks: Ex main list 126 with
four outriders in Tropical Helmets
at gallop and mounted officer.

Serial No: 201W.
Title: Royal Horse Artillery.
Pieces in box: 13.
Remarks: Ex main list 125 with
four outriders all in Review Order
and mounted officer.

'A' Series

'A' Series were introduced in the
1937-40 period.

Serial No: 694A.
Title: Life Guards and Foot
Guards.
Pieces in box: 6.
Remarks: Foot Guards marching
at the slope. All figures fixed arms.

Serial No: 695A.
Title: The Royal Scots Greys (2nd
Dragoons) and Highlanders.
Pieces in box: 6.
Remarks: Both in Review Order.
Highlanders marching at the
slope. See also 32 and 734A.

Serial No: 696A.
Title: 1st (The Royal) Dragoons
and Royal Sussex Regiment.
Pieces in box: 6.
Remarks: Both Regiments in
Review Order. Slope arms.

Serial No: 697A.
Title: British Cavalry and
Highlanders.
Pieces in box: 6.
Remarks: All in Khaki. Cavalry in
shrapnel helmets; Highlanders
charging. Different figure from
11.

Serial No: 698A.
Title: Lancers and East Kent
Regt. (The Buffs).
Pieces in box: 6.
Remarks: Lancers in Review
Order; The Buffs as 16.

Serial No: 699A.
Title: British Cavalry and East
Kent Regt. (The Buffs).
Pieces in box: 6.
Remarks: Cavalry in Service
Dress; The Buffs in Khaki as 16.

Serial No: 700A.
Title: Queen's Royal West Surrey
Regt.
Pieces in box: 8.
Remarks: 3 position firing.

Serial No: 701A.
Title: Foot Guards.
Pieces in box: 8.
Remarks: Marching at the slope.

Serial No: 702A.
Title: Highlanders.
Pieces in box: 8.
Remarks: Marching at the slope in
Review Order.

Serial No: 703A.
Title: North American Indians.
Pieces in box: 8.
Remarks: Crawling.

Serial No: 704A.
Title: Zulus.
Pieces in box: 8.
Remarks: Standing with Shield
and Knobkerrie.

Serial No: 705A.
Title: East Kent Regt. (The
Buffs).
Pieces in box: 8.
Remarks: Marching, Review
Order, slope arms.

Serial No: 706A.
Title: British Infantry.
Pieces in box: 8.
Remarks: Service Dress in peaked
caps; 3 positions firing.

Serial No: 707A.
Title: Cowboys.
Pieces in box: 8.
Remarks: Standing with hand on
holster, kneeling and standing
firing.

Serial No: 708A.
Title: Foot Guards.
Pieces in box: 8.
Remarks: 3 positions firing.

Serial No: 709A.
Title: Royal Navy Bluejackets.
Pieces in box: 8.
Remarks: Marching in bell
bottoms.

Serial No: 710A.
Title: Highlanders.
Pieces in box: 8.
Remarks: In Khaki with steel
helmets, charging with bayonet.
See also 697A.

Serial No: 711A.
Title: North American Indians.
Pieces in box: 8.
Remarks: Braves standing with
knife and tomahawk and standing
Chief.

Serial No: 712A.
Title: U.S. West Point Cadets.
Pieces in box: 8.
Remarks: In Winter Dress.
Marching at slope.

Serial No: 713A.
Title: U.S. West Point cadets.
Pieces in box: 8.
Remarks: In Summer Dress. As
712A.

Serial No: 714A.
Title: U.S. Sailors.
Pieces in box: 8.
Remarks: Marching at the slope.
Peaked caps.

Serial No: 715A.
Title: U.S. Marines.
Pieces in box: 8.
Remarks: Marching at the slope.

Serial No: 716A.
Title: U.S. Sailors.
Pieces in box: 8.
Remarks: Marching at the slope in
White jackets.
See also 1253 and 744A.

Serial No: 717A.
Title: U.S. Marines.
Pieces in box: 8.
Remarks: In Service Dress.

Serial No: 718A.
Title: U.S. Infantry.
Pieces in box: 8.
Remarks: 3 positions firing.

Serial No: 719A.
Title: U.S. Infantry.
Pieces in box: 8.
Remarks: Marching with officer.
In peaked cap.

Serial No: 720A.
Title: U.S. Cavalry and Infantry.
Pieces in box: 6.
Issued:
Remarks: Marching at the slope in
Slouch hats.

Serial No: 721A.
Title: Royal Sussex Regiment.
Pieces in box: 12.
Remarks: Marching at the slope in
Review Order.

Serial No: 722A.
Title: Foot Guards.
Pieces in box: 12.
Remarks: Marching at the slope.

Serial No: 723A.
Title: Highlanders.
Pieces in box: 12.
Remarks: Marching at the slope in
Review Order.

Serial No: 724A.
Title: North American Indians.
Pieces in box: 12.
Remarks: As 703A, 711A and
740A.

Serial No: 725A.
Title: Zulus of Africa.
Pieces in box: 12.
Remarks: Standing with Shield
and Knobkerrie.

Serial No: 726A.
Title: Queen's Own Royal West
Kent Regt.
Pieces in box: 12.
Remarks: 3 positions firing in
Review Order.

Serial No: 727A.
Title: East Kent Regt. (The
Buffs).
Pieces in box: 12.
Remarks: Marching at the slope in
Review Order.

Serial No: 728A.
Title: British Infantry.
Pieces in box: 12.
Remarks: In khaki, 3 positions
firing.

Serial No: 729A.
Title: Cowboys.
Pieces in box: 12.
Remarks: As 707A.

Serial No: 730A.
Title: Foot Guards.
Pieces in box: 12.
Remarks: 3 positions firing.

Serial No: 731A.
Title: Royal Navy Bluejackets.
Pieces in box: 12.
Remarks: Marching in Regulation
Dress.

Serial No: 732A.
Title: Highlanders.
Pieces in box: 12.
Remarks: As 710A.

Serial No: 733A.
Title: Life Guards and Foot
Guards.
Pieces in box: 10.
Remarks: Foot Guards marching
at the slope.

Serial No: 734A.
Title: The Royal Scots Greys (2nd
Dragoons) and Highlanders.
Pieces in box: 10.
Remarks: All in Review Order.
Highlanders at the slope.

Serial No: 735A.
Title: 1st (The Royal) Dragoons
and Royal Sussex Regt.
Pieces in box: 10.
Remarks: Both Regiments in
Review Order. Royal Sussex
marching at the slope.

Serial No: 736A.
Title: Hussars and East Kent
Regt. (The Buffs).
Pieces in box: 10.
Remarks: In Review Order.

Serial No: 737A.
Title: British Cavalry and
Infantry.
Pieces in box: 10.
Remarks: Service Dress in peaked
caps; 3 positions firing.

Serial No: 738A.
Title: British Cavalry and
Highlanders.
Pieces in box: 10.
Remarks: All in khaki. Cavalry in
shrapnel helmets and Highlanders
charging.

Serial No: 739A.
Title: Cowboys.
Pieces in box: 9.
Remarks: Mounted and on foot.

Serial No: 740A.
Title: North American Indians.
Pieces in box: 9.
Remarks: As 724A plus mounted
figures in full war bonnets.

Serial No: 741A.
Title: U.S. Infantry.
Pieces in box: 12.
Remarks: 3 positions firing with
officer.

Serial No: 742A.
Title: U.S. Sailors and Marines.
Pieces in box: 12.
Remarks: Marching at the slope.

Serial No: 743A.
Title: U.S. West Point Cadets.
Pieces in box: 12.
Remarks: In Summer and Winter
Dress.

Serial No: 744A.
Title: U.S. Sailors.
Pieces in box: 12.
Remarks: Bluejackets and
Whitejackets.

Serial No: 745A.
Title: U.S. Marines.
Pieces in box: 12.
Remarks: In Service Dress and
blue uniform.

Serial No: 746A.
Title: U.S. Infantry.
Pieces in box: 12.
Remarks: Marching at the slope
with officer. See also 223.

Serial No: 747A.
Title: U.S. Cavalry and Infantry.
Pieces in box: 10.
Remarks: Marching with
campaign hats.

Serial No: 748A.
Title: The Royal Scots Greys (2nd
Dragoons) and Highlanders.
Pieces in box: 13.
Remarks: As 695A.

Serial No: 749A.
Title: Life Guards and Foot
Guards.
Pieces in box: 13.
Remarks: Foot Guards marching
at the slope.

Serial No: 750A.
Title: 1st (The Royal) Dragoons
and Royal Sussex Regt.
Pieces in box: 13.
Remarks: Both Regiments in
Review Order.

Serial No: 751A.
Title: Lancers and East Kent
Regt. (The Buffs).
Pieces in box: 13.
Remarks: In Review Order.

Serial No: 752A.
Title: British Cavalry and
Highlanders.
Pieces in box: 13.
Remarks: All in Khaki. Cavalry in
shrapnel helmet; Highlanders
charging.

Serial No: 753A.
Title: British Cavalry and
Infantry.
Pieces in box: 13.
Remarks: All with peaked caps.
Cavalry in Service Dress, Infantry
in khaki. 3 positions firing.

Serial No: 754A.
Title: Life Guards and 1st (The
Royal) Dragoons.
Pieces in box: 9.
Remarks: Both Regiments in
Review Order on walking horse. 4
Life Guards and 5 Dragoons. See
also 1 and 31.

Serial No: 755A.
Title: Foot Guards and
Highlanders.
Pieces in box: 16.
Remarks: All in Review Order
marching at the slope.

Serial No: 756A.
Title: British Infantry.
Pieces in box: 16.
Remarks: In khaki with peaked
caps; 3 positions firing.

Serial No: 757A.
Title: Foot Guards.
Pieces in box: 16.
Remarks: 3 positions firing.

Serial No: 758A.
Title: North American Indians
and Cowboys.
Pieces in box: 12.
Remarks: Mounted and on foot
with Chief.

Serial No: 759A.
Title: Cowboys.
Pieces in box: 12.
Remarks: As 707A plus mounted
figures. See also 64N.

Serial No: 760.
Tirle: North American Indians.
Pieces in box: 12.
Remarks: As 740A.

Serial No: 761A.
Title: U.S. Cavalry.
Pieces in box: 9.
Remarks: In campaign hats.

Serial No: 762A.
Title: U.S. Infantry.
Pieces in box: 16.
Remarks: 3 positions firing. In
campaign hats.

Serial No: 763A.
Title: U.S. Infantry and Cavalry.
Pieces in box: 13.
Remarks: All in campaign hats.

Serial No: 764A.
Title: Life Guards and Foot
Guards.
Pieces in box: 16.
Remarks: Foot Guards firing.

Serial No: 765A.
Title: British Cavalry and
Infantry.
Pieces in box: 16.
Remarks: Cavalry in Service
Dress on trotting horse; Infantry
in Khaki with peaked caps; 3
positions firing.

Serial No: 766A.
Title: 1st (The Royal) Dragoons
and Queen's Royal West Surrey
Regt.
Pieces in box: 16.
Remarks: Both Regiments in
Review Order, Surreys three
positions firing.

Serial No: 767A.
Title: The Royal Scots Greys (2nd
Dragoons) and Highlanders.
Pieces in box: 16.
Remarks: Figures as 695A.

Serial No: 768A.
Title: Life Guards and Foot
Guards.
Pieces in box: 16.
Remarks: Foot Guards marching
at the slope.

Serial No: 769A.
Title: Hussars and Royal Sussex
Regt.
Pieces in box: 16.
Remarks: All in Review Order.
Royal Sussex marching at the
slope.

Serial No: 770A.
Title: North American Indians
and Cowboys.
Pieces in box: 16.
Remarks: Mounted and foot
figures.

Serial No: 771A.
Title: North American Indians.
Pieces in box: 16.
Remarks: Mounted and foot
figures.

Serial No: 772A.
Title: Cowboys.
Pieces in box: 16.
Remarks: Mounted and foot
figures with chief.

Serial No: 773A.
Title: U.S. Cavalry and Infantry.
Pieces in box: 16.
Remarks: Marching in campaign
hats, with officer in peaked cap.

Serial No: 774A.
Title: U.S. Cavalry and Infantry.
Pieces in box: 16.
Remarks: In firing positions with
officer.

Serial No: 775A.
Title: The Royal Scots Greys and
Highlanders.
Pieces in box: 19.
Remarks: As 695A.

Serial No: 776A.
Title: British Cavalry and
Infantry.
Pieces in box: 19.
Remarks: Service Dress; Infantry
3 positions firing.

Serial No: 777A.
Title: 1st (The Royal) Dragoons,
Foot Guards and Royal Sussex
Regt.
Pieces in box: 19.
Remarks: All in Review Order.
Infantry marching at the slope.

Serial No: 778A.
Title: Cowboys.
Pieces in box: 20.
Remarks: Mounted and foot
figures.

Serial No: 779A.
Title: North American Indians.
Pieces in box: 20.
Remarks: Mounted and foot
figures.

Serial No: 780A.
Title: North American Indians
and Cowboys.
Pieces in box: 20.
Remarks: Mounted and foot
figures.

Serial No: 781A.
Title: U.S. Cavalry and Infantry.
Pieces in box: 9.
Remarks: Marching with officer in
peaked cap.

Serial No: 782A.
Title: 1st Life Guards The Royal
Scots Greys (2nd Dragoons) Foot
Guards and Highlanders.
Pieces in box: 25.
Remarks: All in Review Order.
Infantry at the slope. Set included
a Marquee.

Serial No: 783A.
Title: Display Box.
Pieces in box: 32.
Remarks: With Royal Horse
Guards, East Kent Regiment,
Royal West Surreys, and
Marquee.

Serial No: 784A.
Title: British Cavalry and
Infantry.
Pieces in box: 25.
Remarks: Cavalry in Service
Dress. Infantry in khaki with
peaked caps running, 3 position
firing and Marquee.

Serial No: 785A.
Title: Cowboys.
Pieces in box: 24.
Remarks: Mounted and foot
figures with large Bell Tent.

Serial No: 786A.
Title: North American Indians.
Pieces in box: 25.
Remarks: Mounted and foot
figures with Chieftain and
Wigwam.

Serial No: 787A.
Title: North American Indians
and Cowboys.
Pieces in box: 25.
Remarks: Mounted and foot
figures.

Serial No: 788A.
Title: U.S. Cavalry and Infantry.
Pieces in box: 24.
Remarks: With officer in peaked
cap and Marquee.

Serial No: 789A.
Title: British Cavalry, Infantry and Highlanders.
Pieces in box: 32.
Remarks: Cavalry in Service Dress with peaked caps and shrapnel helmets; Infantry in Khaki running, 3 positions firing; Officer in peaked cap; Highlanders in khaki charging and Marquee.

Serial No: 790A.
Title: Life Guards, The Royal Scots Greys (2nd Dragoons) Foot Guards and Highlanders.
Pieces in box: 32.
Remarks: With Marquee as 2005. All figures in Review Order. Guards 3 positions firing. Highlanders marching at the slope. See also 695A etc.

Serial No: 791A.
Title: Royal Horse Guards (The Blues), 1st Dragoons (The Royals), Royal West Surrey Regt., East Kent Regt. (The Buffs) and Royal Sussex Regt.
Pieces in box: 32.
Remarks: With Marquee as 1005.

Serial No: 792A.
Title: Cowboys.
Pieces in box: 32.
Remarks: Mounted and on foot with large Bell Tent.

Serial No: 793A.
Title: North American Indians.
Pieces in box: 32.
Remarks: Mounted and on foot, with wigwam.

Serial No: 794A.
Title: Cowboys and North American Indians.
Pieces in box: 34.
Remarks: Mounted and on Foot.

Serial No: 795A.
Title: U.S. Cavalry and Infantry.
Pieces in box: 31.
Remarks: With Marquee. See also 788A.

Serial No: 1081A.
Title: British Bluejackets.
Pieces in box: 8.
Remarks: Marching in Bell bottoms.

Serial No: 1082A.
Title: British Infantry.
Pieces in box: 8.
Remarks: In Battle Dress; Standing and kneeling firing.

Serial No: 1083A.
Title: British Infantry.
Pieces in box: 8.
Remarks: In Battle Dress; with rifles and Thompson SMG.

Serial No: 1084A.
Title: British Infantry.
Pieces in box: 9.
Remarks: In Battle Dress; Charging with officer.

Serial No: 1085A.
Title: British Infantry.
Pieces in box: 16.
Remarks: In Battle Dress with rifles, Thompson SMGs and Officer.

Serial No: 1086A.
Title: British Infantry.
Pieces in box: 20.
Remarks: In Battle Dress with officer. Men in action positions with lying machine-gunners.

Serial No: 1087A.
Title: British Infantry.
Pieces in box: 17.
Remarks: In khaki with peaked caps; firing position with Fort as 1391.

Serial No: 1088A.
Title: Foot Guards.
Pieces in box: 17.
Remarks: 3 positions firing as 708A with Fort as 1391.

'N' Series

'N' Series similar to 'A' but for sale singly. Produced 1938-1940. One item per box, unless otherwise stated.

Serial No: 1N.
Title: Boy Scouts.
Remarks: Walking.

Serial No: 2N.
Title: East Kent Regt (The Buffs).
Remarks: In Khaki 'On Guard' as 16.

Serial No: 3N.
Title: East Kent Regt (The Buffs).
Remarks: In Review Order 'On Guard' position as 16.

Serial No: 4N.
Title: Cowboy.
Remarks: Kneeling with pistol. See also 1252.

Serial No: 5N.
Title: Cowboy.
Remarks: Walking. See also 1831.

Serial No: 6N.
Title: Cowboy.
Remarks: Standing firing pistol. See also 1252.

Serial No: 7N.
Title: Modern Highlander.
Remarks: Charging figure in steel helmet.

Serial No: 8N.
Title: Highlanders.
Remarks: Marching at the slope in Review Order.

Serial No: 9N.
Title: British Infantry.
Remarks: Khaki in peaked cap kneeling firing.

Serial No: 10N.
Title: British Infantry.
Remarks: Khaki in peaked cap lying firing.

142

Serial No: 11N.
Title: British Infantry.
Remarks: Khaki in peaked cap
standing firing.

Serial No: 12N.
Title: British Infantry Machine
Gunner.
Remarks: Khaki in peaked cap
lying firing as 194.

Serial No: 13N.
Title: British Infantry Machine
Gunner.
Remarks: Khaki in peaked cap;
sitting position as 198. Gun and
man separate.

Serial No: 14N.
Title: North American Indian
Chief.
Remarks: See also 22B-24B.

Serial No: 15N.
Title: North American Indian.
Remarks: Crawling with
tomahawk.
See also 703A.

Serial No: 16N.
Title: North American Indian.
Remarks: Standing with knife.

Serial No: 17N.
Title: North American Indian.
Remarks: As 33B. Standing on
guard.

Serial No: 18N.
Title: King's Royal Rifle Corps.
Remarks: Running with rifle in
Review Order. Slightly larger than
54mm.

Serial No: 19N.
Title: British Sailor.
Remarks: Walking wearing straw
hat.

Serial No: 20N.
Title: Royal Sussex Regt.
Remarks: Marching at the slope in
Review Order.

Serial No: 21N.
Title: Zulu.
Remarks: Standing with shield
and Knobkerri.

Serial No: 22N.
Title: U.S. Infantry.
Remarks: See also 227. Slope
arms, slouch hat.

Serial No: 23N.
Title: U.S. Infantry.
Remarks: Standing firing.
See also 1251.

Serial No: 24N.
Title: U.S. Infantry.
Remarks: In Service Dress and
slouch hat, charging.

Serial No: 25N.
Title: U.S. Infantry.
Remarks: Kneeling firing.

Serial No: 26N.
Title: U.S. Infantry.
Remarks: Lying firing. See also
1251.

Serial No: 27N.
Title: U.S. Infantry Officer.
Remarks: In peaked cap.

Serial No: 28N.
Title: Foot Guards.
Remarks: Marching at the slope.

Serial No: 29N.
Title: British Infantry.
Remarks: In khaki with peaked
cap; charging position without
bayonet. Similar figure to 18N.

Serial No: 30N.
Title: Foot Guard.
Remarks: Lying firing.

Serial No: 31N.
Title: Foot Guard.
Remarks: Kneeling firing.

Serial No: 32N.
Title: Highlander.
Remarks: In Service Dress and
Sun helmet lying firing.

Serial No: 33N.
Title: Highlander.
Remarks: In Service Dress
kneeling firing.

Serial No: 34N.
Title: Highlander.
Remarks: In Service Dress
standing firing.

Serial No: 35N.
Title: U.S. Infantry.
Remarks: In peaked cap,
charging. See also 24N.

Serial No: 36N.
Title: U.S. West Point Cadets.
Remarks: In Winter Dress. See
also 226.

Serial No: 37N.
Title: U.S. West Point Cadet.
Remarks: In Summer Dress. See
also 299.

Serial No: 38N.
Title: U.S. Navy Bluejacket.
Remarks: See also 230.

Serial No: 39N.
Title: U.S. Marine.
Remarks: See also 228. Blue
uniform.

Serial No: 40N.
Title: British Infantry Officer.
Remarks: In Khaki with peaked
cap.

Serial No: 41N.
Title: Queen's Royal West Surrey
Regt.
Remarks: In Review Order.
Kneeling firing. See also 2086.

Serial No: 42N.
Title: Queens Royal West Surrey
Regt.
Remarks: In Review Order. Lying
firing. See also 2086.

Serial No: 43N.
Title: Queen's Royal West Surrey
Reg.
Remarks: In Review Order
standing firing. See also 121 and
2086.

Serial No: 44N.
Title: Foot Guard.
Remarks: Standing firing.

Serial No: 45N.
Title: U.S. Navy Sailor.
Remarks: Whitejacket.

Serial No: 46N.
Title: U.S. Marine.
Remarks: as 399.

Serial No: 47N.
Title: U.S. Machine Gunner.
Pieces in box: 2.
Remarks: Sitting position in
Service Dress with peaked cap.
Gun and man separate.

Serial No: 48N.
Title: U.S. Machine Gunner.
Remarks: Prone position, one
piece.

Serial No: 49N.
Title: Royal Navy Bluejacket.
Remarks: At Shoulder Arms.

Serial No: 50N.
Title: Royal Navy Whitejackets.
Pieces in box: 1.
Issued:

Serial No: 51N.
Title: Royal Navy Midshipman.
Remarks: Open jacket and dirk.

Serial No: 52N.
Title: The Life Guards.
Remarks: See also 1.

Serial No: 53N.
Title: British Cavalry, The
Lancers.
Remarks: In Review Order with
moving arm holding lance and
second quality painting.

Serial No: 54N.
Title: British Cavalry. The
Lancers.
Remarks: With sword on moving
arm in Review Order.

Serial No: 55N.
Title: The Royal Scots Greys (2nd
Dragoons).
Remarks: See also 32.

Serial No: 56N.
Title: British Cavalry.
Remarks: Khaki Service Dress.

Serial No: 57N.
Title: British Cavalry, The
Lancers.
Remarks: See also 53N.

Serial No: 58N.
Title: British Cavalry.
Remarks: In Khaki with Shrapnel
Helmet.

Serial No: 59N.
Title: British Cavalry. 1st (The
Royal) Dragoons.
Remarks: In Review Order.

Serial No: 60N.
Title: Royal Horse Guards (The
Blues) Trooper.
Remarks: In Review Order.

Serial No: 61N.
Title: British Cavalry. The
Hussars.
Remarks: In Review Order.

Serial No: 62N.
Title: U.S. Cavalry.
Remarks: Peaked caps.

Serial No: 63N.
Title: North American Indian.
Remarks: With tomahawk.
See also 740A.

Serial No: 64N.
Title: Cowboy.
Remarks: With pistol. See also
759A.

Serial No: 65N.
Title: U.S. Cavalry.
Remarks: See also 266. Slouch
hat.

Serial No: 66N.
Title: North American Indian.
Remarks: On galloping grey
horse.

Serial No: 67N.
Title: Arab on horseback with
scimitar.
Remarks: Same casting as in Arab
sets.

Serial No: 68N.
Title: Egyptian Camel Coprs.
Remarks: See also 48, 115-117,
123, 131 and 918.

Serial No: 69N-70N.
Mixed boxes.

Serial No: 71N.
Title: Highlander.
Remarks: In Service Dress
charging wearing Glengarry.

Serial No: 72N.
Title: British Infantry.
Remarks: In Khaki marching at
the slope.

Serial No: 73N.
Title: British Infantry Drummer
Boy.
Remarks: In Khaki with peaked
cap.

Serial No: 74N.
Title: British Army Bugler Boy.
Remarks: In Khaki with peaked
cap.

Serial No: 87N.
Title: Battle Dress Officer.
Remarks: With pistol, pointing.

Serial No: 88N.
Title: Battle Dress Infantry.
Remarks: Charging with fixed
bayonet.

Serial No: 89N.
Title: Battle Dress Infantry.
Remarks: 'On Guard' position.

Serial No: 90N.
Title: Battle Dress Infantry.
Remarks: Standing firing rifle.

Serial No: 91N.
Title: Battle Dress Infantry.
Remarks: Kneeling firing rifle.

Serial No: 92N.
Title: Royal Navy Bluejacket.
Remarks: In new regulation
uniform.

Serial No: 93N.
Title: Tommy-Gunner.
Remarks: In steel helmet with
Thompson SMG.

Crown Range

Crown Range. All with fixed arms
and second quality painting.
Issued in 1955.

Serial No: 1S.
Title: Foot Guards.
Pieces in box: 6.
Remarks: 3 positions firing.

Serial No: 2S.
Title: Life Guards and Foot
Guards.
Pieces in box: 5.
Remarks: Foot Guards marching
at the slope.

Serial No: 3S.
Title: Highlanders.
Pieces in box: 6.
Remarks: 3 positions. Firing.

146   Nos 4S—25S

Serial No: 4S.
Title: Cowboys.
Pieces in box: 5.
Remarks: 1 mounted. See also
179.

Serial No: 5S.
Title: North American Indians.
Pieces in box: 5.
Remarks: 1 mounted. See also
150.

Serial No: 6S.
Title: Royal Scots Grey and
Highlanders.
Pieces in box: 5.
Remarks: Marching Highlanders
in Review Order.

Serial No: 7S.
Title: Hussar and Infantry of the
Line.
Pieces in box: 5.
Remarks: Hussar in Review
Order, Infantry marching and 'On
Guard'.

Serial No: 8S.
Title: Modern Army British
Infantry.
Pieces in box: 6.
Remarks: In Battle Dress with
officer. Men charging, 3 positions
firing.

Serial No: 9S.
Title: French Infanterie and
Zouaves.
Pieces in box: 5.
Remarks: With mounted officer.

Serial No: 10S.
Title: U.S. Civil War Union
Infantry 1862.
Pieces in box: 5.
Remarks: Action positions with
one mounted.

Serial No: 11S.
Title: U.S. Civil War Confederate
Infantry.
Pieces in box: 5.
Remarks: Castings as 105.

Serial No: 12S.
Title: Royal Canadian Mounted
Police.
Pieces in box: 5.
Remarks: Mounted man and four
marching at slope.

**Double Boxes from here on called
Duo-Crown Range**

Serial No: 21S.
Title: Cowboys and North
American Indians.
Pieces in box: 8.

Serial No: 22S.
Title: Cowboys.
Pieces in box: 8.
Remarks: Mounted and on foot.

Serial No: 23S.
Title: North American Indians.
Pieces in box: 8.
Remarks: Mounted and on foot.

Serial No: 24S.
Title: Foot Guards.
pieces in box: 9.
Remarks: With mounted officer,
marching and 3 positions firing.

Serial No: 25S.
Title: Hussars and Infantry of the
Line.
Pieces in box: 8.
Remarks: Hussars in Review
Order, Infantry Marching and 'On
Guard'. See also 7S.

Serial No: 26S.
Title: The Royal Scots Greys (2nd
Dragoons) and Highlanders.
Pieces in box: 8.
Remarks: Highlanders marching
at the slope in Review Order. See
also 695A.

Serial No: 27S.
Title: Modern Army British
Infantry.
Pieces in box: 10.
Remarks: In Battle Dress with
officer. All in action positions.

Serial No: 28S.
Title: Russian Cavalry and
Infantry.
Pieces in box: 8.
Remarks: Cavalry with cloaks.
Infantry in steel helmets charging.

Tri Crown Range

Serial No: 31S.
Title: Cowboys and North
American Indians.
Pieces in box: 11.
Remarks: See also 185.

Serial No: 32S.
Title: Foot Guards.
Pieces in box: 13.
Remarks: Marching and firing
with mounted officer. See also
24S.

Serial No: 33S.
Title: Modern Army British
Infantry.
Pieces in box: 15.
Remarks: In Battle Dress with
officer in action positions.

Serial No: 34S.
Title: Hussars and Infantry of the
Line.
Pieces in box: 11.
Remarks: See also 7S and 25S.
Infantry marching and on guard.

Serial No: 35S.
Title: The Royal Scots Greys (2nd
Dragoons) and Highlanders.
Pieces in box: 11.
Remarks: Highlanders 3 positions
firing. Tropical dress.

Serial No: 36S.
Title: Union and Confederate
Cavalry and Infantry, 1862.
Pieces in box: 11.
Remarks: See also 2068, 2069
and 46S.

Super Crown Range

Serial No: 41S.
Title: Life Guards and Foot
Guards.
Pieces in box: 14.
Remarks: Foot Guards marching
at the slope with officer and
drummer.

Serial No: 42S.
Title: Royal Scots Greys and
Highlanders.
Pieces in box: 15.
Remarks: Highlanders 3 positions
firing and piper.

Serial No: 43S.
Title: Hussars and Infantry of the
Line.
Pieces in box: 15.
Remarks: As 34S.

Serial No: 44S.
Title: Cowboys and North
American Indians.
Pieces in box: 16.
Remarks: See also 185.

Serial No: 45S.
Title: Modern Army British Infantry.
Pieces in box: 18.
Remarks: In Battle Dress with officer. Action positions with lying machine-gunners added.

Serial No: 46S.
Title: Union and Confederate Cavalry and Infantry, 1862.
Pieces in box: 16.
Remarks: See also 2068, 2069 and 36S.

New Crown Range

Serial No: 51S.
Title: Highland Infantry.
Pieces in box: 6.
Remarks: In action position wearing Tropical Helmets with mounted officer. See also 67S.

Serial No: 52S.
Title: Hussars and Infantry of the Line.
Pieces in box: 5.
Remarks: See also 7S, 25S and 34S.

Serial No: 53S.
Title: Royal Scots Greys and Highland Infantry.
Pieces in box: 5.
Remarks: Highlanders marching in Review Order.

Serial No: 54S.
Title: Foot Guards.
Pieces in box: 7.
Remarks: 3 positions firing.

Serial No: 55S.
Title: Life Guards and Foot Guards.
Pieces in box: 5.
Remarks: Foot Guards marching at the slope.

Serial No: 56S.
Title: Modern Army British Infantry.
Pieces in box: 7.
Remarks: In Battle Dress with officer all in action positions.

Serial No: 57S.
Title: Royal Canadian Mounted Police.
Pieces in box: 5.
Remarks: See also 1349, 591B and 271B. Marching slope arms and mounted trooper.

Serial No: 58S.
Title: North American Indians.
Pieces in box: 6.
Remarks: Sub titled: 'In characteristic War Paint.'

Serial No: 59S.
Title: Cowboys.
Pieces in box: 5.
Remarks: Mounted and Foot figures. See also 184.

Serial No: 60S.
Title: French Infanterie de Ligne.
Pieces in box: 5.
Remarks: Charging and 'On Guard' with mounted officers.

Serial No: 61S.
Title: The Royal Scots Greys (2nd Dragoons) and British Foot Guards.
Pieces in box: 11.
Remarks: Marching and firing.

Serial No: 62S.
Title: Modern Army British Infantry.
Pieces in box: 14.
Remarks: In Battle Dress with officer in action positions.

Serial No: 63S.
Title: The Royal Scots Greys (2nd
Dragoons) with Highland
Infantry.
Pieces in box: 14.
Remarks: Highlanders marching
at the slope. See also 695A and
51S.

Serial No: 64S.
Title: North American Indians.
Pieces in box: 10.
Remarks: Mounted and foot
figures.
See also 208.

Serial No: 65S.
Title: Cowboys.
Pieces in box: 10.
Remarks: Mounted and foot
figures. See also 185.

Serial No: 66S.
Title: Cowboys and North
American Indians.
Pieces in box: 10.
Remarks: Mounted and foot
figures. See also 185.

Serial No: 67S.
Title: The Royal Scots Greys (2nd
Dragoons) and Foot Guards.
Pieces in box: 17.
Remarks: See also 61S.

Serial No: 68S.
Title: Modern Army British
Infantry.
Pieces in box: 20.
Remarks: In Battle Dress with
officer, machine-gunners and men
in action positions.

Serial No: 69S.
Title: Royal Scots Greys and
Highlanders.
Pieces in box: 17.
Remarks: Highlanders wearing
tropical helmets 3 positions firing.
See also 659A.

Serial No: 70S.
Title: Cowboys and North
American Indians.
Pieces in box: 17.
Remarks: Mounted and foot
figures. See also 185.

Serial No: 71S.
Title: Modern Army British
Infantry.
Pieces in box: 15?
Remarks: In Battle Dress with
officer. Men in action positions
with 25 pdr from set 2026.

New Crown Range – 'P' Series
Packed in Bulk for sale singly.
Issued 1956. Second quality
painting.

Serial No: 41P.
Title: Foot Guard.
Pieces in box: 1.
Remarks: Marching at the slope.

Serial No: 42P.
Title: Infantry of the Line.
Remarks: In Review Order 'On
Guard' position. See also 7S.

Serial No: 43P.
Title: Infantry of the Line.
Remarks: Marching at the slope in
Review Order. See also 7S.

Serial No: 45P.
Title: Highlander.
Remarks: In Khaki wearing
Tropical Helmet standing firing.

Serial No: 46P.
Title: Modern British Infantry.
Remarks: In Khaki with steel
helmet. 'On Guard' position.

Serial No: 51P.
Title: North American Indian.
Remarks: With rifle. See also
33B, 74B.

Serial No: 52P.
Title: North American Indian.
Remarks: With knife and
tomahawk. See also 711A, 14B.

Serial No: 56P.
Title: Highlander.
Remarks: In Khaki wearing
Tropical Helmet lying firing.

Serial No: 57P.
Title: Highlander.
Remarks: In Khaki wearing
Tropical Helmet kneeling firing.

Serial No: 58P.
Title: Foot Guard.
Remarks: Standing Firing.

Serial No: 59P.
Title: Foot Guard.
Remarks: Kneeling firing.

Serial No: 60P.
Title: Foot Guard.
Remarks: Prone firing.

Serial No: 64P.
Title: Life Guards.
Remarks: See also 1.

Serial No: 65P.
Title: The Royal Scots Greys (2nd
Dragoons). Remarks: See also 32.

Serial No: 66P.
Title: Royal Horse Guard (The
Blues).
Remarks: See also 783A.

Serial No: 68P.
Title: Hussar.
Remarks: In Review Order. See
also 61N.

Serial No: 70P.
Title: Modern Army British
Cavalry.
Remarks: In khaki with steel
helmet.

Serial No: 72P.
Title: U.S. Cavalry.
Remarks: See also 266.

Serial No: 80P.
Title: Cowboy.
Remarks: Kneeling with pistol.
See also 274B.

Serial No: 83P.
Title: Cowboy.
Remarks: Walking with holstered
pistol. See also 133.

Serial No: 92P.
Title: U.S. Bluejacket.
Remarks: See also 230.

Serial No: 93P.
Title: U.S. West Point Cadet.
Remarks: In Winter Uniform. See
also 226.

Serial No: 96P.
Title: Cowboy.
Remarks: Standing firing pistol.
See also 707A.

Serial No: 98P.
Title: Highlander.
Remarks: Marching at the slope in
Review Order.

Serial No: 99P.
Title: North American Indian
Chief.
Remarks: As 23B.

Serial No: 110P.
Title: Modern Army British
Infantry Officer.
Remarks: In Battle Dress.

Serial No: 111P.
Title: Modern Army British
Infantry.
Remarks: In Battle Dress;
charging position.

Serial No: 112P.
Title: Modern Army British
Infantry.
Remarks: In Battle Dress, 'On
Guard' position. Different figure
to 469P.

Serial No: 113P.
Title: Modern Army British
Infantry.
Remarks: In Battle Dress
standing firing.

Serial No: 114P.
Title: Modern Army British
Infantry.
Remarks: In Battle Dress
kneeling firing.

Serial No: 115P.
Title: Modern Army British
Infantry.
Remarks: In Battle Dress with
Thompson SMG.

Serial No: 116P.
Title: British Bluejacket.
Remarks: Marching in Regulation
Dress. Different figure to 1510.

Serial No: 117P.
Title: North American Indian.
Remarks: With tomahawk. See
also 32B.

Serial No: 118P.
Title: Cowboy.
Remarks: With pistol. See also
34B.

Serial No: 121P.
Title: Royal Canadian Mounted
Police.
Remarks: See also 1349, 271B
and 1373B.

Serial No: 122P.
Title: R.A.M.C. Nurse.
Remarks: See also 137 and 1897.

Serial No: 123P.
Title: Highlander.
Remarks: In Review Order
wearing Tropical Helmet standing
firing.

Serial No: 124P.
Title: Highlander.
Remarks: In Review Order
wearing Tropical Helmet kneeling
firing.

Serial No: 125P.
Title: Highlander.
Remarks: In Review Order
wearing Tropical Helmet lying
firing.

Serial No: 126P.
Title: Zouave.
Remarks: Charging figure. See
also 142.

Serial No: 127P.
Title: French Infanterie de Ligne.
Remarks: 'On Guard' in Review
Order. Similar to Belgian figure.

Serial No: 128P.
Title: French Infanterie de Ligne.
Remarks: Standing firing in steel
helmets.

Serial No: 129P.
Title: French Infanetrie de Ligne.
Remarks: Kneeling firing in steel
helmets.

Serial No: 130P.
Title: French Infanterie de Ligne.
Remarks: Lying firing in steel helmets.

Serial No: 132P.
Title: Belgian Grenadier.
Remarks: As British Guards casting at the slope with different painting.

Serial No: 133P.
Title: Belgian Chasseur à Pied.
Remarks: Charging figure. Similar to Japanese with head change.

Serial No: 134P.
Title: Belgian Line Infantry.
Remarks: On Guard position in Review Order. See also 127P.

Serial No: 135P.
Title: Belgian Horse Gendarme.
Remarks: See also 132P.

Serial No: 136P.
Title: North American Indian.
Remarks: Carrying rifle.

Serial No: 137P.
Title: North American Indian.
Remarks: Crouching with rifle.

Serial No: 148P.
Title: Motor Cycle Dispatch Rider.
Remarks: See also 200, 323, 1608, 1791-1792, 1907, 2011 and 149P.

Serial No: 149P.
Title: Speed Cop.
Remarks: On motor cycle.
See also 239, 319, 621, 659, 775, 776, 808, 824, 1413, 1430, 1477, 1511, 1792 and LB550.

Serial No: 150P.
Title: Pilot.
Remarks: In full flying kit. See also 1894 and 1895.

Serial No: 151P.
Title: Red Army Cossack.
Remarks: Mounted in Review Order. See also 20, 65, 133, 136, 2027, 2028, 2032, 2144, 152P and 28S.

Serial No: 152P.
Title: Red Army Infantry.
Remarks: In steel helmet, charging. As 133P but with Russian style steel helmet.

Serial No: 153P.
Title: Royal Canadian Mounted Police.
Remarks: Marching at slope as 746A but with different painting.

Serial No: 154P.
Title: Cowboy.
Remarks: On foot firing pistol.

Serial No: 155P.
Title: North American Indian.
Remarks: On foot swinging club.

Serial No: 156P.
Title: Highland Officer.
Remarks: In Review Order wearing Tropical Helmet.

Serial No: 120MP.
Title: Infantry Assortment.
Remarks: P series figures for bulk sale.

Serial No: 121MP.
Title: Cavalry Assortment.
Remarks: P series figures for bulk sale.

Circus Figures

Individual items sold as bulk lines with second quality painting.

Serial No: 351 Bulk.
Title: Prancing Horse.
Issued: 1955.
Remarks: Standing on hind legs and tail.
See also 352Bulk.

Serial No: 352Bulk.
Title: Circus Trotting Horse.
Issued: 1955.
Remarks: With hole in back for 355B, 1539.
See also 351Bulk, 1442-1444, 1539.

Serial No: 353Bulk.
Title: Man on stilts.
Issued: 1955.
Remarks: For use with Circus. See also 1442-1444, 1539.

Serial No: 354Bulk.
Title: Clown.
Issued: 1955.
Remarks: With hoop. See also 358Bulk, 447Bulk, 1443, 1444, 1539.

Serial No: 355Bulk.
Title: Equestrienne.
Issued: 1955.
Remarks: To fit on back of 352Bulk. See also 351Bulk, 1442, 1443, 1539.

Serial No: 357Bulk.
Title: Ring Master.
Issued: 1955.
Remarks: In Top Hat and Tails with whip. See also 1442-1444 and 1539.

Serial No: 358Bulk.
Title: Clown.
Issued: 1955.
Remarks: Standing holding baggy trousers. See also 354Bulk, 447Bulk, 1442-1444 and 1539.

Serial No: 359Bulk.
Title: Circus Elephant.
Issued: 1955.
Remarks: Walking wearing a coloured saddlecloth. See also 450Bulk, 901 and 1539.

Serial No: 446Bulk.
Title: Tub.
Issued: 1955.
Remarks: To take 449Bulk or 450Bulk.

Serial No: 447Bulk.
Title: Boxing Clown.
Issued: 1955.
Remarks: See also 451Bulk.

Serial No: 449Bulk.
Title: Lion Tamer.
Issued: 1955.
Remarks: Standing with whip. See also 448Bulk and 1539.

Serial No: 449Bulk.
Title: Performing Tiger.
Issued: 1955.
Remarks: Sitting snarling. See also 448Bulk, 941, 992 and 1539.

Serial No: 450Bulk.
Title: Performing Elephant.
Issued: 1955.
Remarks: Standing on hind legs. See also 359Bulk, 446Bulk, 901 and 1539.

Serial No: 451Bulk.
Title: Boxing Kangaroo.
Issued: 1955.
Remarks: Standing Kangaroo with boxing gloves on forepaws. See also 447Bulk, 902 and 1539.

Miscellaneous Figures

Serial No: 19D.
Title: Jockey on Horse.
Pieces in box: 2.
Issued:
Remarks: For Race Games. 2¹/₄ inches long. Available in assorted colours. See also 96D and 123Bulk.

Serial No: 26D.
Title: Gun.
Pieces in box: 1.
Issued: 1936-1937.
Remarks: Mounted on four wheeled carriage.

Serial No: 27D.
Title: Armoured Car.
Pieces in box: 1.
Issued: 1936-1937.
Remarks: With two integral crew figures.

Serial No: 29D.
Title: Racing Motor.
Remarks: For Race Games.
Available in six assorted colours.

Serial No: 30D.
Title: Yacht.
Remarks: For Race Games.
Available in six assorted colours.

Serial No: 31D.
Title: Cyclist.
Remarks: For Race Games.
Available in six assorted colours.

Serial No: 44D.
Title: Coronation State Coach.
Pieces in box:
Issued: 1936-1937.
Remarks: 8″ long with 8 horse team. See also 1478 and 1503.

Serial No: 86D.
Title: Coronation Chair.
Pieces in box: 1.
Issued: 1936-1937.
Remarks: As 1474.

Serial No: 96D.
Title: Jockey on Horse.
Pieces in box: 2.
Issued:
Remarks: For race games. $3^1/_4$
inches long. Available in assorted
colours. See also 19D and
123Bulk.

Garden Series

01 Flower bed with grass
    border. Straight section.
02 Flower bed with grass
    border. Finishing circular
    section.
03 Flower bed with grass
    border. Return square
    section.
04 Flower bed with grass
    border. Return circular
    section.
05 Flower bed with grass
    border. Half straight section.
06 Flower bed with grass
    border. Finishing corner
    section.
07 Post for stone wall.
08 Garden roller.
09 Crazing paving.
010 Sundial on pedestal.
011 Garden wheel barrow.
012 Stone wall (low).
013 Pergola section. Larch poles
    for use with roses.
014 Rustic Arch.
015 Mound, for single plants.
016 Coloured vase.
017 Garden seat.
018 Interlaced fence with trellis.
019 Rambler rose.
020 Lobelia.
021 Geranium.
022 Torch lily (or red hot poker).
023 Conifer. Dwarf.
024 Sunflower.
025 Poppy.

026 Lupin.
027 Half standard rose.
028 Bush rose.
029 Aster.
030 Hollyhock.
031 Antirrhinum.
032 Dahlia. (Single).
033 Dahlia. (Double).
034 Gladioli.
035 Wall flower.
036 Foxglove.
037 Chrysanthemum.
038 Full standard rose.
039 Delphinium.
040 Hyacinth.
041 Tulip.
042 Crocus.
043 Snowdrop.
045 Narcissus.
046 Sweet Alyssum.
047 Square Tub. (To hold
    conifer).
048 Small flower bed. (to hold 7
    plants)
    Lawn mower with removable
    grass box.
051 Man for 050.
052 Man for 08.
053 Greenhouse.
054 Rockery straight section.
055 Rockery inner return corner.
056 Rockery outer corner.
057 Rockery upper steps.
058 Rockery lower steps.
059 Flower pots. (Assorted
    sizes).
060 Wooden blocks. (For varying
    levels or terracing).
061 Balustrading. (Long
    section).
062 Balustrading. (Short).
063 Post for balustrading.
064 Cold frame.
065 Round flower bed. (Without
    grass verge).
066 Square flower bed. (Without
    grass verge).

067 Lily pond with central figure
     will hold water.
068 Hose on reel.
069 Seed boxes. (7 per packet).
070 Man for 011.
071 Assorted packets of flowers.

Other Miniature Garden
Numbers
28 M.G. Garden shelter.
31 M.G. Garden tree.
    (3 dimensional)
32 M.G. Beginners set.
33 M.G. Double display set.
35 M.G. Giant display set.

Series all between 4-5 inches high,
sold as Garden Ornaments.

Serial No: J1.
Title: Gnome.
Pieces in box: 1.
Remarks: Lying reading book.
See also 2426 and 2436.

Serial No: J2.
Title: Gnome.
Pieces in box: 1.
Remarks: Standing with pipe. See
also J4, J5, 1696, 241Bulk and
487Bulk.

Serial No: J3.
Title: Gnome.
Pieces in box: 1.
Remarks: Sitting with violin. See
also 170Bulk and 171Bulk.

Serial No: J4.
Title: Gnome.
Pieces in box: 1.
Remarks: Standing. See also J2,
J5, 169Bulk, 241Bulk and
487Bulk.

Serial No: J5.
Title: Gnome.
Pieces in box: 1.
Remarks: Standing with flower
pot. See also J2, J4, 169Bulk,
241Bulk and 487Bulk.

Serial No: J6.
Title: Frog.
Pieces in box: 1.
Remarks: With legs extended. See
also J7, 12H and 22H.

Serial No: J7.
Title: Newt.
Pieces in box: 1.
Remarks: See also J6, 12H and
22H.

'H' series figures were large size
70 mm in height.

Serial No: 4H.
Title: Infantry of the Line.
Remarks: Marching at the slope in
Review Order.

Serial No: 5H.
Title: Foot Guards.
Remarks: Marching at the slope in
Review Order.

Serial No: 6H.
Title: Highlanders.
Remarks: Marching at the slope in
Review Order.

Serial No: 12H.
Title: Seagull.
Remarks: For garden use. With
outstretched wings.

Serial No: 16H.
Title: Mickey Mouse.
Remarks: See also 1645.

Serial No: 17H.
Title: Minnie Mouse.
Remarks: See also 1645.

Serial No: 19H.
Title: Donald Duck.
Remarks: See also 1645.

Serial No: 18H.
Title: Pluto.
Remarks: See also 1645.

Serial No: 20H.
Title: Clarabelle.
Remarks: See also 1645.

Serial No: 21H.
Title: Goofy.
Remarks: See also 1645.
Serial No: 22H.
Title: Seagull.
Remarks: For garden use. With folded wings.

'HH' series figures were extra-large size, 90 mm in height.

Serial No: 1HH.
Title: Infantry of the Line.
Remarks: Marching at the slope in Review Order.

Serial No: 2HH.
Title: Foot Guards.
Remarks: Marching at the slope in Review Order.

Serial No: 3HH.
Title: Highlanders.
Remarks: Marching at the slope in Review Order.

Serial No: 4HH.
Title: Assortment.
Pieces in box: 12.
Remarks: 4 each of 1HH-3HH.

Title: Famous Football Teams.
Pieces in box: 18.
Issued: 1936-1937.
Remarks: With Referee, Linesman, Goalposts, Forwards, Half and Full Backs. 28 teams normally produced although others could be had to order. Also sold individually under Bulk numbering.

Serial No: 169Bulk-171Bulk.
Title: Gnome.
Remarks: Decorative figures in various sizes and positions for garden use.

Serial No: 241Bulk-243Bulk
Title: Gnome.
Remarks: Various sizes and positions for garden use.

Serial No: IV-7V. (9671-9676)
Title: Petrol Pumps.
Pieces in box: 1.
Issued: ?
Remarks: IV Shell, 2V B.P., 3V Esso, 4V Mobilgas, 5V National Benzole, 6V Fina, 7V Dominion.

Serial No: 10V. (9680)
Title: Shell Oil Cabinet.
Pieces in box: 1.
Issued: ?
Remarks: 'with sliding front'.

Serial No: 101V-102V. (9681-82)
Title: Stand of 3 Pumps.
Pieces in box: 1.
Issued: ?
Remarks: 101V Shell, B.P., National: 102V Shell, Esso, Mobilgas.

Serial No: 104V. (9689)
Title: Display Box.
Pieces in box: 3.
Issued: ?
Remarks: Stand of 3 pumps;
Shell, National B.P., Garage
Attendant and Oil Cabinet.